Dear People...
Robert Shaw

Dear People . . . Robert Shaw

A Biography

Joseph A. Mussulman

INDIANA UNIVERSITY PRESS
BLOOMINGTON & LONDON

Thornton Wilder excerpts copyright © 1979 by Grant N. Nickerson, Trustee,
Estate of Thornton Wilder. Reprinted by permission.

Copyright © 1979 by Joseph A. Mussulman

Manufactured in the United States of America

Library of Congress Cataloging in Publication Data

Mussulman, Joseph A.
Dear people . . . Robert Shaw.

Discography: p.
Includes index.
1. Shaw, Robert Lawson, 1916–   2. Conduc-
tors (Music)—United States—Biography.
I. Title.
ML422.S52M9   785'.092'4 [B]   78–20401
ISBN 0–253–18457–6   1 2 3 4 5 83 82 81 80 79

For each ecstatic instant
We must an anguish pay
In keen and quivering ratio
To the ecstasy.

EMILY DICKINSON

Contents

Preface

To some of those who knew Robert Shaw in the latter 1930s, it seemed that his achievements could be ascribed to "nothing more than an extraordinary authority of manner. . . . A gift of character, not of dexterity."

From the perspective of the early sixties a much more complex profile prompted a member of the Cleveland Orchestra to write: "He has a shattering wit, a secular imagination, a practical and executive side that belies the seer; he has short hair, is no saint, and—wonder of wonders—speaks a native English. His satire is unrelenting, his humor—as with other great artists—the indispensable safety valve of an uncompromising seriousness. The sacred and the secular are in strained alliance in a mind both religious and highly literary, unexempt from either this world or the other."

Many of those who have known him in the late seventies might recognize in him a paradigm of that rare type called "a self-actualizing humanist." There has always been a centeredness about him, and that center is congruent with the mysterious core of the experience of music. There is that incredible vitality which convinces ordinary people who perform under his direction that they themselves possess the capacity to realize an essential life-force through music. There is his perception of the potential relationships between art and life, and his determination to reveal them to all kinds of people in all kinds of places. There is his altruism toward the whole human race ("I'm *part* of the 'great unwashed' "), and his excruciating yet stoic acceptance of the misery of humanness. There is that guileless courage to confront novelty without fear, even eagerly, and to choose freely among the options. ("Dawgonnit, I don't feel I *have* any manifest destiny.")

His career has threaded itself among some of the most significant episodes in the history of music in the United States since the 1930s: the era of live music on radio, the choral renaissance of the forties and fifties, the florescence of the community orchestra, changes in the recording industry, the evolution of professional concert management, the nourishment of native composers and conductors, the multiplication of music festivals, the development of new avenues of patronage, the emergence of "cultural diplomacy," and the reentry of the South into the mainstream of American musical life. It has so far spanned an era in which, while nationalism became a principle rather than a cause and internationalism became a new intellectual and economic force, the United States at last produced all the conditions of a genuinely indigenous musical culture.

The best of Robert Lawson Shaw's career may be yet to come.

I.

Dear People . . .

1.

The Fred Waring Glee Club

As a freshman at Pomona College, majoring in philosophy and literature, Shaw was elected by the members of the Glee Club to substitute for their ailing director. Two years later the administration offered him a stipend of $500 to conduct the forty-five-voice male chorus while Professor Lyman took a yearlong leave of absence.

In the spring of 1937 Fred Waring and his Pennsylvanians moved onto the campus with a Warner Brothers crew to shoot some scenes for the musical film *Varsity Show*, starring Rosemary Lane and Dick Powell. All the students served as extras, and even the Glee Club made an appearance with the band—although the singing was dubbed in later by Hollywood musicians. One evening the college held an official banquet for the actors, with the Glee Club providing the entertainment.

Impressed by Shaw's compelling, clean-cut "collegiate" manner, his contagious enthusiasm, and his spirited interpretation of the music, Waring offered him a permanent job with the Pennsylvanians.

Robert said no thanks, he was going to be a minister.

A year later, considerably in debt to the college and needing money for seminary in the future, he decided to accept Waring's invitation for, say, six months. His initial impression was that he was supposed to sing with the group, but Waring soon set him straight. His job was to audition and train a special glee club of about twenty "boys" for a new radio series scheduled to begin in October. His salary was to have been a comparatively generous fifty dollars per week, but negotiations brought it up to seventy-five. Waring sent him $150 in travel money, but the twenty-two-year-old Californian, habituated to thrift by Depression-era life as a minister's son, made the trip at excursion rates—day coach to New Orleans, boat to Broadway—and handed his new boss sixty-seven dollars in change.

> When I was in college at Pomona in Southern California there were four major and influential American choral traditions. There was the Christiansen-Lutheran-St. Olaf tradition, which brought a vibratoless pseudo-Gregorian tone to a pseudosacred literature located somewhere between folk song and "The Rosary." There was also the Williamson-Westminster-Wasp tradition, which brought a convulsive operatic vocalism to every piece of music it touched, from folk songs to Bach cantatas. There were the leisurely, lively, good-humored, and all-but-improvised folk and student songs of Marshall Bartholomew and the Yale singing groups. And there was the tradition planted—so far as I know—only by Archibald T. Davison and nourished (at that time) by G. Wallace Woodworth, the focus of which was the extraordinary polyphonic literature of the Medieval, Renaissance, and early Baroque periods, transcribed for male voices and sung for purposes totally other than credit, recruitment, profit, or prizes.
>
> Pomona College fell somewhere between New Haven and Cambridge; and when I started college in 1934 Pomona had just won the last of the national glee club competitions way "back East" in St. Louis, with a di Lasso motet, a Nathaniel Dett spiritual, and a highly communicative school song sophisticatedly derived from a fragment of American Indian chant.

However, when young Shaw entered the Fred Waring studios that morning in 1938, he knew practically none of the current academically sanctioned choral techniques or vocal methods. His musical credentials consisted of several years in the Pomona College Glee Club, a week or so of classes under John Finley Williamson at Occidental College, which he had managed to squeeze into his schedule the preceding summer, a few piano and voice lessons, a semester of music theory, and an unusually musical family background. His principal strengths were an incredibly lucid inner conception of an ideal choral sonority and the ability to inspire the kind of confidence that moved Waring to hire him in the first place.

The newspaper announcement of auditions brought a lineup of some eight hundred men, all incredulous at the prospect of being paid for singing in a chorus anywhere outside the Broadway theaters. Shaw painstakingly sorted out the applicants in a grueling two-week process involving half a dozen callbacks for comparing and matching voices and evaluating general musicianship. He was looking for voices of superior range and flexibility, able to sing any interval, in tune, in any rhythm, on any syllable, at any tempo. Stentorian "operatic" voices were unusable. Finally he settled upon twenty-four singers, among whom were a few ex-Pomona classmates and some other West Coast natives.

The average age of the group was a youthful twenty-six years—four years older than Shaw himself. Most were trained vocalists holding degrees from colleges and universities all over the United States, though they had temporarily been accountants, photographers, farmers, clerks, radio announcers, athletic coaches, composers, arrangers, and conductors. Since no one was paid until the broadcasts began, each man had to have enough cash on hand to last through five weeks of rehearsals.

For up to six hours daily Shaw coached the group, bolstered by advice and encouragement from Waring. He needed the support, for he was occasionally stricken by intimations of inadequacy. He could "read music" after a fashion, but he had to learn scores laboriously, note by note, and he was never sure he was hearing all there was to be heard. Still, he had an intuitive sense of the effect he wanted at any given moment, and he drew on his "extraordinary authority of manner" to get it. Often, when the dictates of his inner ear outdistanced his ability to articulate them, his vocabulary became colorfully laced with unministerial expletives. After all, so far as Robert knew, judging from Waring's example, that was the way a professional got the job done.

Waring's career had begun in Tyrone, Pennsylvania, around 1916, when Fred, his brother Tom, and two high school cronies formed a combo called "Warings' Banjazzatra" to play at local dances and parties. The boys couldn't read music and used their instruments— piano, drums, and two banjos—merely for rhythm accompaniments to their improvised vocal harmonies. Within another ten years the band had grown in size, versatility, and renown, but Waring retained the practice of having the men put down their instruments every so often and sing as a glee club.

That very feature, distinctive as it was, caused them to fail thirty-two consecutive auditions for radio shows: the networks and the advertising agencies doubted that choral music, even in the popular idiom, would appeal to a sufficiently large audience. By the time they finally succeeded in 1933, Waring had realized that the singing needed more polish. Since the instrumentalists wouldn't have tolerated "voice lessons," and he knew nothing about the subject anyway, the only practical recourse was to refine the delivery of the words.

Gradually he evolved what he called his "tone-syllable technique" of enunciation, in which "all of the beauty of all of the sounds of all of the syllables of all of the words" was spelled out phonetically. To assure a sinewy legato, *l*, *m*, *n*, and *ng* sounds were prolonged and emphasized, and, in consideration of the microphone's sensitivity, explosive consonants were suppressed.

Waring also overcame the inherent weakness of radio as a medium—the absence of facial expressions and bodily gestures to enhance verbal meanings—by insisting that when singing the men concentrate on the message and the emotional import of each song.

His methods worked well enough, but he decided to supplement the orchestra with a glee club made up of bona fide singers. When he observed Robert Shaw at work with the Pomona College Glee Club, he knew he didn't have to look any further for the right person to organize and conduct it.

Shaw nourished the Waring Glee Club on the best available music in print, such as Randall Thompson's "Tarantella," and Waring allowed him to perform some of it early in the 1938–39 season on the half-hour weekly show the Pennsylvanians broadcast for Grove's Bromo-Quinine. Most of it was unsuitable to the "pop" format of the show, however, so on Sunday afternoon, December 11, Shaw and the Glee Club presented a special choral service at the Reverend Harry Emerson Fosdick's Riverside Congregational Church in New York City. It was an especially memorable occasion for Shaw; he held Fosdick in high esteem and had often used the noted preacher's published sermons as models for his own when he substituted for his father in the pulpit.

The audience was amazed by the surpassing tonal beauty and rhythmic precision of the singing. A reviewer for the *Jersey Journal* wrote enthusiastically that

> the unusual demonstration of the vocal attainments very definitely establishes the Waring Choir as one of the country's foremost and elevates it definitely above a mere radio singing group. That Shaw should have developed such an artistically competent group in such a short time seems almost incredible. Here's a comparative youngster who most certainly is destined to make outstanding contributions to the music of the world with the passing of the years. ... Fred Waring, who was present but took no part, must have been extremely proud. The service was emphatic confirmation of Fred's judgment that in young Shaw he has a vocal-directing "find."

Back in California, in the communities where their father occupied various Disciples of Christ (Christian Church) pastorates and teaching positions—Fresno, Red Bluff, Santa Barbara, Stockton, Ontario, Eagle Rock, and San Diego—people called them "the singing Shaws." The mother, Nelle Lawson Shaw, established her reputation long before the children began to arrive. The music she sang was commonplace at best, but she was no ordinary singer. She had a magical way of establishing a mood, and seemed to pull her listeners through the music with her.

> My mother and grandmother occasionally would sing duets. —Nothing like the *Christe eleison* of Bach's *B Minor Mass*. But I seldom rehearse that piece without hoping for the unbelievable coincidence of time, tone, and temperament that used to characterize their concert.
>
> And I wonder, now as then, how it was that their musical utterance (it was always called "the message in song")—undoubtedly as poor in literature or philosophy as the "spoken word" which followed—could have seemed so much more palatable—less offensive.
>
> Returning some years later, after a life of professional music— and amateur sin—in New York to the West Coast, I wondered how Mother's voice would sound to these more sophisticated ears and tougher heart.

That Sunday she sang "The Ninety and Nine"—about the Master Shepherd and his One Lost Lamb—of an aesthetic order of merit which, if it had been formed in solid rather than sound could have appropriately adorned the Babyland of Forest Lawn Cemetery. —And I wept.

One by one the children took their places among "the singing Shaws"—first Holly, then Robert, Jim, Anne, and finally John. Years later, Robert recalled: "The young parents and their passel of kids gathered around the parlor piano 'harmonizing' from an album of 'sheet'-music collected during World War I just past: 'Good morning, Mr. Zip, Zip, Zip . . .' 'There's a long, long trail a-winding . . .' 'Over there . . .' There must have been a score of 'fight' songs we knew from memory and could sing in four parts."

They sang in church, at the doors of shut-ins, travelling together in the car. (You might as well sing in the car, since there's not much else to do. And you might as well learn to harmonize, since Mother and Holly are matchless on the melody, and Father teases you into it by improvising a bass.) Camping on the beach, they would mark the sun's descent with the undulating trochees of

> Day is dying in the west;
> Heaven is touching earth with rest;
> Wait and worship while the night
> Sets her evening lamps alight
>   Through all the sky.

And then in the dusk, by the light of the campfire, they would intone the even meter of "Now the day is over."

To be sure, life was not all sweetness and sunset. "Be ye kind one to another" was a stern imperative laid down by the Reverend Father, but in his absence perdition reigned betimes. Holly, occasionally left in charge when the parents were away, would be quite helpless to placate quarrelling brothers whose natural grievances had been held in check for weeks, and the day wasn't over fast enough to suit her.

Every time the Reverend Shirley R. Shaw moved to a new parish, he took along a larger and better nucleus for the volunteer choir. Or better yet, a director. That talent ran in the family, too. Father was leading "the message in song" at a church conference in Santa Cruz when he met Nelle, and later, while finishing his studies at

Jim, Anne, Reverend Shaw, John, Nelle, Robert, and
Holly

Robert, Nelle, and John in the mid-forties. Photograph by Robert C. Frampton

Pomona College, he directed the choir at the same church in Glendora where Robert and the next two children earned part of their college expenses in the same capacity, their twenty-five-dollar-a-month salaries donated by a longtime friend of the family.

Undoubtedly the family musical experiences honed all the young Shaws' innate sensitivities to pitch and balance, which in turn once tempted Robert into a rather sophisticated musical prank. At a church choir rehearsal in Ontario he and Jim deliberately tormented the youth sitting between them by taking turns singing sharp and flat, frustrating their victim to utter exasperation and bringing the rehearsal to a halt. Word of the dastardly deed reached father Shaw. The next day Robert cornered Charley Ross, the director, and explained that there was a crucial high school football game that afternoon and if Mr. Ross didn't accept the brothers' apologies for breaking up the choir rehearsal their father wouldn't let them attend. A few hours later, Robert was in the grandstand leading the cheers.

More often, Robert put his "extraordinary authority of manner" to constructive use. On the last day of junior high school in Eagle Rock, when his history teacher had some urgent paper work to finish, he led the class in songs, keeping all thirty-five restless teen-agers under complete control for a solid fifty minutes. Still later, when attending religious conferences at Asilomar on the Monterey Peninsula, he would herd the delegates together for rock-ringing sing-alongs. One of his cohorts with a voice powerful enough to match his leadership was John Raitt, who twenty years later was to star on Broadway as Billy in Rodgers and Hammerstein's *Carousel*.

Intermittently Robert acquired some formal training in music. He played drums in junior high, and during his high school years in Ontario he received a few voice lessons from Charley Ross in return for his participation in the church choir. But regular lessons were clearly impractical, with Father making a scant $200 a month. "All the churches of my early growing up were, I suppose, poor churches, with Wednesday evening suppers and Friday evening movies. . . . It seemed to me quite natural that a good deal of emphasis should be placed on Heaven, for certainly, for a lot of people—of which we were not nearly the least blest—there was precious little to be had hereabouts. I suppose I took it for granted that salvation was assuagement for poverty."

To be sure, a clergyman's lot was hardly prosperous even in the comparatively affluent years before the Depression, and after the Crash it deteriorated precipitously. The Shaw family cultivated the knack of sublimating as many earthly desires as possible, and wills were tested by leaving the collection box open in the house. You took from it what you needed, but if you were wise you first petitioned for divine guidance and then consulted the rest of the family. "One morning I couldn't stand it any more. I sneaked a dollar out. I bought silver bells and sour balls and wieners and just ate and ate. I guess I spent my twelfth, thirteenth, and half of my fourteenth year sweating that out of my conscience."

As soon as he graduated from high school Robert went to work in a bakery, wrapping bread ten to twelve hours a day, for $6.12 a week. He soon switched to a better job in a steel mill, where his $6.50 pay check just covered the cost of breakfast for the seven-member family for a week. After the National Industrial Recovery Act was launched in 1933, a new job assembling electric irons almost doubled his salary. "I got twelve dollars a week," he recalls, "and, as they say in New York, some change." And his work week was down to forty-eight hours.

All the children grew up with an affinity for Father's pulpit, seizing every available opportunity to read scripture from its lofty vantage, reveling as much in the resonant poetry of the Good Book as in its comfort and inspiration. Under the Reverend Shaw's coaching the boys' suasive skills were also cultivated, so that by the time Robert was out of high school he could toss off a prize-winning oration on "What It Means to be Human" or a frivolous defense of profanity entitled " 'Damns of Distinction' or 'Cusses that Count.' "

The first of the young Shaws to spin off into orbit was Holly. After graduating from Pomona she entered a radio "amateur hour" and won a contract with the CBS network. Radio was the perfect medium for a singer who, like her mother, could convey a mood purely through the tone of her voice, and she quickly rose to stardom. On through the forties she was heard successively as "Vivien" on the "Hour of Charm" with Phil Spitalny and his All-Girl Orchestra, on CBS's weekly "Invitation to Music," on the "Saturday Night Serenade," and on many special broadcasts. In addition, she was a frequent headliner at Radio City Music Hall. In 1939 she played a leading role in Jerome Kern's musical *Very Warm for May*. The show was something less than a hit, but it contained one of the best ballads of the decade, "All the Things You Are," which Holly sang so beautifully that Kern said he felt as if he had written it especially for her.

When Robert matriculated at Pomona in 1934 he entered an environment more yeasty than that which Holly had encountered. Dubbed "the Oxford of the West," Pomona had been founded in 1888 as a college of the New England type, dedicated to the liberal arts and guided in general by Christian principles. By the midthirties, however, it was jumping with issues, full of speeches, meetings, and leaflets—hardly the frivolous playground for the idle or the rich depicted by Hollywood in movies like *Varsity Show*.

Robert was thrust among a generation of young men and women who were inclined to regard the Great Depression not as the mortal agony of "the American Way of Life" but rather as an evolutionary cataclysm through which society could be purged of its outworn habits—the ushering in of an era of challenge and opportunity. The experimental ideas being churned up by the New Deal were making a powerful impression on the undergraduate mind, and "social consciousness" was the popular catch-phrase of the day. He wasn't interested in political strategies but his passions were aroused by the moral and ethical issues implicit in them.

Politics, teaching, or other careers that offered opportunities to serve one's country or to mold future generations were most attractive to college students of the thirties. The Christian ministry was a somewhat less desirable calling, not only because of its financial insecurity but also because institutional religion was at odds with the prevailing atmosphere of religious liberalism.

At vesper services in the college chapel at Pomona, the Sermon on the Mount might give way to Robinson Jeffers's "Roan Stallion" in order to emphasize the contrast between civilized lusts and the power and beauty of nature, to the imagery of Emily Dickinson to illustrate the relationship between the natural and the spiritual orders of being, or to Sandburg's *The People, Yes* to point up the divinity of the common man.

In the classroom, William James's *Varieties of Religious Experience* was apt to be supplanted by Hartley Burr Alexander's *God and Man's Destiny*, in which "the primary dogmas of Christian teaching are shown to make sense in modern thought and to have reality in modern life, and in modes supported rather than disputed by the sciences of nature and the progress of historical understanding."

Alexander was in his final and physically declining years as professor of philosophy at Scripps College in the latter thirties.

One recalls strange fragments of classroom experience.

I can remember one lecture in which he called to our attention the metaphysical reflections of the numbers and functions of man's anatomical members: decimal systems, decalogues, Unity, Duality, and Trinity. It was then that I perceived that if man only had been born three-legged, "Onward, Christian Soldiers" would have been a waltz.

On another occasion when I was questioning a near failing grade on a paper which had caused me more concern and effort to greater accomplishment, I felt, than anything in my college experience, he replied gently, "Mr. Shaw, you must have misunderstood the assignment. You were asked to write on 'What is Christianity?' Not 'What does it mean to you?' and not 'What do you think it ought to be?'"

On a later essay, Professor Alexander wrote: "I am impressed by your thinking, and like perhaps equally well both its puzzles and its insights. Certainly you go directly to central problems."

Only gradually did Robert become aware that his faith was being winnowed from his religion. Only little by painful little did it dawn on him that when you entered his father's church to profess your love for the Lord thy God, you checked your mind at the door.

It used to bother me that I couldn't understand the argument of the sermons. I couldn't find a subject, predicate, and object within any appreciable area of adjacency.

In my childhood church I do not think I ever heard a sermon in which the preacher did not stop, his voice broken by his own emotion, to wipe away a tear or blow his nose. Almost always they ended, "Won't you come? He is waiting.... Softly and tenderly ... while we sing the last verse ... Won't you come?"

About that time God began to die. He'd been made that way; and every time the Christ was whittled down by common sense or natural science or not-really-so-ancient history, God died a little.

Actually, to Robert's way of thinking it was not God but the institutional church that was dying; God was only undergoing a kind of shape-shifting, and by sheer force of intellect the emerging image could be fixed and informed with spirit.

What with his demanding curriculum, his volunteer pastoral work, and his part-time jobs—in the commissary or grading papers for the department of religion—he had little leisure for recreation. Once in a while he played tennis. In his junior year he won a fullback's slot on the football team—though he had never played the game before—only to have his nose broken early in the season. He was a strong and graceful swimmer, but holidays at oceanside were rare.

Robert could have acquired as good a musical background at Pomona as at any other first-rate liberal arts college. Having boasted a school of music since 1893, the college offered its nine hundred students, plus registrants from Claremont and Scripps colleges, instruction in applied music, music history, theory, composition, orchestration, and music education. There were two mixed choruses, two glee clubs, a band and an orchestra, and the calendar was crowded with performances by those groups as well as solo recitals and chamber music concerts. In addition, the musical environment was enriched with concerts by stars like Lily Pons or Joseph Szigeti, the Vienna Choir Boys, the Don Cossack Male Chorus, or the Los Angeles Philharmonic. But the only musical pastime Robert indulged in regularly was singing with the prize-winning Men's Glee Club.

Shaw quickly assimilated the disciplines of radio broadcasting and learned to operate within the technological limitations of the medium. For instance, the system would not respond well to sudden and extreme contrasts in loudness, nor would it transmit fortissimo singing without distortion, so a carefully modulated succession of dynamic levels within the scope of pianissimo to mezzo forte had to be maintained. Moreover, both the standard RCA-44 microphone and the average home receiver carried bass and mid-range frequencies best, so shrillness of tone had to be avoided.

Waring's arrangers were producing scores in five to eight or more parts, often extending from low D-flat in the bass part to high B-flat in the tenor, plus three-part female obbligatos, or "punctuation," in a pyramidal sonority. Shaw was thus forced to sharpen his already acute capacity for aural discrimination in order to assure that every note of every chord was perfectly balanced with respect to both loudness and color. To provide continuity of timbre and volume, especially in the baritone and second tenor lines, he frequently called upon "roving" voices in each section to reinforce a few notes in an adjacent part.

In the early broadcasts by the Glee Club, when they were mostly singing published four-part choral compositions from traditional repertoire, the men stood in the time-honored formation with all first tenors together next to the entire second tenor section, and so on. One microphone was placed above the group, fifteen to twenty-five feet away, to assure the best pickup. But this did not provide ideal balance between the chorus and the band, so another microphone was placed within six feet of the singers, making the problem of balance within the chorus still more critical. The show originated from the Vanderbilt Theater, and Waring would monitor rehearsals by direct line from his office at 1697 Broadway, advising Shaw which voices to move closer to the mike or farther from it. It didn't matter if the singers in each section were separated from one another so long as the sound that came over the air was the one Waring wanted listeners to hear.

It is regrettable that we cannot aurally retrace the evolution of the Shaw-Waring sound during the first five years, but no commercial recordings exist. Waring had recorded some 265 tunes between 1923 and 1932, but he discovered that they were being used by small independent radio stations to compete with his own live network shows. When legal efforts failed to stop the practice, Waring quit making records for nearly ten years. The only way to hear new arrangements by the Pennsylvanians on radio was to listen to their live broadcasts. As a result, they became one of the highest-paid groups in the industry.

In the spring of 1939 Waring farmed out Shaw to producer Billy Rose to prepare a chorus for the water spectacular *Aquacade*, starring Eleanor Holm, at the New York World's Fair, and to teach the "aquabelles" to swim in time to the music. "What was funny," Shaw once said, "was that while drying myself off after rehearsals I always got the most remarkable ideas for sermons!"

No sooner had that show opened than the Pennsylvanians' broadcasting was stepped up to a year-round schedule. On June 19 CBS premiered the first "Pleasure Time" show, sponsored by Chesterfield cigarettes. The fifteen-minute program, aired five nights a week in the time slot opposite NBC's popular comedy "Amos 'n' Andy," was performed once for the East and Midwest, and again an hour later for West Coast listeners. Within a year the show was commanding one of the largest audiences in the history of American broadcasting and was named the finest quarter-hour in radio by the National Poll of Radio Editors. "Pleasure Time" was on the air continuously for the next five years.

Although radio listeners seldom heard Robert Shaw's name, his reputation as a choral conductor was well known and respected in professional circles. Still, he was extremely self-conscious about his lack of formal training in music. The demands of a daily broadcasting schedule allowed no time for the cultivation of a choral "method"; all technique was but a matter of expediency and had to arise out of the music itself. He felt he had to work twice as hard as his singers in order to use their talents to capacity and to meet Waring's exacting standards, and thus his job consumed nearly all his time and energy. Yet he was no drudge, and he occasionally found time to enjoy himself in the company of his friend and college classmate Jake Jaqua, an aspirant to the New York business world.

Jake's sister, Eleanor, and Hollace Shaw were then sharing an apartment with a tall, dark, snappy-eyed girl named Maxine Farley, a graduate of George Washington University currently employed as a "very junior executive" in table linens at Macy's department store. Maxine's first meeting with the young musician didn't inspire instant affection, for Bob and Jake entered the apartment on all fours, barking like dogs. But there was an unmistakable attraction between the two, and an intense courtship followed. A few weeks later Robert borrowed Jake's fraternity pin to seal the engagement, and in October of 1939 he and Maxine were married. Together they paid off his loan at Pomona College, and when Billy Rose sent Bob to San Francisco in the spring of 1940 to prepare another *Aquacade* for the World's Fair there, the Shaws stayed on through most of the summer while course-work for a bachelor's degree was completed.

Back in New York even Robert's social life was usually connected with music. He joined The Lambs, America's oldest and most celebrated theatrical club, at the suggestion of Fred Waring, who was then president. He immediately organized a glee club of fifty of the members to entertain at the club's "Gambols." In April of 1941 the Lambs Glee Club, with Broadway composer Frederick Loewe as accompanist, presented its first annual spring concert. Repertoire extended from classics like "Onward Ye Peoples," by the Finnish composer Jean Sibelius, to arrangements of popular tunes like Hoagy Carmichael's "Star Dust" and Jerome Kern's "All the Things You Are."

Waring always stressed youthfulness in personnel and programming. He carefully cultivated a "collegiate" image for the Pennsylvanians and frequently dedicated his broadcasts to specific colleges or universities, including in each instance one of the school's traditional songs. When Colby College in Maine wrote asking him to compose a song especially for them, he was quick to oblige and subsequently announced that he would be willing to do the same for any other school. He and his staff of composers and arrangers were flooded with more than 350 requests, and they managed to satisfy nearly a hundred of them. In 1941 Shaw helped write a new fight song for his alma mater, which was sung on "Pleasure Time" during Pomona's homecoming weekend.

High school choral conductors listened to "Pleasure Time" with special interest. Radio had become an important performance outlet for their groups. Home-grown talent was proudly aired by every local station, and some of the best choirs in the nation were invited to appear on the network series "Music and American Youth," sponsored by the Music Educators National Conference under the supervision of Peter Dykema.

But few of them were equipped to cope with the peculiarities of the medium. No matter how enthusiastically a performance might be applauded in the school auditorium, it was apt to be a comparative failure when heard through a loudspeaker. Even the most skillful studio engineer was unable to capture the concert-hall ambience that relied heavily on the visual charm of youthful singers.

Waring's style made it sound easy. Although conservative educators like Noble Cain deplored the "strange harmonies" and the "unvocal habit" of prolonging m's and n's, high school choral conductors began to adopt some of the more easily imitated features

The San Francisco *Aquacade* Glee Club

Conducting the first Fred Waring choral clinic. Photograph by Ray Levitt

of the Glee Club's style and begged Waring to share more of his ideas with them.

Shaw and Waring discussed possibilities for extending the Pennsylvanians' operations into the educational field. Waring established a publishing company, Words and Music, Inc. (later Shawnee Press), to meet the demand for editions of the choral arrangements made famous by the Glee Club. The first catalog contained several contributions by Shaw, including a lullaby, "Sleep, Baby, Sleep," and the perennially successful spiritual "Set Down, Servant." Waring also began inviting local conductors to bring their choirs to his production studios, where he would coach them in the fundamentals of his choral technique. Finally, one of his chief assistants, Ennis Davis, suggested extending the invitation throughout the country, and in the spring of 1945 the first three-day choral clinic for conductors was held in New York, with Shaw as the principal clinician.

The annual clinics were so successful that a series of week-long summer workshops was set up near Waring's estate, Shawnee-on-Delaware, in Pennsylvania. Before long the curriculum had to be expanded to embrace elementary education methods, church music, piano, band, and orchestra. Shaw was a key person in Waring's plans for expansion, but when he left for the Navy in April of 1945, he terminated his contract with the Waring organization and never renewed it.

2.

The Collegiate Chorale:
"A Melting Pot That Sings"

BY THE SPRING of 1940, Robert was growing restive. Rehearsing several hours a day, week after week, he had discovered more about choral technique than he could have learned at any music school in the world. On the other hand, his abilities as well as his sensibilities now exceeded both the demands and the rewards of the repertoire he had to work with, and he was strongly impelled to reach out in new directions.

He decided to try to apply his technique to music of a different kind, and in the fall of 1941 organized a Chapel Choir of twenty-five professional singers who were interested in performing sacred choral music. The eleven women included his sister, Holly, and Patricia Neway, who ten years hence was to star on Broadway as Magda in Gian-Carlo Menotti's opera *The Consul*. Among the men, mostly Waring Glee Club members, were Don Craig, Paul Owen, and Gordon Berger.

The Chapel Choir's first public concert took place November 16 on the Tuesday evening recital series at the Barbizon, a sedate hotel for women on 59th Street across from Central Park. The program consisted of motets by Vlockmar Leisring, Tomás Luis de Victoria, Alexander Gretchaninov, and Johannes Brahms; some folk songs; and some Negro spirituals. A special feature was the first performance of an anthem, "I will lift up mine eyes unto the hills," by

Frank Cunkle, organist and choirmaster at All Angels' Episcopal Church in Manhattan. To mollify listeners stricken with the current taste in Protestant church music Shaw included the saccharine Latvian hymn "My God and I."

The Chapel Choir never sang together again, for Robert had already become engrossed in a new enterprise that was consuming every bit of his spare time and energy. Gordon Berger, formerly director of choral organizations at the University of Oklahoma, had moved to New York early in 1941 to join Waring's Pennsylvanians. Purely for the fun of it, he had started a community chorus of about sixty young singers at Norman Vincent Peale's Marble Collegiate Church. In September Berger invited Shaw to guest conduct one number on a concert, and Shaw instantly became so enthusiastic about the group that Berger offered to share with him the job of developing it. Together they decided on a new name for the group—The Collegiate Chorale. Properly speaking, the word *collegiate* in the church's name referred to a collegium of ministers, not an educational institution, and the noun *chorale* denoted the tune of a German Lutheran hymn, but the phrase sounded youthful and euphonious, and it was different enough to attract attention.

Berger and Shaw set out to recruit more members. On October 7 they placed a two-line ad in the newspapers announcing auditions at the Waring studios. At the same time Shaw sent a letter—on Waring's stationery—to local alumni of the "all-city" choruses conducted annually by Peter Wilhousky, supervisor of vocal music in the public schools:

> Under the sponsorship of the Marble Collegiate Church of Manhattan, I have undertaken the responsibility of forming and directing the Collegiate Chorale, a mixed choir of one hundred fifty young singers, amateur and professional, to be selected by competitive auditions.
>
> The purpose of the Collegiate Chorale is the development of artistry and musicianship among its members, as well as the pleasure it may afford them and their audiences. Its attention will be very largely directed to the a cappella literature of the Christian tradition. But, in addition, there will be an emphasis upon contemporary American music, with reference to radio techniques, modern interpretations, and the general artistic demands of the field of professional entertainment.

Lured by what appeared to be an invitation from Fred Waring, nearly 500 people showed up for the auditions. Using the same meticulous procedure he had employed in selecting singers for the Glee Club, and applying only slightly less rigorous standards, Shaw finally chose 185 of them.

One of the most conspicuous features of the Chorale was the proportions among the sections: three basses for every two tenors, three altos for every two sopranos, and twenty more men than women. Another was its youth: ages ranged from seventeen to seventy, but the average was twenty-six. Shaw was immensely proud. He could tell it was potentially "a very hot musical instrument."

Rehearsals got under way on a Monday evening early in November. Shaw waded into the music with the same intensity that had inspired his fledgling Glee Club only three years before. Sweat rolling down his face, stripped to undershirt, baggy trousers and stockinged feet, he raced on at the frenzied pace of a revivalist. By the end of the first hour the church fairly trembled at the roar of sound that arose from the undercroft. By the end of the rehearsal the charismatic current that flowed between conductor and chorus had ignited a spirit so volatile that everyone must have sensed they were attending the birth of an epoch.

After the second rehearsal Dr. Peale summoned Shaw and presented a few requests in behalf of the Consistory: Trim the group to 100 members; be sure that fifty percent are members of the Marble Collegiate Church; drop the Catholics, the Jews, and the Negroes; and . . . oh, yes, kindly refrain from profanity during rehearsals.

Shaw hadn't given a thought to the racial and religious diversity of the group until Dr. Peale mentioned it, whereupon it struck him as a rather admirable thing. He and his flock abruptly moved, name and all, to more hospitable quarters. "This shall be for music" was their motto. "These songs for love of singing!"

After rehearsals Shaw and a few of the gang would bound off down the street to the nearest late-night beanery for a lively postmortem over sandwiches and beer. The talk was always about the music, the music, the music. It took Robert hours to come down from the emotional high. He felt he had to find a way to inspire every member of the Chorale with the spirit of these informal sessions. Late on the night of Monday, December 8, 1941, he dashed off a letter to the members.

Although the nation had been plunged into war scarcely thirty-six hours before, it was to be "business as usual" for the Collegiate Chorale. Robert encouraged his singers to study their scores in advance of the next rehearsal, and reminded them that Fred Waring was personally interested in their progress. He spelled out the words to all their Christmas pieces in "tone-syllable" fashion— "bray-ee kfo-uh tho-oo bee-oo-tee-uh sevN-LiL Lah-eet, aN duh-shuh riN THuhM Mo-uhrN-NeeNG"—and enclosed instructions on how to practice.

> I figured it might be well if you could see the lyrics of all our Christmas music blocked out in a modified sort of phonetic pro-nunciation, on the theory that what you know won't hurt you, and time's gettin' short, and Waring'll be at rehearsal probably next week, and here it is Thursday.
> H-oh-ool-dee-oo-uhr ha tseer roo-ee goh-oo !!!
>
> bah bshaw

This was the first of a series of almost weekly letters to the Chorale, many of them beginning with the salutation "Dear People."

The Chorale's first engagement was a broadcast of Christmas music over the NBC network on December 21, 1941. Little notice was taken of it, for the nation was still in the grip of emotional aftershock from the Japanese attack on Pearl Harbor.

> December 22, 1941
> I don't feel at all evangelistic about it, but I am pretty convinced that there is a considerable place for a group like yours in a time like this.—And I do not refer to the implementing of political morale.
> What I have hazily in mind is this: The next few years may prove to be pretty brutal.—And if somewhere during that time there is a group of 200 young people with—let us say—a real devotion to great music and flawless artistry, and with the sensitivity which music such as we sang yesterday demands, a group capable of responding to the less tempestuous virtues, with over all a feel-ing of friendliness and reasonable human regard—that is pretty important.
> I'd like to feel that the Collegiate Chorale helped to preserve those attitudes in the days of *our* years.
>
> Sincerely,
> Bob Shaw

A couple of short private engagements took place in January and February, with no response from the critics. In professional circles, however, word quickly got around that a new star was aborning in the constellation of New York choral organizations. Influential people began visiting rehearsals to see what was going on. Leon Barzin invited the Chorale to sing with the National Orchestral Association in March, and Leopold Stokowski booked them for an appearance with the NBC Symphony under his direction in April.

The Collegiate Chorale's first official public appearance took place at the Riverside Congregational Church on Sunday, March 8, 1942. That morning Robert led the chancel choir in F. Melius Christiansen's arrangement of "Beautiful Saviour" and Will Mc-Farlane's creaking Mendelssohnian anthem, "Ho, Everyone that thirsteth." At the vesper service that afternoon the resident choir joined with the Collegiate Chorale in two excerpts from Bach's *Christmas Oratorio*, while the Chorale's own program consisted of Tom Scott's arrangement of John Jacob Niles's "I am a poor wayfarin' stranger," Franz Wasner's arrangement of "Angels we have heard on high," Christiansen's piece again, and Shaw's own setting of the hymn "Sun of my soul." Also sung were Vlockmar Leisring's "Lift up your heads, O ye gates;" "Corpus Christi," by the twentieth-century Englishman Peter Warlock; and "Here is thy footstool," by the American composer Paul Creston. Again the press was indifferent.

The appearance with the National Orchestral Association on March 28, however, was definitely newsworthy. The concert was part of Barzin's annual "Winners Series," featuring recipients of prizes in composition and solo performance. It opened with a Bach chorale prelude transcribed by Ernest Lubin, recipient of the Joseph Bearns Prize in composition. Arthur Carron, recent winner of the Metropolitan Opera Auditions of the Air, sang an aria from *Hiawatha's Wedding Feast*, by the British Negro composer Samuel Coleridge-Taylor. The orchestra played *Pastorale and Tarantella*, composed in 1941 by Paul Creston, and the Chorale sang the same composer's *Three Chorales from Tagore*. The climax of the concert was the premiere of Charles Haubiel's dramatic cantata, *The Vision of St. Joan*, by the orchestra, the Chorale, and the St. Thomas Choir.

The critics' most enthusiastic comments were reserved for the Collegiate Chorale. Francis Perkins of the *Herald Tribune* wrote: "The Collegiate Choir [perhaps he couldn't bring himself to misuse the word *chorale*] was formed last November with the aim of giving non-professional singers an opportunity to gain choral experience and training corresponding to those of professional organizations. Judging by yesterday's singing, Mr. Shaw has fulfilled his purpose with noteworthy success." Noel Strauss of the *Times* remarked that the Chorale had "reaped prolonged ovation for its remarkable singing, characterized by exceptional freshness and purity of tone, fine balance and blending, sharp attacks and releases, sensitive treatment of nuance, and rare expressiveness." *PM*'s Henry Simon was elated. "Robert Shaw conducted in a violent and unconventional manner," he said, but "made it at once apparent that here is a new, major chorus."

The critics confirmed their initial judgments after the NBC Symphony broadcast on April 14, when the Chorale and the Eva Jessye Choir sang William Grant Still's *And They Lynched Him on a Tree*. Stokowski, who also conducted the Chorale and orchestra in excerpts from *Boris Godunov*, wrote Shaw a note of appreciation: "I am deeply impressed by what you have done as a conductor and by the ideal spirit that is in your chorus. . . . You have an entirely new approach to choral music, which gives everything you do freshness and originality. It is fundamentally different from the conventional chorus singing and conducting, and brings out new beauties and new expressiveness in the music."

The cumulative excitement aroused by the first few performances of the Collegiate Chorale was so overwhelming that neither audiences nor critics concerned themselves much with the precise methods Shaw used to bring it about. Among the Chorale members, though, were many who had studied or were currently studying voice, and, given the disparity of pedagogies they represented, Shaw could hardly avoid antagonizing some of them at one time or another. Having encountered that problem before, in the early days of the Glee Club, he had learned that it is unwise to tamper with a trained singer's vocal technique, and he tried to avoid any such implications. Nevertheless, some of the Chorale members were bound to become defensive about their own pet theories, so Shaw wrote them all a letter to set the record straight, and to suggest that he was planning to compound the intellectual diversity of the organization by introducing more of the same.

April 15, 1942

Just in case—

The Collegiate Chorale operates on the assumption that in matters of music and artistry, its members are sufficiently imaginative and intelligent to seek a complete catholicity of theories and techniques—no matter how widely divergent—and make an evaluation which is at least individual and aware of other points of view.

The point is that we're interested in developing minds, not reflexes; creative artists, not automatons. And so we need a department of hot and cold, not a department of lukewarm. That's democracy, and it's pretty important these days.

Knowledge may be a dangerous thing; but that's no reason to inoculate oneself against it. Love, I hear tell, is dynamite; but nobody dodges *it*.

I say this because it would be too bad if anyone should carry the idea that the Collegiate Chorale was sponsoring a vocal heresy. The only thing the Collegiate Chorale sponsors is *dramatic integrity*; that happy condition which exists when choral tone fulfills—not limits—the text and spirit of song. Neither weight lifting nor watchmaking is the concern of our singing—but mood and meaning.

Shaw was determined to make the Collegiate Chorale more than just the best amateur chorus in the country. He set in motion a broad educational program, assisted by a few of his close friends and associates. Gordon Berger taught a course in ear-training and sight-singing; Frank Cunkle, organist and choirmaster at All Angels' Episcopal Church (whom Shaw had asked to compose a cantata on passages from Sandburg's *The People, Yes*), offered a course in music theory. Leo Rosenek coached German lieder, and Elemar Nagy, opera staging. Lectures were scheduled by prominent New York critics such as Henry Simon of *PM* and Robert Lawrence of the *Herald Tribune*. Andrew Summers, a folk song collector and dulcimer player, spoke on "How to Sing an American Folk Song." There was a rotating plan whereby the men of the Chorale—one from each section, in groups of four—might attend the daily rehearsals of the Waring Glee Club, sit in with the professionals, and perhaps even sing with them on the broadcast of that particular day. Shaw promised "for all incipient arrangers and composers in the Chorale, the printing and performance of any works which establish their distinction and worth." Finally, he announced, "if you wish it—I am prepared to form a sort of 'Varsity Choir' of thirty-two members, chosen by competitive auditions every six months from among the general Chorale membership, to do additional work in advanced choral fields."

On May 30 Fred Waring held the final competition in his nation-wide college male glee club contest, and the Collegiate Chorale made a guest appearance. Once again they stole the show. "Coming on toward midnight," wrote Henry Simon, "with only serious music after a long, light program, they got more shouts and whistles of approval than even the Pennsylvanians themselves."

Soon after the United States entered the war, the *Musical Courier* editorialized that "the American credo, as it will be increasingly and ever more strongly voiced by the united people of this country, as it is given greater incisiveness by being allied with music, promises to carry its message even to the ears of enslaved nations. They are eagerly waiting for such reassurances, and the musician— when it is all over and the final results are tabulated—may be found to have made one of the most potent contributions to the winning of freedom."

Service bands, orchestras, and choruses were organized, often with combinations of talents that could not have occurred otherwise. They boosted morale on military bases and, via radio broadcasts, inspired the folks on the home front as well as men and women overseas. Civilian amateur and professional musicians provided free concerts at the camps and in USO centers; symphony orchestras and concert managers offered free or reduced-rate tickets to service men and women. Altogether, more Americans were being exposed to more music than ever before.

Naturally, professional musical activity was subjected to certain hardships. Taxes were imposed on concert tickets, and wartime assessments reduced the abilities of major guarantors to support orchestras and opera companies. Rationing on a "points" system of commodities such as fuel and tires limited the mobility of audiences; strictures on rail and air travel affected the schedules of touring artists.

Almost daily, organizations like the Collegiate Chorale lost men to the draft and women to jobs in industries. Shaw could not predict from one rehearsal to the next what the makeup of the group would be. On top of that, requests to help out in the war effort quickened the Chorale's schedule to a burdensome pace: a Mac-Arthur Day–Flag Day Rally in Central Park Mall on June 14; a broadcast for the Greater New York War Bond Pledge Campaign on June 21; another broadcast for the Federal Security Agency's "I Hear America Singing" series on July 5; a war-industry awards celebration at Madison Square Garden early in August.

Although letters poured in, effusive with praise, Shaw sensed an approaching crisis. "Frankly," he replied to one correspondent, "I was rather chagrined at the performance of the choir. We may have assayed too much and too difficult music in too short a time. At any rate, while I felt the program did have a dramatic unity and some moments of excitement and inspiration, the choral standard was considerably below that which we have set for ourselves. I shall not make that mistake again." Early in July he remarked to the Chorale that after eight short months of its existence only 58 of the original 83 women, and 33 of the original 102 men were still with the organization. New members were added regularly, but since performances crowded out rehearsals there was seldom a time when all the singers knew all the music.

It was more than just a matter of the performance schedule, the turnover in personnel, or the difficulty of the music. In mid-July, determined to infuse the organization with a new sense of identity and purpose, he analyzed the situation.

> The setup is universal: Boy meets girl, birds sing, papers are signed and inaugurate the delirious days of delight. But in a week or two weeks, a month or two months, a year or two years—depending upon the relative vitalities—there passes the first "fine free careless rapture," and with its passing ends a very romantic and beautiful thing. (Of course it does not pass forever. Its return is occasional and probably most welcome. But—this "fine free careless rapture" cannot be depended upon to assume the full responsibility of the companionship.) And at this point one of two things happens: (1) The marriage falls apart or (2) the people discover more permanent bases for their relationship. And these latter bases are the product of reason and profound spiritual intuition, and very often realized only after considerable personal travail.

Well, something like that has happened to the Collegiate Chorale. The first all-embracing flush of passion is about spent; and right now is the time when we discover whether that was all we ever had, and fold—or whether our union is more fundamentally based and gives promise of further development.

Then he outlined several "maturing purposes and ends" for the Chorale. One was "the complete exploitation of the choral instrument" in terms of musical discipline, technique, and style. Another was "by performance of the distinguished musical literature of other peoples and other times to disclose to American audiences the strains which go to make the American culture and the broader human culture." But the most important was "the discovery and performance of worthy new American choral music."

I had no idea six months ago that this would come to be one of the major aims for the choir's existence. So it's an idea pretty new to my thinking—but solidly embedded.

The function and future of the Collegiate Chorale, he said, was implicit in its very makeup.

I conceive the Chorale's purpose to be considerably broader than any of the comparable choral organizations. And the fundamental difference hinges around the absolutely unique parallel of our choir to the motley straining virile bottled "giant" that is the American people.

You see, we're a sort of musical montage,
A melting pot that sings. . . .

Half of us speak two languages because
the mothers and fathers of two thirds of us
were born in foreign countries.

You could count on the fingers of one hand
the states we don't come from.

If you're looking for democracy
set to music
The Collegiate Chorale . . . that's us
We're it.

The moment when Shaw and the Collegiate Chorale set out to advance the cause of American choral music was an auspicious one, made so by conditions that had been evolving for half a cen-

". . . a melting pot that sings"

tury or more. By the early 1940s there were nearly two hundred music schools in the United States, the majority of which had been established since the turn of the century. Colleges and universities of all sizes were granting degrees in performance and music education, and most were offering courses in composition. Classic European models were the pattern for more than two dozen major independent conservatories, such as the David Mannes School of Music in New York, the Cleveland Institute of Music, and the San Francisco Conservatory. Among the largest and most renowned of the conservatories were those created by individual benefactors: The Institute of Musical Art in New York, established under Frank Damrosch in 1904 with a bequest of $500,000 from banker James Loeb; the Juilliard Graduate School, established in 1920 with a $20-million gift from cotton merchant August Juilliard; the Eastman School of Music, founded in 1921 with a $4.5-million gift from inventor and industrialist George Eastman; and the Curtis Institute of Music in Philadelphia, built by Mrs. Mary Louise Curtis Bok Zimbalist and named in memory of her father, publisher Cyrus Curtis.

A number of important composition departments were staffed by leading American teacher-composers—Roy Harris at Juilliard, Howard Hanson and Bernard Rogers at Eastman, Walter Piston at Harvard, Charles Haubiel at New York University—many of whom were alumni of Nadia Boulanger's classes at the American Conservatory at Fontainebleau near Paris. There was an even larger number of Europeans, some of whom were more respected for the rigor and discipline of their teaching methods than for the worthiness of their own compositions. There were Italians like Rosario Scalero, who taught at the Mannes School and then at Curtis, and Giuseppe Randegger, who directed the Atlanta Musical Club from 1893 to 1897, taught at colleges in Kentucky and Tennessee, and finally opened his own conservatory in New York City. There were Adolf Schmid from Germany, Gaston Dethier from Belgium, and Bernard Wagenaar from Holland, each of whom taught at Juilliard at one time or another. Ernest Bloch of Switzerland, the first director of the Cleveland Institute, taught at the San Francisco Conservatory in the late twenties. In another ten years or so graduate music education in America was topped off by the arrival of a new contingent of Europeans, refugees from the totalitarian juggernaut: Ernst Toch, Paul Hindemith, Darius Milhaud, Arnold Schoenberg, Béla Bartók, and the Russian composer Arthur Lourié; Felix Wolfes left Germany in 1938 and became assistant conductor at the Metropolitan Opera House. And Julius Herford of Berlin, who was to play a major role in Shaw's career, was stranded here in 1939.

The first beneficiaries of the country's thriving new educational institutions were the aspirant composers born shortly before or after World War I. Some were native New Yorkers, like William

Schuman, Paul Creston, and Norman Dello Joio, but others were drawn there from the far corners of the country and beyond, like Samuel Barber of Westchester, Peter Mennin of Erie, Pennsylvania, Charles Bryan of McMinnville, Tennessee, Gail Kubik of Coffeyville, Kansas, and Henry Brant of Montreal, Quebec. There were also several refugees among them—Lukas Foss's parents left Berlin with their fifteen-year-old son in 1937, the same year that young Jacob Avshalomov, born in China of Russian parents, fled from the Japanese invasion of Manchuria.

Schuman studied with Schmid and Wagenaar, Haubiel and Harris; Dello Joio was tutored by his godfather, the Italian immigrant Pietro Yon, as well as by Wagenaar and Hindemith; Creston studied with Randegger, Dethier, and Yon; Foss resumed his studies under Herford and also worked with Scalero and Hindemith. Bryan received most of his education at the Nashville, Tennessee, Conservatory of Music, and Kubik was a graduate of the American Conservatory in Chicago.

Few could make their livelihoods as composers, so most entered the teaching profession. Schuman taught first at Sarah Lawrence College. When he left in 1945 to assume the presidency of the newly reorganized Juilliard School, Dello Joio took his place. At Juilliard Schuman hired Brant and Mennin—and Shaw. Foss was staff pianist for the Boston Symphony Orchestra from 1944 until 1950, and Creston spent his entire career, from 1934 on, as organist at St. Malachy's Catholic Church in New York. In 1947 Bryan went to Peabody to teach, and Avshalomov went to Columbia University.

Meanwhile they vied for honors: Creston, Schuman, Foss, and Dello Joio won Guggenheim fellowships; Barber and Mennin received the prestigious Joseph H. Bearns Prize for composition; Foss and Avshalomov won the New York Critics Circle Award; others gained a measure of prestige, and occasionally a little money, from awards from organizations such as the National Federation of Music Clubs and its affiliates.

Most important of all were opportunities to be heard and to be tested in the refining fire of public audition. Commissions from such agencies as the League of Composers, the Alice M. Ditson Fund, the Koussevitzky, Juilliard, and Coolidge foundations, or from the few orchestras and ballet companies that had the resources for it, were especially coveted, for they assured that a work would be performed, and perhaps reviewed, by professionals. From 1936 to 1941 the CBS Radio Network sponsored the Columbia Composers Commission, underwriting six new concert works each year to fulfill a need for music expressly tailored to the acoustical and temporal limitations of the medium.

The Federal Music Project of the Four Arts Program was established in 1935 under the aegis of the Works Progress Administration, and throughout the six years of its existence hundreds of new compositions by Americans were premiered by WPA "relief" orchestras throughout the country. In 1940 New York's municipal radio station, WNYC, initiated an annual American Music Festival, occupying most of the available air time during the eleven days between Lincoln's and Washington's birthdays; for ten years, the works of as many as fifty different American composers were programmed in each festival.

On the whole, conductors of the established symphony orchestras were not especially hospitable toward new music, though there were a few notable exceptions. Pierre Monteux, at San Francisco from 1935 to 1952, was well known for his championship of contemporary music; as a young man in Paris he had conducted premieres of such landmarks as *Le Sacre du Printemps* and *Daphnis et Chloë*. Leopold Stokowski, too, maintained a long-standing reputation as an innovator. But it was to Serge Koussevitzky more than anyone else that Americans owed thanks for the encouragement of native compositions. While he led the Boston Symphony Orchestra, from 1924 until 1949, he introduced nearly seventy-five major new works by Americans. His protégé, Leonard Bernstein, followed suit during his tenure as volunteer conductor of the New York City Symphony from 1945 through 1948.

Finally, there were numerous leagues, alliances, and other associations whose purpose was the encouragement and support of American music by one means or another, such as the American Composers Alliance, a licensing organization founded in 1938 by Aaron Copland, Roy Harris, Bernard Wagenaar and others; the American Music Center, a score library and information center; and the League of Composers.

Thus at the beginning of the 1940s American musical life had become in many ways the most varied and vital the country had ever seen. To be sure, not all the degrees, professorships, prizes, and premieres put together could assure American composers of more than a minute percentage of the total performance time available in all media put together. But at least there was some hope for their orchestral music.

The field of choral music was virtually closed to the serious composer. Many of the best-known amateur and student choirs—the New York Oratorio Society, Ifor Jones's Bethlehem Bach Choir, Hugh Ross's Schola Cantorum, John Finley Williamson's Westminster Choir, Father William Finn's Paulist Choir, or Nicolai Montani's Palestrina Choir of Philadelphia—were devoted to a limited type of repertoire. Few were interested in contemporary art music, and fewer still were capable of performing it. The professional touring choruses such as the Trapp Family Singers, Serge Jaroff's Don Cossack Choir, and the Negro choirs of Eva Jessye and Hall Johnson were in the field of show business.

If a composer entertained any hope at all of writing successfully for school and adult amateur choral groups, he had to accept the stylistic limitations inherent in the amateur choral tradition, and he thereby entered one of the most competitive commercial markets in the world of music. At one end of the scale were the numerous editions of Renaissance motets and madrigals by Archibald Davison, Sir Edmund Fellowes and similar conductor-scholars; at the other were the made-to-order genre pieces for high school choirs, written by journeymen composer-educators like Noble Cain. In between were the editions of Russian liturgical music made by Lindsay Norden and Winfred Douglas, the stylized Spanish folk songs arranged by Kurt Schindler, the simple settings of Central European folk songs by the Trapp Family's conductor, Franz Wasner, and the Negro spirituals suitably whitened by John Work, William L. Dawson, Harry Burleigh, Nathaniel Dett, or Hall Johnson. Wallingford Riegger, a composer of the older generation born in Albany, Georgia, and an otherwise successful and widely respected artist, wrote only a handful of choral works of his own but ground out, under at least nine pseudonyms, arrangements and transcriptions of hundreds of works by others, from Palestrina to Vincent Youmans.

Clearly, there was a need for an organization that could do for choral music what the BSO under Koussevitzky was doing for symphonic music—as Shaw expressed it, "an instrument available to all serious American composers which should be technically equal to their most stringent demands and sympathetic without reservation to their mood and talent."

December 9, 1942

Present Indicative—or
The Chorale Courier goes stream-of-consciousness:
When I was trying to state the purpose of this choir some months ago, among the literary conceits and verbosities there was apparently the germ of an idea which later crystallized (became set . . . defined . . . bounded . . . dead . . . could be . . .) into some slogan sequences enraptured of an *American Ideal in Song* unquote.
A lot of times those look to me like all words and no ideas. A lot of times I wonder whether The Collegiate Chorale isn't just a pretty plaything, buttressed by epigrams, egotism and eroticism.
For along the lines of some of those slogans we made a few program commitments, and I presume the pressure will prove the sincerity of the intent—as well as who among us share it.

One of the commitments was to William Schuman. Schuman, six years older than Shaw, had gotten a rather late start as a composer, but since the performances of his first symphony and string quartet and his *Four Canonic Choruses* on a Composers Forum Laboratory concert of the WPA in 1936, he had had works premiered by Koussevitzky and Artur Rodzinski, earned two Guggenheim fellowships, the first New York Critics Circle Award, a commission from the League of Composers, an Award of Merit from the National Association for American Composers and Conductors, and within another year was to win the first Pulitzer Prize in music. In mid-1942 he had begun looking around for a chorus to perform some of his works on a Town Hall concert and, wanting something even better than his own chorus at Sarah Lawrence, or the Schola Cantorum, had dropped in on a Collegiate Chorale rehearsal.

He was struck by a remarkable paradox: on the one hand, Shaw's naïveté—he was rehearsing a Brahms motet with impeccable Waring tone-syllable diction, but with no apparent understanding of the implications of contrapuntal texture—and on the other, the wondrously visceral quality of his conducting and the resultant tonal vitality and rhythmic urgency of the group's singing. He returned a week or two later with Koussevitzky, who was similarly impressed, but who also was amazed that any group of adults would willingly endure such tyrannical treatment from a conductor.

In turn, Shaw was taken by Schuman and his wife to Carnegie Hall to hear Koussevitzky conduct Beethoven's *Eroica*. He was moved to tears, saying it was the most beautiful thing he had ever heard.

When Schuman asked if the Chorale would perform some of his choral works on the Town Hall concert, Shaw replied, "Sure, if you'll conduct them."

"No," said the composer, "you must conduct. But first you've got to find a good teacher and learn a few more things about music."

"All right," said Shaw, "will you take the job?"

Schuman declined, but recommended a certain gifted conductor and pianist who had been teaching at the Mannes School since fleeing Germany in 1940, and who had recently been engaged by the Met. Both teacher and pupil were performers at heart, and equally impatient with pedantries. Valiantly, they stuck it out for four lessons. Fourteen years later, Robert Shaw and George Szell were to enter into a more permanent and productive, though similarly tenuous, contract.

The Collegiate Chorale's performance schedule lightened somewhat in the fall of 1942—only a Brahms Requiem for All Angels' Episcopal Church in return for the privilege of rehearsing in one of the Sunday school rooms, and a Christmastide radio broadcast— but Shaw was as busy as ever. So seldom was he home at daughter Johanna's bedtime that he made her recordings of two stories from A. A. Milne's *The House at Pooh Corner*. One of those, "In Which a House is Built for Eeyore," was rerecorded, issued commercially in 1945, and soon won an award as an outstanding children's record.

The Chorale began meeting twice a week—once for rehearsal and once for the new educational program. The latter session was divided into two segments, the first given over to courses in sight-singing, ear-training, harmony, music history, and general musicianship, and the other to informal lectures by some of the organization's new friends: Dimitri Mitropoulos, Edward Tatnall Canby, Martha Graham, and William Schuman.

The Chorale's identity crisis evidently behind it, things improved —or at least Shaw was sometimes pleased. In the late night hours after the NBC broadcast of Christmas hymns and carols on December 21 he was so mellow with pride that he couldn't wait to write the members an affectionate letter:

Dear Friends—

I'm always pretty confused by the Christian festive seasons. There seems such a disparity between incident and commemoration, between the simple story of the Nativity, and the encrustations of our time and society and merchandising. The thing that makes it most confusing is that sometimes there appears among all the trappings someone or some group that seems to act with the directness and simplicity of the beginnings. —Like last night.

In such instances I feel decidedly inarticulate, because all the good words I know are standing off with their tongues in their cheeks. "Watch the words go down! We are a nation of word-killers. All the great words are dead." [A paraphrase of a passage from Edna St. Vincent Millay's *Conversation at Midnight*.] Too much handling in too many markets. Used so easily so long there are none left for matters of worth. —Like last night.

I do have a sort of Christmas wish. It's pretty much like that of last year. At that time we had just entered the war, and the days ahead looked rather grim. —Nor do they look much happier now. The defense even of democracy is a brutal business.

What I felt then, and what I now feel is that if somewhere, in all the seemingly necessary brutality, there can be even a small group of people concerned with the fruits of men's dignity, I don't think *that*'s non-essential. I think it's so essential that we can do no less than match the passion and completeness of those who are now caught in the more bitter engagement.

Most of you don't remember Holden Bowler. He was one of the first men to leave the Chorale for the armed service, overseas from almost the beginning, a beautiful baritone voice, and—well—the kind of mind that wrote from God knows where:

"You can't deny that it *is* a big and important piece of work you are doing. . . . You've picked the best and the worst time in our generation to try it. I think you can hold enough together to bring it through this mess—the idea won't tarnish, it's *solid*! . . . I only hope I can live long enough to do and help advance the fine things that are beginning to come from it."

Good night,
R. Shaw

The concert of Schuman's works took place on Wednesday evening, January 13, 1943. It opened with one of the Brandenburg Concertos, played by the Saidenberg Little Symphony under Daniel Saidenberg, and concluded with a first performance of Schuman's Concerto for Piano and Small Orchestra, with Rosalyn Tureck as soloist. Between the two instrumental works the Collegiate Chorale sang Schuman's "Choral Etude," "Four Canonic Choruses," "Holiday Song," and "Requiescat."

At the close of the concert Virgil Thomson, the *Herald-Tribune*'s critic, moderated a free-for-all discussion between Miss Tureck and Schuman, Saidenberg, and Shaw, as well as members of the large, knowledgeable, and enthusiastic audience. Schuman's music, characterized as it was by energetic rhythmic patterns arising out of his earlier experiences as a jazz musician, popular song writer, and Tin Pan Alley song plugger, had been stimulating, and the dialogue was lively. Once again, though, Shaw and the Collegiate Chorale were the focus of attention.

As Louis Biancolli reported, Mr. Shaw, "whose first-rate chorus was generally regarded as the night's real news," was asked how he could justify working for Fred Waring's outfit and leading "serious music" at the same time.

" 'I think Mr. Waring tries to say in the music of entertainment what we are trying to say here in serious music,' he said, getting the night's biggest ovation. 'Fred tries to make sense and tries to make it simple and honest.' "

The whole evening was a high point for Shaw, the Collegiate Chorale, and American music, even though there had been time for only four full rehearsals of Schuman's rather demanding pieces. *Time* magazine exclaimed:

> Conductors who can rouse both their musicians and their audiences to frenzied enthusiasm are born, not made. . . . But last week in Manhattan's Town Hall a budding U.S.-born conductor had Manhattan's surliest critics holding their breaths with excitement. . . . The critics were excited not so much by Conductor Shaw's musicianship as by the way he held the minutest control over his singers. Gesticulating with feverish intensity, Shaw suggested a cross between Arturo Toscanini and an over-wrought college cheerleader. By the time he had finished, a hand-picked audience agreed that his Collegiate Chorale was one of the finest in the U.S.

In contrast, composer and teacher Isadore Freed was vexed. "The parted stage curtains revealed an entirely novel seating of the new chorus," he wrote in a letter to the *New York Times*. "Basses, sopranos, tenors and altos were scattered all over the stage in small unconnected units. The total sound was distributed throughout the hall as a constant mass. For this reason Schuman's canons, excellent bits of vocal part writing, did not come off as canons at all. One could not follow the outlines of each part." He remarked that one might as well put performers "in the boxes and (why not?) even in the hall itself alongside the audience."

Freed went on to say that "the director of the new chorus undoubtedly has ideas he is a superior choral trainer and his dynamic personality dominates his group." As a result, he concluded, "the singers act like a group of performing seals."

At the next rehearsal Shaw reacted good-naturedly to Freed's diatribe by having everyone bark and bob like seals. A few days later he wrote a brief exegesis of his theories, which also appeared in the *Times*.

Music is primarily an aural art, he said, and except for rare antiphonal choruses, and much rarer antiphonal orchestral works, the direction from which the sound comes is a negligible consideration. Moreover, he said, there is an optimum arrangement of voices unique to each piece of music and to each stage in its preparation. In contrapuntal works, for example, he found the best results were obtained "when two, three, or four voices of a single section were placed together—a 'leader' and two or three 'followers'—thus yielding out of one hundred sixty voices ten to sixteen choirs of sixteen to ten members each." Practically speaking, the mixing of voices had the advantage of facilitating blend and balance, as well as improving intonation.

Aside from whatever instructive value he could derive from it, Shaw didn't let negative criticism bother him very much. After all, no critic in the world would have castigated him or the Chorale as severely as he himself could. At the first rehearsal in February the democratic foundations of the organization were strengthened, giving more specific powers to the membership and leaving almost none to its conductor. The process was treated by the members with self-conscious lightheartedness, which in turn caused Shaw immediately to relieve himself of some more pent-up feelings with uncompromising urgency.

February 8, 1943

In case anybody asks you—

It gripes from Genesis that the things I'd like to write tonight must sound cheap and weak and sentimental. I'd like to scream them. I'd like to write with my fists . . . . . and all the words I know are the clichés of generations of preachers.

We kidded around a lot tonight with nominations and voting. It was good fun . . . . . and a hell of a lot smarter than trying to fumble through the grade-school-popularity-poll-class-election. We have at least an organization capable of administering this body for the balance of this season.

But I doubt that very many of you realized the nature of the responsibility you assumed.

This choir no longer belongs to one man. It belongs to each of us everyone. And what it does or fails to do from now on is your credit or your fault.

I wish you could know the strength of the dissenting opinion on the constitution which was so easily accepted tonight. Men who've handled the affairs of musical and educational organizations for many years have dubbed it everything from foolishness to suicide. They say that no group can conceive and sustain the vision and passion and regimen necessary to either artistic or financial success. The artist, they say, is one.

What they don't see—and what I'm afraid you don't see—and what you *must* see is that the Collegiate Chorale is not a glee club or a stock company. You don't *join* the Collegiate Chorale. You *believe* it. It's very damn near a religion. It's a way of life. Either you feel the fellow next to you is an important human being, and you like him, and you try desperately to understand how he feels about what he sings about, and pool your creative passions to make something a damned sight bigger than either of you could make alone—or this isn't your kind of choir. Either the music you sing is torn out of you—or you ought not to be singing.

We sing too damned much just for the fun of it. Not near enough for the *must* of it. . . . I don't think anybody should sing if he can help it. I'd like to belong to a choir that sings because it just can't help it.

It seems to me that the Collegiate Chorale is a lot bigger now that it belongs to everybody. It says that the great music of great men is within the ken and affections of common people who mean to make it so. And it says that there is a community of creative spirit no less than a community of political system. And to me it says that this union of spirits before goodness and beauty and truth is as close as men come in this life to the ends for which they were born. This establishes their humanity.

You don't join the Collegiate Chorale. You believe it. —And if you don't believe it, please don't come next Monday night.

R.S.

Nothing was more likely to soothe hurt feelings on either side than another crucial performance situation. Three days later, on February 11, 1943, Jan Peerce, the leading Metropolitan Opera tenor, notified his manager at two o'clock in the afternoon that he was too sick to fulfill his engagement on the Town Hall Endowment Series that evening. An hour later Shaw was located at the hospital where Maxine had just given birth to their second child, Peter Thain, and asked if the Collegiate Chorale would substitute for Peerce. He raced to the nearest phone, and at 7:45 P.M. forty singers were gathered for a warmup; at 8:30 they were on stage. "We'll just rehearse in front of you for a while," Shaw told the audience.

The next day, Henry Simon wrote:

If you preferred believing your judgment of the performance of that group, you'd say they had been preparing this event half a year. They sang part of a Brahms motet, a group of works by William Schuman, some good and some bad religious music, and a crackerjack arrangement of a Negro spiritual. Some of these, it's true, the whole Collegiate Chorale of 150 voices had done before, but never this particular group of 40. Once Mr. Shaw asked the chorus, "How many never have seen this music before?" A dozen hands went up. At the end he asked, "How many are singing with us for the first time tonight?" I counted seven.

It was hard to believe. One just doesn't achieve such precision, such diction, such balance and spirit without months of practice. *One* doesn't, but Bob Shaw does.

There was no time for "months of practice" on anything. Within the next few weeks the Chorale had more performances than rehearsals: a broadcast on the Fourth Annual WNYC American Music Festival; a second appearance on the Gabrilowitsch Memorial Series with the National Orchestral Association, this time singing a new Requiem by the contemporary French composer J. Guy Ropartz; a Red Cross benefit show at Madison Square Garden; a "production" of the *St. Matthew Passion* under Stokowski; and, on April 13, a concert at the Museum of Modern Art featuring premieres of Paul Hindemith's *Six Chansons* and Aaron Copland's "Lark," and the first New York performance of Milhaud's *Two Cities*, all for unaccompanied chorus.

Stokowski, who was notorious for his bold and sometimes tasteless emendations of the works of Bach, had conceived the *St. Matthew Passion* as "something like a Greek drama" in twelve scenes. Robert Edmond Jones, the noted Broadway director, designed the staging, which consisted of multilevel platforms and ramps in front of a depthless blue cyclorama, on which were projected the three crosses and some stars. To the sides of the stage were arrayed the Collegiate Chorale (in light so dim they could hardly see their scores) and the soloists, including Lucius Metz, Gerhardt Pechner, Eleanor Steber, and Jennie Tourel. The role of Mary Magdalena was mimed by Lillian Gish, the famous movie actress of the silent era. Christ was represented by a moving shaft of yellow light which, in Olin Downes's opinion, "furnished no particular raison d'etre for the group of hooded figures [choreographed by George Balanchine] who thrashed about like the Ku Klux Klan when Jesus was captured and taken away."

Some of the critics were awed by the "strangely beautiful and moving exhibition," to which the resurrection scene was "a breathtaking conclusion." The *New Yorker* liked "the way the harpsichord seemed to melt into the rest of the orchestra at the end of the recitatives." Downes, though, was outraged by Stokowski's treatment of the score, which had been mercilessly cut in order to fit the work into the dimensions appropriate to a comfortable evening's entertainment. "More could have been heard," he said, "had it not been for the extremely lachrymose and dilatory tempi and the unblushing sentimentalism in interpretation, which almost uniformly prevailed, so that the B-minor aria with the violin solo sounded like the meditation from *Thaïs*."

From a purist's point of view the whole affair was a travesty, but Shaw was too preoccupied to brood over such matters. In addition to conducting the Collegiate Chorale and preparing the Glee Club for Waring's broadcasts, he was taking piano lessons, studying music theory, and shaping up a chorus of sixty singers from the Chorale to audition for a radio sponsor. He hardly had time to accept, on April 16, 1943, the engraved parchment scroll from the

Leopold Stokowski, Shaw, and Fred Waring

National Association for American Composers and Conductors naming him "the year's most important American-born conductor, as evidenced in his direction of the Collegiate Chorale."

The highbrow critics who were the self-styled guardians and heralds of progress in the nationalization of our musical culture habitually viewed orchestral conducting as a profession dominated by Europeans. American conductors, they held, had so far failed to make any important contributions. What they meant by American was "American-born," and what they considered "an important contribution" was the leadership of some major orchestra, in turn definable by its annual operating budget and the length of its season, not to mention its artistic standards. In January of 1943, *Time* had declared that "of the men who conduct the 17 big U.S. symphony orchestras, only one (the Kansas City Philharmonic's Karl

Kreuger) is U.S.-born. More native talent undoubtedly exists but is not used."

Toscanini, Koussevitzky, and Stokowski—an Italian, a Russian, and a Polish-Irish-Englishman—led the field of foreigners. Eugene Ormandy occupied the podium in Philadelphia, Frederick Stock in Chicago, Pierre Monteux in San Francisco, Artur Rodzinski in Cleveland, Otto Klemperer in Los Angeles, Dimitri Mitropoulos in Minneapolis, and so on. True, Kreuger was born in New York City and raised in Kansas, but his heritage, his educational background, his early experience, and his style of conducting were thoroughly Viennese.

Actually, the foreign-born conductors of the "big 17," with superior players at their command, adequate rehearsal time, and long concert seasons, were in positions to do as much for the cause of music in America, and American music, as anyone could have— more, in fact, than the conductors of the other two-hundred-odd, smaller orchestras in the country. Despite the limitations inherent in their situations—the conservatism of boards of directors, benefactors, and concertgoers, and the need to maintain their individual repertoires of standard works—some of them, like Koussevitzky, were constantly on the lookout for new works by American composers, and most of them actively encouraged aspiring young American conductors.

But how was the American conductor's absence from the spotlight to be explained? Ever since the middle of the nineteenth century one theory had been that our "national temperament" lacked the "dictatorial element" that the born maestro must have. Another was that the "society ladies" who allegedly ruled most of the orchestra managements were partial to exotic personalities and gave prowess with the teacup as much weight as prowess with the baton. The excuse most often heard was that America, unlike Europe, had no small-town opera companies where young conductors could practice their craft.

Preoccupied with the desire to rationalize our national failure to produce any virtuoso conductors, the apologists virtually ignored the appearance during the thirties of an impressive number of American—or thoroughly Americanized—conductors whose influence on our musical life, though all too brief, was in certain respects more substantial than that of all the foreign stars put together. Their principal medium was radio.

There was Howard Barlow, from Plain City, Ohio, who conducted the first nationwide radio broadcast for CBS in 1927 (with André Kostelanetz as his assistant), served as the network's musical director for many years, and in 1943 moved to NBC as conductor of the Firestone hour. Frank Black, a Philadelphian, was named musical director at NBC in 1928, and regularly conducted his own orchestra on network broadcasts. Erno Rapee, a Hungarian who resigned his assistantship with the Dresden Opera orchestra because he was not given enough to do, came to the U.S. in 1912 to conduct theater orchestras for S. L. Rothafel's huge "Roxy" chain, and in the thirties conducted NBC's "Music Hall of the Air." Another naturalized American was Alexander Smallens, who was brought to this country from Russia as a child, began his career as assistant conductor of the Boston Opera Company, and became known to radio listeners as conductor of the Lewisohn Stadium concerts and the "Ford Sunday Evening Hour." Werner Janssen, of New York City, began conducting on Cleveland's radio station WTAM; in 1940 he organized his own orchestra in Hollywood, with which he frequently performed new works by American composers on his network broadcasts. Philip James, born in Jersey City, founded the Bamberger Little Symphony under the patronage of Bamberger's Department Store and presented some two thousand different works on his hundreds of radio shows. Chicagoan Alfred Wallenstein, urged by Toscanini to abandon the cello and take up the baton, made his conducting debut on radio in 1931 and two years later became musical director for the Mutual Network, also leading his own Sinfonietta in weekly broadcasts.

Each of these men had to possess the talent and the technique to handle a wide variety of musical styles with skill and taste. Each was expected not only to conduct light classical music, arrangements of popular songs, and incidental music for radio dramas, but also to be equally at home in the serious classical idiom.

Alfred Wallenstein, for example, confronting the need for variety in programming and the demands of the rigid time-frames of radio broadcasting, not only used the best-known standard works but also resurrected many long-forgotten pieces of comparable value. He also directed a Sunday evening series of all the church cantatas of J. S. Bach that were then in print; he led a series of Mozart operas, some of which had never before been heard in this country; he devoted one sequence of programs to the piano concertos of

Mozart and another to modern American choral works. The performance of contemporary American music was facilitated by the fact that the networks, unintimidated by the prejudices of patrons and cash customers, were ready and willing to pay the necessary royalties.

Few of these men developed public images that approached the stature of the ones whom the critics most admired, even though they were occasionally privileged to appear before major orchestras as guests. And most of them still do not qualify for more than passing mention in directories of the "great" conductors. American-born or not, they didn't have the peculiar credentials that made them newsworthy. They were so busy satisfying the omnivorous appetite of the medium for more and more musical material that they rarely had the chance to evolve original interpretations of the usual concert-hall fare. There was little tolerance for tyranny and no leisure for temper tantrums in the studio, nor was there any need to balance either budgets or teacups.

The vicissitudes of commercialism, the advent of the long-playing microgroove record, and the arrival of FM radio transmission eventually eliminated their kind from American musical life. In the meantime, throughout the thirties and well into the forties, the names of these men were household property from coast to coast, border to border, and were identified by millions of listeners with treasured musical experiences.

By the time Robert Shaw appeared on the scene the function of radio as a patron of live music had passed its apogee, and studio orchestras were beginning to decrease in number. The foreign conductors were still in charge of the "big 17," and the young men faced a bleak future. Only the extremely gifted and thoroughly prepared hopeful had much chance of even finding an orchestra to practice on.

The things that made the critics optimistic about Shaw's prospects as an orchestra conductor were obvious to them. To begin with, he had temperament. Henry Simon noticed it: "On the stage he appears to get his remarkable results through kinaesthetic exhortation and silent prayer. In rehearsal there's just as much unconventional gyration, but the prayer isn't silent, and it's sprinkled with an admixture of good cussing out, cajoling, and old-fashioned drill." Perhaps Simon wasn't aware how ashamed Shaw was of his explosive lapses from equanimity. Anyhow, the other half of the story made better newspaper copy.

He also showed qualities that made him seem approachable by nonmusicians: his boyish good looks, his ready wit, his "aw, shucks" shyness, and his unassuming, informal air both on and off the stage. Besides, there was the clipped rhythm of a name that sounded genuinely mid-American.

Nevertheless, although Stokowski and Koussevitzky both offered to teach him more about conducting, and Wallenstein invited him to lead the Sinfonietta as a guest, Robert knew he was not ready. "Ask me again in three years, Mr. Wallenstein," he replied.

There were other reasons for Shaw to postpone further involvement in orchestral conducting. He was still deeply committed to the entertainment field; his reputation as a choral conductor was rapidly expanding; and he was all but obsessed with the possibilities of choral music as an instrument of democracy.

He was indebted to Waring for the experience he was gaining as director of the Glee Club, as well as for Waring's encouragement and material support of the Collegiate Chorale. Above all, his job with the Pennsylvanians was helping him keep the Chorale afloat, since he received no salary for conducting the amateur organization and often paid its bills out of his own pocket. But when the Chorale, sharing the program on a Lewisohn Stadium Concert with Paul Robeson and the New York Philharmonic under Alexander Smallens, sang its unaccompanied triple-choir arrangement of Cole Porter's "Begin the Beguine"—a Waring-style "vochestration" replete with peppy "tropical splendor" and the Andrews Sisters' brand of vocal jazz, Shaw became uneasily aware of an underlying absurdity. Here were 200 people singing to 20,000 listeners, out-of-doors on a hot summer evening, "Dah-rleeNG, Ah-ee Luh-vyoo"—the kind of music, as he later remarked, that "should only be sung in private by consenting adults in pairs, preferably one of each sex."

On the other hand, his connection with the entertainment field was strengthened in the fall of 1943 when Billy Rose hired him to prepare the chorus for *Carmen Jones*, a Broadway parody of Bizet's *verismo* opera with new lyrics by Oscar Hammerstein II and a new orchestration by Robert Russell Bennett. Shaw's forty Negro singers were given six weeks to learn their parts; at the end of the first five days, even though few of them could read music very well, they had everything memorized. To utilize the rest of the rehearsal time, Rose and choreographer Eugene Loring worked out some dance routines, but that only spoiled the singing. Shaw experimented with directional effects, placing singers in the wings and the orchestra pit as well as on stage. Only by sheer brute force was Rose able to restrain him from putting some of them in the audience—*pace* Isadore Freed. "Are you *crazy?*" Rose screamed. "*Actors* in seats for which *people* will pay four-forty?" Finally it was decided that the best thing to do was line up the singers in front of the footlights and just let them sing. The critics thought it was the best chorus ever heard on Broadway, and opera buffs who condescended to come were amazed that it didn't sound like the Metropolitan's at all!

As news of his successes with the Chorale, the Waring Glee Club, and on Broadway spread across the country, he began receiving more and more requests to explain his methods to other choral conductors. Modestly, even reluctantly, he consented, but he was unaccustomed to the role of a pedagogue and his approach was refreshingly straightforward and unorthodox. In July of 1943 he accepted an invitation from a group of twenty Southern California school and church choir musicians to lead a ten-day seminar at Occidental College, using a seventy-five voice demonstration group recruited from the area by Howard Swan. At the end of the first session he shrugged and said, "Gentlemen, that's all I know. What'll we do for the next nine days?" What they did was turn out a stunning performance of a program of contemporary choral music and incidentally establish the basis for a new community chorus in Los Angeles. In St. Louis the following spring, conducting a demonstration chorus of high school teachers, he told the onlooking members of the Music Educators National Conference: "We've been handicapped by inhibitions, but we're losing 'em. You may not like what we're doing up here, but that's the way we're doing it. We're not interested in the beauty of tones. We're just trying to get the story of the words across. We just try to do what the composer intended." In only a few hours he prepared the chorus for an inter-American radio broadcast that brought him still more invitations to conduct similar clinics.

His belief in the ethical power of choral music became a surrogate for the religious calling he had forsaken, and he preached his gospel with a missionary zeal. The ancient search for cosmic unity through music had gained new relevance in the liberal 1930s, and the eminent music critic and commentator Olin Downes had written: "Art can not only represent but become religion. Here is release and sublimation and unfoldment of the spirit. Here is sanctuary and fulfillment in a realm where aggrandizement of self is not destruction of a brother, but indeed the contrary. What does more than music toward true communication and the demolishment of the invisible barriers between man and man, those barriers which are hardest of all to level?"

Shaw conceived a plan for developing workers' choruses on a national scale, using an expanded Waring educational program to seed industries with exhibition concerts, pro tempore conductors, music, and organizational advice. He went to Washington to discuss his idea with a sympathetic group of high-level officials in President Roosevelt's administration. Shaw claimed it would not only help win the war but also meliorate the postwar adjustments that would have to be made between management and labor. The president, however, was preoccupied with battlefront emergencies, and found no time even to reply.

One evening in the early winter of 1943 the Shaws were entertaining some visitors who innocently confessed to not having read Carl Sandburg's *The People, Yes*. It was two o'clock in the morning, but Robert refused to let them go home until he had read aloud nearly the entire book, finishing somewhere around six. "Isn't this what I'm trying to say with the Chorale?" he demanded of his limp audience. "Getting Negro and White, Jew and Gentile, all singing together, all striving for the mighty harmony? Isn't that the first step toward solidarity? And what I've done here, can't I do elsewhere?"

3.

Choral Renaissance in America

FOR A YEAR or more Shaw had been deliberately assessing his strengths and weaknesses as a musician, and he had arrived at a reasonably clear notion of what he needed to learn. Meanwhile he had been relying on the Collegiate Chorale's "musical consultants" when he wanted help—William Schuman, Felix Wolfes, Frank Cunkle, and several others. Late in the summer of 1943, at Schuman's suggestion, he decided to apply for a Guggenheim fellowship for a year of intensive study. An early draft of the application proposed "a program of studies in musical theory, orchestration, repertoire, score analysis, piano, and vocal techniques." When the grant was received the following April it was for "a study of music theory and the techniques of instrumental and choral conducting, and to prepare a book on the development of symphonic choruses for the performance of modern choral music."

The idea of a book had been urged upon him by participants and observers at the choral clinics and seminars he had led, as well as by Collegiate Chorale members and admirers. It sounded like an excellent suggestion at the time, for choral conductors everywhere could hardly contain their curiosity. Although once or twice a year ever since then he has "started" the book, it has not yet been finished.*

*Shaw's choral techniques have been summarized, however, by Howard Swan in his essay "The Development of a Choral Instrument," in *Choral Conducting: A Symposium*, ed. Harold A. Decker and Julius Herford (Englewood Cliffs, New Jersey: Prentice-Hall, Inc., 1973).

He is of course quite capable of expressing the myriad objective details of his choral "method" in ways that anyone can comprehend. His first premise—a revolutionary one in the early forties—is that a performer is subservient to the composer. Or, as he once put it in a letter to the Collegiate Chorale, "This choir is, and ought to be, interested in singing as a means to music, and not music as a means to singing." A corollary is that the conductor is indebted to the performer; the integrity of the individual singer is paramount.

Beyond that, his "secrets" are ultimately elusive, for they reside in those mysterious dictates of his inner ear, which guide his judgments from the beginning of the audition to the end of the performance. Besides, he prefers to speak in the context of a specific musical situation rather than a hypothetical case, and he does so with his own inimitable way of making a point.

After one particularly frustrating rehearsal with the Collegiate Chorale he tried once more to put on paper what it was he had expected to hear, and how it could have been brought about. Although the letter began on a disarming note of self-abasement, it continued with a blistering summary of the group's sins of commission and omission:

> Normally I would feel very embarrassed at rehashing this material, particularly for the older members—but not after tonight! I have never heard in any rehearsal such snafued enunciation or such careless, perverse and dispirited rhythm. Mind you—these are things we should be able to take for granted.
>
> As a matter of fact, I've written to you so many times about it that I'm damned sick and tired of the whole subject. It all sounds like SLOGANS. —Or the "Infatuation with the Sound of Own Words Department."

He worked on the letter for hours, at last winding up the four intense, single-spaced typewritten pages with the dramatization of a simple principle:

> I can think of a couple of emphases that haven't been emphatic enough up to now. The first is that little notes are just as important as big notes, that they have places and that they should be put in their places. Sixteenths and eighths and quarters are not just things that come between bigger things. They are not "introducings" or preparations or pick-ups. I get a horrible picture, from

the way you sing, of little bitty eighth notes running like hell all over the place to keep from being stepped on. Millions of 'em! Meek, squeaky little things. No self-respect. Standing in corners, hiding behind doors, ducking into subway stations, peering out from under rugs. Refugees.

Dammit, you're all a bunch of Whole-Note Nazis. And dots! Poor little dots! Oh—(I can't stand it!) I just thought of a *double*-dot!

Look—This is a democracy. Little people count. They're included in the census. Eighth notes can vote. They carry ID cards. They belong.

Dialogue—

Sixteenth-note marches up to a bar. "Gimme a glass o' beer."

Collegiate Chorale—"I'm very sorry, my little man, that's only for whole notes."

Moral—

Hell—give 'im a drink.

It's daylight. Good night.

Robert

His study of orchestral conducting was purely pragmatic. All he really wanted to do at the time was to learn to coach an orchestra well enough to be qualified to conduct accompanied choral works himself instead of always teaching notes that others were to conduct. He assembled a thirty-five-piece ensemble from the CBS, NBC, and New York Philharmonic orchestras for the premiere of Lukas Foss's cantata, *The Prairie*, in May of 1944. Never before had he conducted an orchestra. Realizing the futility of trying to bluff a bunch of professionals, he cheerfully dispensed with conventional podium protocol and said to them, "You know your instruments better than I do, but I know the score and what I want out of it. Let's work along. If you can help my beat, fine."

Twenty-year-old Foss had studied in Berlin under Julius Herford, who was known throughout Europe as a concert pianist and choral conductor of superior gifts. Herford had been brought to Columbia University as a guest lecturer for two years beginning in 1939, but during his visit the turn of political events in Germany made it prudent for him to remain here indefinitely, even though he had no prospect of a permanent job. For the next few years he barely managed to sustain himself and his family by free-lancing as a teacher and pianist, until Foss introduced him to Shaw during rehearsals of *The Prairie*.

Shaw, Lukas Foss, and Julius Herford, 1953. Photograph by John Gass

It took but a brief acquaintance to convince Shaw that this was
the man with whom he should spend his year on the Guggenheim
fellowship. "I want to take lessons from you," he said. "I want to
begin at the beginning and learn everything—harmony, counter-
point, the piano."

Herford was delighted. He was as much a maverick in higher
American music education as Shaw was in the choral field. With

the theories of Heinrich Schenker and Ernst Kurth as his point of departure, he taught score study as a holistic, contextual discipline, tracing musical meaning to the unique structure of a given work.

The two began with a seemingly ambitious program of five lesson hours a week, but before long they were working ten nonstop hours a day. Moreover, the study of the classics that Shaw had requested gave way to analysis of the music the Chorale was currently working on.

The relationship was an invigorating one for both. Whenever Herford came down to earth he announced to all and sundry that he was learning as much as he was teaching. He discovered that Shaw could discern the emotional implications of the printed score whether the mechanical factors were clear to him or not. He was also impressed by his pupil's fanatical attention to detail.

Their association continued well beyond the end of the formal period of study, and a few years later Herford broadcast a message to his musical following in Germany via the State Department's Voice of America radio network: "I have found in this country a great choral conductor, Robert Shaw. It is he who has convinced me at last that in music there is really only one world."

In the late spring of 1944 Shaw temporarily gave up his responsibilities with the Waring Glee Club to allow time for study with Herford, but otherwise his schedule was nearly as crowded as ever. He conducted ten rehearsals and a concert by the Bound Brook Community Chorus (which he had helped establish the previous year), and led choral clinics at Northwestern University, New York's High School of Music and Art, the Minnesota Music Educators Association, and the University of Tulsa. He assembled a professional chorus consisting mainly of Collegiate Chorale members to record portions of the sound track for a documentary film, *The Roosevelt Story*. He prepared the chorus for a new Billy Rose production, Cole Porter's *Seven Lively Arts*, which opened on December 7, and coached the glee club scene for Olsen and Johnson's madcap revue, *Laffing Room Only*, for a December 24 opening. In February of 1945 he initiated his career as an RCA Victor Red Seal Recording Artist.

In August of 1944 the Chorale took up permanent residence in the New York City Center for Music and Drama. The City Center had been established in late 1943 at the instigation of Mayor Fiorello La Guardia in an effort to do for the performing arts what museums and libraries had done for painting and literature—democratize their audiences. The long-range plan included an educational program as well as performances, but the immediate goal was simply to provide concerts, opera, and ballet at prices within reach of the largest possible audience.

The city had recently acquired the Masonic Shriners' Mecca Temple on West 55th Street by tax default, refurbished it for a mere $60,000, and turned it over to a nonprofit corporation headed by Newbold Morris, president of the City Council. Within a year its tenants consisted of Leopold Stokowski's New York City Symphony, an opera company, a ballet company, the National Orchestral Association, the Dessoff Choir, and the City Amateur Orchestra, as well as other organizations related to the performing arts, such as the Dalcroze School of Music, the Naumburg Foundation, the American Music Center, and the New York Singing Teachers Association. Rent amounted to the tenants' proportionate shares of the building's annual taxes of $28,000, with the understanding that admissions to performances would be kept at the lowest reasonable figures. The scheme served to satisfy some proponents of government patronage while avoiding the conservatives' anathema of direct subsidy.

That fall the Collegiate Chorale resumed its normal, frantic pace: the annual Herald Tribune Forum; two appearances with the Boston Symphony Orchestra in Lourié's *The Feast During the Plague*; and its first concert in the City Center's 2,800-seat auditorium, consisting of the Fauré Requiem, Beethoven's *Choral Fantasia*, and three works by Giovanni Gabrieli (tickets, 90¢, $1.20, $1.80).

The climax of the 1944–45 season was reached on April 28, when the Chorale joined forces with the Waring Glee Club, the Waring orchestra augmented to symphonic strength, and soloists Eileen Farrell and Robert Merrill to present the premiere of the first work commissioned by the Chorale (but paid for by Shaw): Norman Dello Joio's symphony for voices and orchestra based on Stephen Vincent Benet's epic poem, *Western Star.*

The program opened with Waring conducting a group of patriotic songs and several Negro spirituals, after which he announced

Norman Dello Joio at the piano, with Fred Waring, Richard Laderoute, Shaw, and Robert Merrill. Photograph by Metropolitan Photo Service

the late-breaking but premature report that Germany had surrendered to the allies. (The surrender actually took place on May 4.)

In that incredibly emotion-charged atmosphere Shaw stepped to the podium to conduct Dello Joio's new work. The next day Henry Simon explained regretfully: "There is doubt that the greatest music ever written could have satisfied the expectation and emotion of that moment. And that the new work did not measure up to the tremendously dramatic setting of its first hearing can hardly be blamed on its composer. For it is a substantial, sincerely written and highly creditable piece of music. One would like to hear it again under less extraordinary circumstances."

A few days later, on April 30, Shaw was inducted into the Navy. In July of 1944 his brother Jim, an Army chaplain, had been killed in action on the island of Owi in the South Pacific, whereupon Robert had withdrawn his declaration as a conscientious objector. When he arrived at the Naval Training Center at Sampson, New

York, he was directed to organize and conduct a chorus for a series of weekly radio broadcasts. He auditioned recruits as they stood in line for their physicals by having each sing a few bars of the national anthem. He worked late every night making plans and writing arrangements for the chorus, and was up before dawn every morning to lead the calisthenics. Before long Able Seaman Shaw was afflicted with a debilitating combination of exhaustion and allergy to the dye in his wool uniform. In July, after many days in the hospital, he was given a medical discharge.

Scarcely allowing himself time to recuperate, he set up another strenuous season of engagements with the Chorale—averaging more than one a month—plus an appearance as guest conductor of the New York City Symphony and a long list of recording sessions for RCA. The first order of business, however, was the preparation of the Chorale for a September performance of Beethoven's Ninth Symphony under Arturo Toscanini.

The Finale of the Ninth is a monumentally difficult work. Extreme tessituras for first one part and then another tax the abilities of the most competent performers to sing softly in very high passages, or loudly in very low ones. Shaw explained to Toscanini his customary expedient of naming a few singers in each section as "roving centers," and asked permission to apply it. "Anything that makes the score sound right, *is* right," Toscanini assured him, adding: "You know, I have never had a good performance of this work. Sometimes the chorus is bad; sometimes the orchestra is bad; many times the soloists are bad. And many times *I* am terrible."

Shaw was determined that the Chorale should do its very best. On September 17, 1945, he wrote to them:

> I don't believe I have any right to insist on a particular vocal method, to at least the confusion, if not the possible detriment, of those of us who are seriously studying their own private vocal methods—and paying good money for it.
>
> However—now that we have most of the notes and most of the syncopations and most of the dynamics—the fact remains that we do not have the vocal vigor that the Beethoven demands. We do not have the screaming magnificence and mass of tone. Stacked up against that particular score (which is admittedly as rough as they come) our tenors are adolescent and/or sexless, our altos have not passed puberty, our sopranos trip their dainty ballet of colora-

tura decorum, and our basses woof their wittle gway woofs all the way home. There is no astringency. There is no majesty.

People, the flesh must not be weak. Beethoven is not precious, he's prodigal as hell. He tramples all over nicety. He's ugly, heroic; he roars, he lusts after beauty, he rages after nobility. Be ye not temperate. Enter ye into his courts on horseback.

Which, being freely translated, means: Get your backs and your bellies into it. You can't sing Beethoven from the neck up—you'll bleed. Quit sitting back on your soft little laurels. Get your feet on the floor. Get elbow room. Spread your back. Keep your neck decently erect and your throat open. Don't lead with your chin. And give with the part of your gut that ties onto your ribs. Make your body do part of the work. And, oh yes! Get lots of sleep. Read lots of good books. Drink lots of milk and orange juice. Think good clean thoughts. Love your neighbor—and Allah be praised.

Robert

Toscanini visited the next rehearsal. The Chorale had been frantically polishing up details for a solid hour, tense with the expectation that *Il Maestro* would lead them through a long and arduous session, perhaps launching into one of his famous rages. However, he declined Shaw's proffered baton with "No. You conduct, I listen."

Nervously the Chorale proceeded, their eyes glancing furtively from Shaw to the venerable Italian master as the latter walked slowly back and forth across the rear of the hall. During the final measures Toscanini quickened his pace and approached the podium. Before the echoes of the final chord had died away, he flung his arms around Shaw and kissed him on both cheeks, saying tearfully, "It is the first time that I hear it sung! I'll see you at Carnegie Hall." Then, having been present only seventeen minutes, he turned and left, as the astonished chorus and its conductor gaped in disbelief.

A short while later Toscanini showed up at a friend's house, where Samuel Chotzinoff, manager of NBC's Music Division, was dining. Surprised, Chotzinoff asked if the rehearsal had been called off. "When he told me that the rehearsal had taken place, I began to fear that all had not gone well and that he had, as sometimes happens, left in displeasure. 'On the contrary,' said Toscanini. 'The chorus was wonderful. They went through the music just once. I found nothing to criticize. As for Robert Shaw, I have at last found the Maestro I have been looking for.'"

The performance on the 25th, a benefit for the Italian Welfare League's War Orphans Committee, was an unqualified triumph. The orchestra was superb, and magic issued from the voices of the soloists, Norma Andreotti, Nan Merriman, Jan Peerce, and Lorenzo Alvary. "But most of all," wrote Louis Biancolli of the *World-Telegram*,

> it showed like sunshine in Mr. Shaw's young choir. . . . Last night's choral singing was the best I have ever heard in Carnegie Hall. The power and impact of Beethoven's outcry never seemed so urgent. The massed tone was bright and solid. Sky-high sequences sounded like voices from above.
>
> I have watched this chorus grow in the last two years. No other choral unit or choirmaster has hurtled so fast into deserved fame. Young Shaw has stamped the chorus with a fervid zeal. And a high standard, too. Last night it outdid itself. When greater singing is heard, the Collegiate Chorale will do it.

The day after the performance Shaw wrote to the Chorale:

September 26, 1945

Dear People:

> I just couldn't be any happier than I've been in the past twenty-four hours. —And you must feel just about the same way. To have been there in front of him, watching him work—you must have been walking on clouds, too.
>
> It was wonderful, wonderful—the mass of tone, the bite of the rhythm and enunciation, the spirit of vehemence and confidence, and faith that felt like faith, and joy that sounded joyful. —And all the newspaper superlatives don't add up to his smile of pleasure and thanks.
>
> If only you could have seen him afterwards—. It's hard to tell you without making it sound cloying and sentimental. You certainly saw that child-like, pure, angel's countenance—a grace which served in him only as virility and strength; the illusion of height without being tall; the capacity (in his reading) for roughness and vulgarity without ever hinting at ignobility. In his dressing room afterwards, wrapped in towels, and sweat pouring down his face and chest, most of the sternness gone from his eyes, only this wonderful unselfconscious childlike smile; then, in his half-Italian and half-English—that sounds like Italian—"Caro maestro—I am very happy."

This and subsequent collaborations with Toscanini left an indelible impression on Shaw. The master's linear approach to texture, which made every vertical relationship audible over a wide range of dynamics; his unswerving tempos which heightened the tensile resilience of the smallest rhythmic figure; his expressive delineation of phrases; and above all, his intuitive understanding of a composer's intentions ("to hear it as if before it was written") —these qualities confirmed the viability of Shaw's own proclivities and stimulated his thinking in new directions.

Forthwith the Chorale plunged headlong into music for the remainder of the season, pausing only momentarily to approve a new constitution embodying Shaw's changing vision for the organization. For some of the singers, however, the exhilaration of September 25 was short-lived, and a current of unrest began to arise as they labored to surmount the unfamiliar complexities of Samuel Barber's *A Stopwatch and an Ordnance Map*, Schoenberg's *Friede auf Erden*, and Stravinsky's *Symphony of Psalms*. They blanched at the prospect of learning a new work by Paul Hindemith. On October 16 a spokesman for the dissidents addressed their grievances to their conductor:

O Shaw, gifted leader of our brilliant choir,
Hearken to our tale of grief and sadness:
Though we do drink our orange juice,
We remain stupefied by those crippled 19ths,
And their swarm of homeless flats and sharps.
True, there is great honor in singing next century's music.
But can mortal ears exult to the epsom salt
Of Dello Joio, Barber, Schoenberg, Stravinsky and Hindemith?
We shout and strain and heave, yet there is no joy.
The memory of Beethoven and Toscanini fades quickly away.
We yearn for juicy steaks a la Mendelssohn, Bach, Handel and
     Brahms,
But we live in penury and no red points.
The love of singing is no longer with us,
For there is bitterness in our mouths. (From epsom salt, Bob.)
O Shaw, gifted leader of our brilliant choir,
Have mercy on our tender guts.
                                   Sincerely yours,
                                   Ludwig Wolfgang Jones

Shaw fired off a reply to whomever it might have concerned, pointing out that, in terms of actual performance time throughout the season, the classics had it over the moderns "at least 3 to 2, and maybe 2 to 1." More importantly, he reminded his readers, the Collegiate Chorale was one of the few choruses in the country interested in the performance of contemporary music.

> I'm not talking about *next* century's music. Who's interested in *this* century's music? . . .
>
> The Collegiate Chorale is dedicated to the proposition that this century and this people have a voice and a song and something to say. Our whole reason for being together is tied up in that faith. And while some of the things we may do are alien to the very great tradition of our European heritage, we can only be very humble and hungry before the beginnings of the new American song. . . .
>
> We were not always this concerned with today's music. In the early months . . . we spent our time on the conventional college glee club sort of repertoire. One of the surprising accompaniments of the swing toward the new song has been the accelerated interest in the real masterworks—of Bach, Beethoven and the Titans. They seem quite surprisingly to go hand in hand. Every time we tried to find a healthy new voice we found a healthy, fresh, old voice.
>
> We're not going to turn our backs on these works and these men. Their gifts are certainly not antiquarian or stale. But at the same time—it's about time that the sick, unhealthy emphasis of musical art as a vehicle for personal exploitation is recognized here in America. And that it be given back to the composers.
>
> If that's a twenty-five year job, then it's the job of our generation—and the job of the Collegiate Chorale.
>
> Robert

Shaw's business correspondence has always been sparse and to the point. But in his letters to the Collegiate Chorale—and, later on, those to his choruses in Cleveland and Atlanta—his whole self is present and accountable, replete with convictions and anxieties, ambitions and frustrations, realities and ideals. One began:

> Dear People:
> This is Monday night—after that late rehearsal—and I want desperately to talk to you. I wish it were possible to sit with each of you for an hour or two and just talk Collegiate Chorale—because I'm worried about it.

He was perpetually worried about it, and the Collegiate Chorale letters were worksheets in which he tried to resolve some of the dilemmas inherent in the institution that was growing up around him:

—His desire to give as many singers as possible the opportunity to experience a wide range of repertoire, versus his realization that the varied stylistic demands of that repertoire necessitated his maintaining a "small choir" of the most talented singers within the larger organization, despite the attendant psychological and personal conflicts. ("We believe that music is peculiarly a doer's art, and its benefits are in direct proportion to active participation.")

—His determination to preserve the amateur status of the Collegiate Chorale, while faced with the obligation to keep it solvent by accepting professional engagements. ("We believe that the choral instrument should assume a position of respect and musical responsibility commensurate with the distinction of its literature and comparable to that of the major professional orchestras.")

—His commitment to music as a way of life, versus the popular attitude toward it as a supplement to everyday existence. ("We believe that music is more a necessity than a luxury—not simply because it is 'therapeutic,' nor because it is the 'universal language,' but because it is the persistent focus of man's intelligence, aspiration and good will.")

Many of his letters reviewed basic technical principles and procedures for the edification of new members or put them in other words for the benefit of the old:

> Let's begin with the chorales [in Bach's *Christmas Oratorio*]. There are two fundamental faults in our singing of these: enunciation and rhythmic quality. With respect to the former we need to remind ourselves that enunciation is not simply a technique—but also a spirit. It is not enough to follow the rules—to which all of us have now been exposed. Good enunciation comes with the *desire to communicate*—and that is not a technique but an attitude—a *spirit*. That is to say—unless each of us really *loves* each little sound, the "disappearing" vowel in a diphthong, the hummed consonants, the exploded "t," the final "d"—unless each detail is precious to us—no set of rules can ever be effective. It ought to be written in blood or fire—it sounds too passive in pencil. Take any of the chorale texts: "How can I fitly meet thee?" Say it quietly often enough to induce a semi-hypnosis—and then ponder how miraculously the little sounds have become a part of the spirit of the text. Taste the *texture* of even a single word. "Fitly . . . . fitly . . . . fitly." —Naught but the spirit giveth life.

Other letters document his personal growth as a musician. In the letter of February 14, 1946, he recounted four experiences that had taught him one important thing. First, there was the performance of Beethoven's Ninth under Toscanini.

> Toscanini's Beethoven was great not primarily because he could get more (from his performers) but because he could hear more (in the music). . . . There was over all his passion a mantle of sadness and defeat, as though (I think) he heard sounds and relations and forms in his own study which he could never actually achieve in performance.
>
> That must have been very nearly my first consciousness of the conductor's art as synonymous with the art of hearing, of listening.

Next was Stravinsky's *Symphony of Psalms*, with the composer himself conducting.

> We had just finished a performance of that work with the New York City Symphony [on January 21–22]. And I think all of us were greatly impressed by Leonard Bernstein, his superb musicianship, his intimate knowledge of the score (to the point of memorization), his enthusiasm, and his vital, vigorous interpretation of the Psalms.
>
> The radio performance [over CBS on January 30] was a different thing. Here was one of the great musical figures of our time, and one of the time's heroic pieces—his piece. And *he* had the score in front of him. He allowed himself a bare minimum of interpretative gesture. His rehearsal was calm and precise; a word here, an explanation there. But *always*—the score. Always listening. Nonviolence—and more listening.

The third lesson came with the Bach motet that the small choir had sung for the New Friends of Music on February 3. (It was a "railroad-rhythmic version" of Bach's *Singet dem Herrn ein neues Lied* —a distinctively "Americanized treatment," said one reviewer, which was "giddy and exciting, having somewhat of the sect-group revival spirit about it, more earthy and physical than reflective or devout in nature. A touch more and those on the mourner's bench might have been sent.")

> It is a work of frightening difficulty. . . . And a couple of weeks prior to the concert we had rugged rhythm and a fair-to-middling sonority—but very little Bach. What we had was not a motet—but a contest.
>
> Fortunately, we also had friends, among them musicians, and among the musicians Julius Herford. He attended a rehearsal, and after we had sung it through, I turned to him. "It seems to me," he

said kindly, "that if we all did a little less singing and a little more listening, we'd have more Bach."

The fourth experience was his encounter with a paragraph in Hermann Scherchen's *Handbook of Conducting*: "To conduct means to make manifest—without flaws—that which one has perfectly heard within oneself."

> In the early days of the Chorale I felt it was our business to grab an audience by the shoulders, shake well, and say "Look here, we *believe* this! You've gotta believe it, too!"
>
> I'm ready to qualify that now to this extent. It seems to me that if you really believe in the integrity and worth of a piece of music, then you must believe that it speaks or ought to speak ideally with a directness and persuasiveness far beyond your own "poor power to add or detract." And your only valid endeavor is to *get out of the way of the music.*
>
> It seems to me that some sort of a troth has to exist between a performer and his music whereby the performer says, "Bach (or Brahms) is here. Let's listen."

The season of 1945–46, which had begun so auspiciously with Beethoven's Ninth, continued from pinnacle to pinnacle. Barber's *Stopwatch* and Schoenberg's *Friede* were dispensed at the Christmas Concert in Carnegie Hall in mid-December, along with settings of carols by Peter Warlock and Ralph Vaughan Williams, and J. S. Bach's *Magnificat*. Then came the Stravinsky, followed by the NFM concert. On February 17 and 18 the Chorale sang the Brahms Requiem with Shaw—fists clenched to prevent his nervousness from showing—conducting the New York City Symphony. The consummation was reached on May 14 in the City Center, when the Chorale premiered its second major commission, Paul Hindemith's *When Lilacs Last in the Dooryard Bloom'd*, at the first annual Sponsors' Concert.

It was Julius Herford who had urged Shaw to contact Hindemith about the possibility of writing something for the Chorale. Hindemith had been driven from Germany by Nazi harassment, had settled at last in the United States in 1940, and was now teaching at Yale. Through a mutual acquaintance Shaw gained an introduction to the composer and asked him if he would accept $1,000 for a commission. The outcome was a titanic opus, which Shaw regards as one of the great choral utterances of the twentieth century.

Hindemith had already written one song with piano accompaniment using a portion of Walt Whitman's threnody on the death of Abraham Lincoln. Moved by the horrors of World War II as well as by the death of President Roosevelt on April 14, 1945, Hindemith proposed to extend the song with choruses and other solos. When finished, his "Requiem for Those We Love" comprised four sections in eleven episodes for mezzo-soprano, baritone, chorus, and orchestra.

The commission was confirmed in the fall, but Hindemith didn't begin serious work on it until February; the last orchestra part was delivered a little more than three weeks before the performance. Shaw went over the score with Herford note by note, phrase by phrase, until he acquired a thorough comprehension of "the excitement of design and plan and line."

Early in May Shaw wrote a long article for the *New York Times* reiterating the Collegiate Chorale's commitment to contemporary choral music, emphasizing Hindemith's importance among living composers, and explaining the significance of the new Requiem. "It is the work of a profoundly organized musical mind. Tonalities, and rhythmic and melodic motives have insistent and conscious significance. The smaller sections of the work have their own logic and construction, and there is a grand and unifying architecture throughout." He also revealed the extent to which his own musical perceptions had grown through his contact with the work.

> And the thing that has been fresh and exciting to those who have been studying and rehearsing it has been the discovery of the vitality and spiritual eloquence of form itself. What we have faced—many of us for the first time—is the awareness that logic does not militate against the expressiveness of music. The fact that music is built with mind and craftsmanship and a sense of order, the fact that its construction is calculable upon earnest study, does not in any way decrease the degree of its "inspiration" or leave it emotionally sterile. For there is a spiritual quality to pattern itself, the awareness of which may be one of the chief qualifications of the mature artist.
>
> Paul Hindemith's "Lilacs," I feel, has disclosed that if music is to have life, it will be gained by an increasing awareness of the beauty and spiritual quality of the informing architectures.

Preparing for another performance nearly twenty years later, this time by the Cleveland Symphony Orchestra and Chorus, he reflected further:

> By tradition those forms which can carry the largest amount of text per musical minute are *recitative* and *arioso*. With incredible virtuosity, Hindemith has managed to set the whole of Whitman's *Lilacs* in only slightly over an hour—and still give us a sinfonia, marches, double fugues, arias, dramatic choruses and a chorale. —And the miracle is . . . that though it is one of Whitman's "loaded" poems, Hindemith has enriched enormously Whitman's language—its intellectual content, its emotional variety, and its introspective subtlety.

A week or two before the first performance Hindemith attended a Chorale rehearsal, sitting off in a corner with the score before him and a set expression on his face. Mack Harrell was supposed to have sung the baritone solos, but his contract with the Metropolitan Opera interfered, so Shaw called on a bass-baritone by the name of George Burnson, a young Californian with a beautiful voice but limited experience. Burnson had so much difficulty with the part that finally Hindemith, exasperated, summoned Shaw. "For the love of God," he whispered, "find out what notes that young man can sing, and I will write them!" The value of the experience of working with Hindemith and Shaw was not lost upon Burnson, who subsequently set out to study in Europe, and not long afterward became one of the most famous bass-baritones in the world, under his new name—George London.

At the close of the rehearsal Shaw reassured the weary sufferers "of the bleeding throat" that the composer was moderately happy about their interpretation. "He likes it," Shaw said with a straight face. "He thinks it's good music."

The critics were not all of a similar accord. Several recognized its power and majesty, but one or two found it overlong and "perilously tiresome." Shaw himself admitted that it was indeed "a sometimes 'gray-brown' work, . . . somewhat dense and opaque, occasionally clotted or knotted, and not overly festive."

Hindemith, however, was indifferent toward others' opinions, favorable or not. As Shaw recalled on the occasion of still another performance, by the Atlanta Symphony Orchestra and Chorus in 1974:

"Why should I?" he replied to the invitation to attend the world premiere. "Do you think you can *perform* it as well as I can *hear* it?"

It was not, I think, that music should remain on the page, unperformed. Rather for Hindemith it was that the economic and social adjuncts of present day performance had little or nothing to do with music's meaning. He finally agrèed to come to the premiere of *Lilacs* not to accept the audience's tributes, although he was then one of the most revered figures in the musical world, but because an earnest group of amateurs had spent long and loving hours on his most recent love's labor.

Today, not only is the musical language a good deal more scrutable, but its quietness and understatement, its willingness to encounter sorrow and invite solitude, offer at least a note of caution to a society affluent principally in inhumanity, the big lie and flatulence.

Hindemith was much man. As was Lincoln—who also was wry and self-deprecatory. Whitman may sometimes have filled his words with too much wind—but not on this occasion; and one did find him in the hospital wards tending gangrene and despair.

Vote yes for *Lilacs*. Vote hundreds of times each day. Each vote one note. Given enough right notes we might even validate universal suffrage.

Lilacs was repeated over the air on June 2, with Shaw conducting the CBS Symphony. Since it was an unsponsored program, and the network's budget severely limited the size of the chorus, he relinquished his own stipend in order to secure extra voices.

Immediately after the broadcast, Shaw and twenty selected members of the Collegiate Chorale boarded a train for Lenox, Massachusetts, and the sylvan precincts of Tanglewood—the Berkshire Music Festival.

In the summer of 1934, on a private estate known as Tanglewood, nestled among the Berkshire Hills near Lenox, the first series of concerts was performed by sixty-five members of the New York Philharmonic; two years later Tanglewood became the principal summer home of the Boston Symphony Orchestra.

In 1940 the Berkshire Music Center was established under the direction of Serge Koussevitzky. Though only six weeks long, and not a credit-granting institution ("Credit! Vass iss credit?" demanded Koussevitzky. "It iss a credit to *come* to Tanglefoot!"), the center is nevertheless one of the finest graduate-level schools anywhere, with emphasis on performance in orchestras, choruses, chamber ensembles, and opera groups. In addition, there are frequent lectures by men and women prominent in the arts and letters as well as music.

When Shaw went to Tanglewood for the first time in 1946, Aaron Copland was there to teach composition, Gregor Piatagorsky to coach chamber music, and Olin Downes to lecture on music criticism. Other guests included Howard Hanson, William Schuman, and Edward Weeks, essayist and editor of the *Atlantic Monthly*. Shaw's assignment was to teach classes in choral conducting, along with Hugh Ross of the Schola Cantorum, and to prepare the chorus for a performance of Beethoven's Ninth Symphony.

As if the summer weren't full enough with work at Tanglewood alone, he took on a guest conducting appearance with the NBC Symphony. Shaw had already made his debut as an orchestra conductor the preceding May 30, when he led the Naumburg Orchestra, made up of musicians from the New York Philharmonic and other local symphonies, in Beethoven's First Symphony, overtures by von Weber and Rossini, and Borodin's *Polovetsian Dances*. The concert was one of three provided annually since 1905 to the people of New York City on the major civic holidays—Memorial Day, Fourth of July, and Labor Day—by the wealthy clothing manufacturer, banker, and music patron, Elkan Naumburg. It took place on the Mall in Central Park from the bandstand Naumburg had given to the city in 1923. Because of its informal, somewhat festive character, the event attracted little notice from the critics. Not so the mid-August broadcast by the NBC Symphony, when Shaw conducted Beethoven's Second Symphony, the Fifth Symphony of William Schuman, and Peter Mennin's *Festival Overture*. Robert Bagar reported in the *World-Telegram*: "What particularly impressed me was his naturalness, the well-co-ordinated, well-paced flow of the music in each case. I thought there existed certain resemblances between Mr. Shaw's and Arturo Toscanini's conception of the Beethoven Second. Mr. Shaw should be encouraged in this latest predilection. He is a sincere musician with considerable gifts and an infinite capacity for taking pains, which, we may conclude with Thoreau, 'is the hallmark of genius.' "

The talk between Shaw and "the gang" that summer at Tanglewood usually came around to the Collegiate Chorale—whether it

Shaw and Paul Hindemith

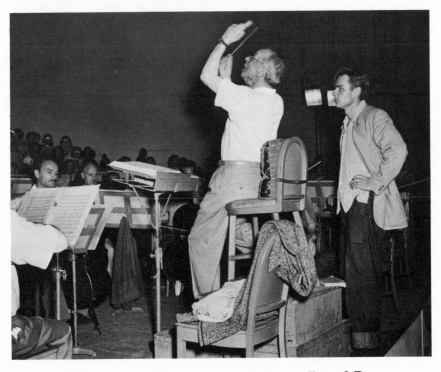

Serge Koussevitzky conducts the recording of Beethoven's Ninth at Tanglewood, August 1947. RCA Victor Records Photo

should be expanded, or whether all energies should be directed toward the development of a smaller professional touring choir. When rehearsals resumed in the fall no decisions had been reached, but ideas were taking shape that were to mature within the next year or two.

Meanwhile, Shaw's presuppositions about music in general, and choral music in particular, continued to evolve. For instance, by November the axiom that musical form symbolizes musical spirit had been transmuted into a new one with broader ramifications:

November 19, 1946

We have, almost from the beginnings of the Chorale, assumed the function—if not the particularized truths—of that relationship, and now with a frightening clarity and in a flood of specific detail I begin to understand that music is spirit.

We began years ago by assuming that song was a story—it had a tale to tell, an argument to deliver, or a mood to convey. Its function was dramatic. Song was drama. Our first understandings of spirit in music were limited then to understandings of text; and our techniques centered around systems of enunciation and a practical speech discipline, if also text was seen to qualify tone and sonority.

We understood spirit, too, as synonymous with our own corporate enthusiasm for the music we sang. It was very evident in concert performance that here was a group of people who loved to sing together and who somehow believed their song.

But at this point and from this time on the Collegiate Chorale begins. I have never felt so sure of anything in my life. The hours after rehearsal last night, though mixed and jumbled, begin to resolve. The ends for which we have assembled take shape; the pace and manner of their achievement grow more conscious and clear.

I believe that the essential musical properties—harmony, melody, rhythms, tone and dynamics—under whatever critical microscope —are to be understood finally and only as relations of qualities.

I believe that form in music is a symbol of relations and values, not a blueprint of construction technique.

I believe that intervals have quality; that good intonation is the result of sensitivity to truth and untruth in tonality.

I believe that the voice is fantastically responsive to musical understanding, and that in every instance the sense of what must be precedes the how.

And I am no longer so concerned about the inability of any choir (including the Chorale) to master the long line of a long piece in a single sitting; for there are a hundred miracles in every measure worthy of the whole of a man's understanding.

I believe, then, that spirit in music is not the wholesale emotional orgasm that weeps appropriately in public, but rather the marshalling of one's keenest, most critical consciousness—till one hears in terms of values and the movements of values, until the most pedestrian minutiae of pitch and rhythm are heard inwardly in relation to adjacent minutiae; and finally in relation to wholes of form, tonality and intent.

The process of arriving at such a perception was no less strenuous than the effort to carry out its musical implications in a way that could be recognized and appreciated by a listener. The preparation and performance of the B Minor Mass, which climaxed the season, was one of the most conspicuous examples of that effort. To begin with, Shaw analyzed the score in infinite detail before the first rehearsal, determining the expressive import of every possible relationship. Then he deployed his forces in proportions approximating those typical of the baroque era: the small choir of the Chorale, consisting of but sixty voices, was matched with an orchestra of only thirty-five players, including harpsichord and organ. In the solo and duet movements he reduced the accompaniments to single instruments or at most two on a part. As a result, observed Virgil Thomson,

> the accompanied solos, really small chamber ensembles, took their place in the choral framework of the *Mass* very much as the concertino group in a concerto grosso is set off against the larger instrumental body. The work became thus a dialogue, an antiphony, each kind of music being both beautiful in its own way and comfortable to hear, the two kinds giving amplitude and perspective to the expression of the whole. . . . Rhythmic courage, tonal exactitude, pretty balances and sweetness all around allowed the proportions of the work to take on full majesty without any heaviness.

Shaw's success in getting the performers out of the way of the music and allowing the composer to speak for himself disappointed other critics, who were perhaps conditioned by Stokowski's sentimentalization or the Oratorio Society's massive sonorities. "There was need of definition of mood, of assertion beyond statement," wrote one, and it seemed to another that Shaw's accomplishment "was all in the objective, intellectual phase of the endeavor."

From then on, for quite a few years, critics tended to be sharply divided in their perceptions—and judgments—of Shaw's work, some hearing in it the intellectual, others the emotional, side of the conductor. One recognizes the rationality of a Hindemith, another the sensibility of a Herford; one senses the fastidiousness of a Szell, another the passionate abandon of a Toscanini. It was to be some time before they actually heard Shaw. And all the while Shaw himself struggled mightily over the same ambivalences. His prologue to that letter of November 19, 1946, was indicative:

> Half-ideas are transient-shaped,
> Or else they must dissolve somehow each into each.
> If only they would stand completely still
> Until one found the words their size.
> "I see, your measurements are thus and thus—
> That's clear enough."
> You inventory your entire stock—
> "Now this should fit"—and turn to find
> It really doesn't fit at all.
> You have a cubed suit
> For a sphered thought.
>
> You were sure that thought had corners.

In many ways it was a lonely struggle, but Shaw was surrounded by a small group of individuals who in one way or another shared it with him, people in pursuit of similar ideals who were willing to be absorbed into Shaw's endeavor in order to turn them into realities. Foremost was Julius Herford, who, now a companion and a partner as much as a teacher, was acknowledged as music consultant for all the major concerts and recordings, such as that of the B Minor Mass. Then there was the coterie from the Chorale, "the gang," who not only helped carry out the logistical end of that operation, like soliciting contributions from sponsors, but also were friends and confidantes with whom he could engage in informal dialogues that were mutually instructive—Florence Kopleff, Clayton Krehbiel, Charlotte Bieg, Tom Pyle, and a few others. The beer sessions after rehearsals would go on for three or four hours. "Those were the real learning situations," one of them remembers, "just to hear him talking and asking questions that ranged over everything in the world."

In 1946 the Institute of Musical Art and the Juilliard Graduate School were merged into the Julliard School of Music, and in the fall Shaw was named director of choral music by the new president, William Schuman. Unsuited to formal classroom teaching techniques, Shaw turned his conducting classes into high-powered bull sessions, and remained himself as much a student as a teacher.

Shaw daily reexplored and retested the concepts that had been germinating in his own mind—conducting as the art of listening, choral singing as a democratic art—concepts whose fruition was accelerated by the open and aggressive intellect of these people whom he eagerly confronted. Every idea that came up, like every experience he ever had, was examined for its potential viability as part of a working hypothesis.

The question of the future of the Collegiate Chorale, for instance, was ultimately resolved when, after numerous conversations around and about the subject, Shaw discerned ways in which the implications of its brief, phenomenal history could be put into action. As the 1947–48 season opened, he assessed the situation for the enlightenment of the membership.

> The Collegiate Chorale is no longer a community chorus. It is not simply that your progress and your so-called technique are a subject of national interest and criticism—there's not a choral director in the country who isn't aware of your programs and their critical success or failure. In terms of membership about 30% of you are in New York and in this choir to study. You do not expect to make New York your home. Some of you expect solo careers, others plan to teach, others conduct—and this is a part not only of your recreation, but your education. You do not know where you'll land.
>
> To you people, the Collegiate Chorale must say, "Help yourself— and if it is helpful—help others." . . . And to the others who are rather permanently settled here—we must accept the responsibility of the perpetuation of this training-ground and this "mother earth." It is now for this purpose, too, that we exist: to make it possible for such specifically talented and professional musicians to be with us for a season or two and to leave with our best wishes, to extend our common work.
>
> That introduces—or rather it recognizes what already exists— an element of transiency and professionalism to our membership. I say that is a good thing—and for all of us who are resident and non-professional—this is the chief avenue by which we can extend our program and our musical faith. The amateur will help provide the education of the professional—and the little child shall lead them. That's a big responsibility—you doctors and lawyers and private secretaries—and you've got to assume it.

The third factor that qualifies the Collegiate Chorale is that it is a musical organization. That is rather unique among choruses. Most of the finer choirs exist in connection with some school or church—with the attendant mixture of motives. Industrial, community and adult choruses most frequently (and there are exceptions) are recreational or social ventures.

The Collegiate Chorale is not a social club—though you are welcome to make friends or get married if you are so moved (3 in the last 3 years—and I can see more on the connubial horizon). It is not an inter-racial chorus—though you would be strapped to find a more polyglot personnel. We're not trying to prove that democracy works—not any more. We're trying to make music—together.

The outcome of countless hours of deliberation was an elaborate scheme to erect a Choral Arts Foundation, designed "to widen the horizons of the choral art and to help it achieve a mature and responsible position in American musical life." It was announced that beginning with the 1947–48 season the Collegiate Chorale would present a subscription concert series; an educational division of the foundation would offer formal courses in "the literatures and techniques of the choral craft," with emphasis on the study of musical structure; and the extension division would undertake the publication of music as well as a periodical on choral art, the organization of community and industrial choruses, the organization of a group of associate conductors available for festivals throughout the country, the establishment of a rental library of choral music, and the continued commissioning of new music, "with added attention to shorter works suitable for public school performance."

Two phases of the foundation were already under way. First, the Chorale, in association with the Jacob Riis Neighborhood Settlement and the First AME Zion Church of Brooklyn, had helped organize the Brooklyn Chorale, providing conductor, accompanist, and music, plus assistance in setting up audition procedures and plans of membership, function, and government.

Second, the educational program had been intermittently operating since its beginning in 1942. Now, for a small tuition fee, courses in the rudiments of choral musicianship, including sight-singing, theory, and the like, were offered by Vladimir Ussachevsky of Columbia University; methods of score study and structural analysis were to be given by Julius Herford, then a member of the

Juilliard faculty; a conducting seminar was directed by Shaw; courses in German Lieder, opera literature, and contemporary art song were coached by Leo Rosenek, Walter Taussig, and William Jonson; and at intervals eminent guest lecturers were to appear before the whole Chorale.

For a time it appeared that another objective of the Choral Arts Foundation might become a reality: the establishment of a resident professional chorus comparable to a major symphony orchestra in quality and purpose. A series of six low-priced concerts by a thirty-voice ensemble of Chorale members, plus a chamber orchestra, was projected for the 1947–48 season, to be underwritten by the New Friends of Music, performed at Hunter College, and broadcast over WABF-FM. As usual, Shaw preferred to use soloists from the chorus, being opposed to the hiring of big-name virtuosos merely to attract customers. The music, mostly new to American audiences, was chosen by Shaw and Herford together, and was to consist of six Bach cantatas, six Mozart masses, and assorted works by Hindemith, Ravel, Copland, Diamond, Krenek, Schuman, and Ives.

Unfortunately, anticipated costs exceeded the available resources of both the New Friends of Music and its benefactor and president (and president of the radio station), Ira A. Hirschmann. Even Shaw, who had personally covered the $3,400 deficit the Chorale had incurred with its Sponsors' Concert the previous season, was helpless. The series was abruptly cancelled in November.

The foundation limped along for a few more years. The list of sponsors contributing from twenty-five to one hundred dollars grew from forty-six to one hundred thirteen names in three seasons, and read like a rollcall of the most magical names in American music and society: Leonard Bernstein, Walter Damrosch, Charles Ives, Jacob Javits, Otto Kahn, Fiorello H. La Guardia, Elsa Maxwell, Wilfred Pelletier, John Raitt, Richard Rodgers, Gustav Schirmer, Jr., William Schuman, Mme Olga Samaroff Stokowski, Deems Taylor, Maestro Arturo Toscanini, Fred Waring, Mrs. Cornelius Vanderbilt Whitney, and many others. Yet all their gifts and good wishes were not enough to support the Chorale *and* the foundation. The Board of Governors held an auction to raise money, offering such treasures as a few measures of autograph manuscript from Walter Piston's *The Incredible Flutist* (the bid for which was won by a Chorale member). A couple of grants were received from the Juilliard Foundation to help with commissions. There was even some talk of affiliating with a college or school, but nothing came of it. The momentum of the 1947–48 season dissipated, and the grand plan failed to materialize. Events were drawing its prime mentor farther and farther away from active involvement in it.

The most permanent and far-reaching work of the Collegiate Chorale was that carried on by those who helped themselves—and helped others. The annual membership turnover of 40 to 50 percent, which had been a plague in the early days, was now almost a cause for pride. Men and women came from every corner of the country, revolved in the orbit of Shaw's influence for a season or two, and then moved on. Many became choral conductors in churches, schools, colleges, and universities. There were those who merely borrowed some of the more colorful and imitable characteristics of Shaw's conducting, along with a few of his more incisive aphorisms. The majority, however, discovered that what they had learned would work with any group of singers, whatever the age or competency.

There were many lessons to be learned through an association with Shaw, not the least of which were industriousness and concentration, for he covered an astounding amount of repertoire in a given period of time. Within the eighteen months between the fall of 1946 and the spring of 1948 he conducted some twenty-five choral scores that were new to him, from a Palestrina Mass and Ives's *Harvest Home Chorales* and *67th Psalm* to the B Minor Mass. He led the Juilliard Chorus in Bach's *St. John Passion* and Mozart's Requiem. He conducted the Collegiate Chorale and the CBS Symphony in Beethoven's *Missa Solemnis*, and the Boston Symphony Orchestra and Tanglewood Chorus in Stravinsky's *Symphony of Psalms*. There were world premieres of Hindemith's *Apparebit Repentina Dies*, Copland's *In the Beginning*, Malipiero's *La Terra*, and Charles Bryan's *The Bell Witch*.

To fill out the schedule there were repetitions of some of the above under varying circumstances, plus performances of Blitzstein's *Airborne Symphony* and Stravinsky's *Oedipus Rex* with the New York City Symphony under Bernstein; preparation of another Beethoven Ninth for Toscanini (televised in April of 1948); Easter Sunday CBS broadcasts of "The Son of Man," with script by Archibald MacLeish and music selected from the B Minor Mass and the two Bach Passions; guest conducting at the Potsdam Festival (Hindemith's *Lilacs*), at Pomona College, in Los Angeles, and the All-Kentucky High School Chorus; and the regular round of incidental performances by the Chorale at testimonial banquets and forums.

At odd moments he was learning to play the violin and the trumpet, getting ready for a radio series and a concert tour and— briefly—competing in a ping-pong tournament.

The Collegiate Chorale sang the Ives pieces in April of 1948, after working on them for more than two months. At the end of January, following the initial reading of the *Chorales*, Shaw had written:

Well—
    The Ives *Chorales* are at least *different*.
    I keep thinking of what Martha Graham said the other evening concerning contemporary music. She spoke of being in a Carnegie Hall audience surrounded by people who sat in calculated rapture while the established repertoire was played, but who, at the first note of a contemporary score, climbed into their high dudgeons and departed. —Whereupon Graham gets mad. "They have no right to be sore—they don't even understand the music. Who do they think they are! Such vanity!"
    I'm still plenty perplexed by this set of Ives' pieces (though not nearly so much by the *Psalm* which we'll do next Monday—simple and purty)—but I do think Graham's frame of mind is the one that counts. It isn't smug music, and no smug chorus is ever going to perform it, and no smug audience is going to like it.
    Actually, the sounds are very exciting. Most of you are so immersed in the struggle for your own lines that you don't get to hear the over-all avalanche. And while I can't yet figure the pieces mentally, the sum total is very exciting emotionally.
    I can remember Bill Schuman saying of some works that he didn't particulary admire intellectually, "so what—when I listen to it, it gets me; and anything that *excites* me is good music." —which makes me wonder if the first of us to "get" the Ives won't be those of us who are the less "intellectual" musicians. —Not that the ability to read won't help—but that this music is a little like a forest fire, and you have to be willing to go up in smoke to be a part of it. —Remember the good old days when we first did William Schu-

man's *Free Song* (alongside of the Ives a *Sweet and Low*)? There was plenty of misgiving and misapprehension then—but since we didn't know from nothin' we just sang our throats out.

It would be awful if the Collegiate Chorale ever became a respectable institution and thought before it sang. 'Might as well bring a towel and a change of clothes to rehearsal Monday. We'll have the Red Cross there to bank the blood.

Robert

Shaw invited Ives, then seventy-four and in ill health, to attend the performance, but the composer's wife, Harmony, sent regrets, adding: "He does hope to meet you and to shake the hand of a man who isn't afraid to tackle a hard job."

II.

The White-hot Years

4.

The Robert Shaw Chorale

EVERY SUNDAY EVENING at eight—fall, winter, and spring—since 1936, millions of radio listeners had tuned in NBC's lively half-hour comedy featuring ventriloquist Edgar Bergen and his wooden-headed companions, Charlie McCarthy, Mortimer Snerd, and Ersel Twing. Any act that could win the chance to try to sustain those listeners' loyalties to time and station through the summer months could also test its ability to meet the competition of a regular broadcasting season.

The Robert Shaw Chorale, consisting of thirty singers and a pianist, mostly from the "small choir" of the Collegiate Chorale, got its chance in 1948 when the show's sponsor, Standard Brands, Inc., hired it to replace the Edgar Bergen show with a nine-week series beginning Sunday, June 6. The half-hour programs contained madrigals by Monteverdi and di Lasso, hymns and Bach chorales, part-songs by Brahms, familiar Broadway tunes arranged by Henry Brant, folk songs and spirituals, and nine Choral Profiles by Gail Kubik—settings of poems from Stephen Vincent Benét's *Book of Americans*. The weekly signature was a Waring-flavored singing commercial for Royal Pudding.

In certain respects it was an ideal time to embark on such a venture. Shaw's RCA Victor Chorale had recently won first place in the vocal ensemble category in *Musical America*'s annual radio poll of daily newspaper music editors and critics in the United States and Canada. Also, the exposure might help assure the success of the first Robert Shaw Chorale tour, which had already been booked for the fall of 1948. Finally, there was still a slim chance that the good-music era of radio was not yet over, and that between recording, touring, and broadcasting, Shaw would be able to keep a professional chorus working the year around.

"How the show fares will be watched closely by the trade," *Variety* magazine remarked, "for Standard Brands, it's understood, attaches unusual significance to the program. SB reasons, for one thing, that when television hits its big-time programming stride and takes over the comedy-novelty act roster of shows, it's the type of musical show it is experimenting with this summer that will survive in the AM program picture."

Unfortunately, such hopes were doomed by the networks' increasing reliance on audience-preference surveys in determining program policies, and by the sudden diversion of radio's profits toward the development of television broadcasting. Toscanini remained on NBC until his death in 1954, but CBS's "Invitation to Music" was terminated in the spring of 1948, although the previous year it had won the George Foster Peabody Citation for bringing to the air "compositions and composers who deserve but might not otherwise have received the hearing." Several other less sophisticated series were likewise withdrawn from the air, to be replaced by low-budget quiz shows and other egregious stuff. In 1953 *Musical America* suspended its annual radio poll because in nine years so few new programs of high artistic merit had been developed that the same programs and the same network, NBC, turned up year after year as winners. Radio's role as a systematic purveyor of "good music" came to a virtual end in 1959 when the thirty-one-year run of the "Voice of Firestone"—never a repository of the sublimest classics, to be sure, but several cuts above rock and roll—was ended not because the sponsor was unwilling to continue footing the bill, but because ABC wanted the program's prime time for a show with a better popularity rating. Only Texaco's regular Saturday afternoon Met broadcasts remained secure.

People who looked forward to the possibility that television might assume the responsibility for carrying the art of serious music to the nation were encouraged when the NBC Symphony and the Philadelphia Orchestra were heard and seen on different networks on the same Saturday afternoon in March 1948. However, that was the first time in three years any live symphonic music had appeared on video, and viewers could not fail to notice that the new medium was far more compatible with the action and drama of opera than with the static aspect of the concert and recital stage. Proof was seen in the first full-length telecast from the Metropolitan Opera in November of the same year, plus the subsequent successes of Samuel Chotzinoff's NBC-TV Opera Company, established in 1949 and climaxing with the first classic television opera, Menotti's *Amahl and the Night Visitors*, in 1951.

Neither operas nor concerts were afforded the continuity on television that they had enjoyed on AM radio in the old days. Moreover, the intermittent scheduling of most such events on television only served to intensify the competition between mass-appeal and limited-appeal programs (protests flooded in when Toscanini preempted the Lone Ranger), and to create conflicts with live concerts, which local managers were powerless to predict or counteract.

For a while it appeared that FM broadcasting, which had increased significantly between 1940 and 1947, would provide an alternative outlet for live musical performances. Proponents of the new medium were convinced that its high fidelity quality, free of atmospheric noises and fading, would enable it to compete with AM stations on the basis of programming rather than wattage, and that the motto "FM means Fine Music" would prove itself true. At the close of World War II there were only 48 FM stations in operation; by the spring of 1948 there were 435 on the air, with an additional 580 under construction, and license applications pending with the Federal Communications Commission for another 70. At that point, the boom began to bust.

The networks remained fundamentally committed to the concept of AM broadcasting because they already owned the most powerful stations across the country and were thus capable of reaching a larger audience in behalf of their advertising clients than was possible via FM. Nationwide hookups of FM stations could not be effected without losing the benefit of the 15,000-cycle frequency range—exceeding AM's by 10,000 cycles—that was their main appeal to begin with. In addition, there were legal battles over patents, which delayed the manufacture of FM receivers.

Some AM stations tried to satisfy the demand for FM transmission by broadcasting AM programs simultaneously over the other frequency, but Petrillo insisted that double forces of live musicians be employed, which few stations could afford. Ultimately, independent FM station owners found themselves trapped into competing with their AM rivals within the narrow scope of popular program appeal rather than technical quality. The Long Playing record, introduced by Columbia in 1948, facilitated the broadcasting of classical music, inasmuch as an entire symphony or string quartet could be played without interruption, but the idea was so new and the library of serious music so limited that FM station managers were reluctant to try it for several more years.

Concert management, though exempt from some of the vicissitudes of radio and television, is a highly speculative business. During most of the nineteenth century it was solely in the hands of colorful entrepreneurs like P. T. Barnum, Max Maratzek, and James Henry Mapleson, who independently and personally promoted concerts wherever there was some chance for profit. All too often, they were compelled to accept full financial responsibility for their errors in judgment. Successful impresarios earned their reputations at the cost of such great travail that the desperate ones who fled town with the proceeds of a sold-out house could gain a kind of folk-heroship.

In the late 1880s the pattern began to change. Artists' agents set up shop in New York and sold their wares to a new breed of speculators, the booking agents, who established themselves in other metropolitan areas and assumed all the risks. Still, profits made from one concert could be wiped out by the next.

Then, in 1921, Harry P. Harrison, formerly general manager of the Redpath-Chicago Lyceum Bureau, and Dema Harshbarger, formerly head saleswoman for the rival Century Lyceum Bureau, conceived a booking procedure that revolutionized American concert life. It served to expand the market for travelling virtuosos, gave the management industry a degree of economic stability, and somewhat relieved musical performance of the onus of crass commercialism at the box office. By 1930, after various refinements in technique and some high-level power plays, there were two such booking companies in operation, the Civic Concert Service and the

Community Concert Service. Each was a subsidiary of an artist agency: Civic was owned by the National Concert and Artists Corporation, Community by Columbia Concerts Corporation.

Instead of booking artists one at a time and relying on separate publicity campaigns, Civic and Community organized audiences in advance for an entire series of four or five concerts. A volunteer association of a town's leading musical devotees was set up to solicit "memberships." No reserved seats or single admissions were available; everybody paid the same price for the series. The membership drive began in the spring, and the goal was to fill every seat in the largest auditorium in town. When it was finished in the early fall, and the cash was in hand, the association contracted with its parent agency for the best artists it could afford. Commonly this meant one major star and three or four lesser lights. Field representatives sent out from the New York offices gave pep talks to membership committees and offered guidance to local chairmen in everything from publicity, bookkeeping, and house management to the etiquette of extending hospitality to visiting artists.

The organized audience plan was efficient enough to survive the Depression years, and by the end of the thirties both Civic and Community were enjoying yearly increases in bookings. The wartime prosperity of the early forties and the closing of the European market permitted continued growth. By the end of the war the two combined were controlling nearly 90 percent of all professional concerts given in the United States and Canada. But as inflation began to permeate the national economy and mobilization for the Korean conflict got under way, the picture darkened. In the winter of 1949 all management agencies were suffering as much as a 25 percent decline from the previous year's business.

Nevertheless, by 1952 three times as many concerts were being given annually in the U.S. and Canada as in all the rest of the world, and the total concert audience in North America had doubled in twenty years. It was clear that the scope of the industry was now almost commensurate with the size of the territory. "The growth of interest in the art has been so great that even television can't kill it," crowed NCAC president Marks Levine.

In the mid-fifties the hegemony of the two great empires began to dissolve under the onslaughts of internal dissension and public scandal. In 1954 Ward French, then president of Community, was fired because he expressed objections to his firm's monopolistic practices. The publicity left a scar on Community's public image. In 1955 a U.S. attorney filed suit against Columbia, Community, NCAC, and Civic on charges of conspiracy and restraint of trade because they had privately agreed to refrain from trespassing in one another's territories. The defendants pleaded *nolo contendere*, paid a fine, and promised to keep their business transactions open to inspection and all dealings open to competition. But the scar became uglier.

Soon hundreds of organized audiences were won away by independent managers. The newcomers, located not only on the East Coast but also in the West, the Midwest, and the South, limited themselves to running organized audience circuits and providing talent from any and all sources. In 1961 David K. Sengstack, president of the Summy-Birchard music publishing company in Evanston, Illinois, bought Civic from NCAC, thus leaving Community the only booking agency in the business directly connected with a management agency.

The trend toward decentralization had been gaining momentum ever since the mid-forties, and Shaw had reacted to the rising public sentiment favoring decentralization in a speech he made in 1946. He declared that the problem was not to be solved merely by dispersing material resources, emphasizing his point with a parody of the opening chorus from T. S. Eliot's play *The Rock*.

> The fundamental question is not that of "decentralization" but that of music. What do we *decentralize*? New York?
>
>> The endless cycle of recital and concert
>> Endless opera, endless virtuosi,
>> Brings knowledge of sound—but not of music.
>> Knowledge of the performer, but not of the creator.
>> Knowledge of techniques and ignorance of the why.
>> Where is the life we have lost in living?
>> Where is the music we have lost in singing?
>
> We decentralize—We cut up, divide, and apportion. Who gets the Metropolitan Opera Company? Who gets Carnegie Hall? Who gets Teachers College? Who gets Juilliard Graduate School? Who gets the church music in New York? Who wants it?
>
> New York City may have more music—but it's accountable to the law of averages, not to the law of the spirit. Music is not to be

weighed in terms of concerts per second, as members per union, or sopranos per cubic foot. Music is a quality of the human spirit. And I have seen more music in Lincoln, Nebraska, with 400 high school students singing William Billings, and upstate New York with 300 college students murdering Bach, and Eagle Rock, California, with 30 choral conductors criticizing each others' methods and attitudes, than I have in most of eight years in New York City—which included several trips as far north as 122nd Street.

The significant miracle would be the changing of the water into wine, not the pouring of the liquid into more and smaller bottles.

The first Robert Shaw Chorale tour was an exercise in faith and perseverance on the part of Shaw, Walter Gould of the independent James A. Davidson agency, and Davidson himself.

Shaw had already tried unsuccessfully to sell Columbia on the idea of a tour, but the star system was the basis of the concert industry, and Columbia, like NCAC, was interested only in attractions that possessed qualities capable of beguiling the greatest number of concert-goers. Soloists were the easiest to sell; with high fees and low travel expenses, they could also return the most in commissions.

Group attractions were less profitable, and few of them could meet the common standards of stardom. The Don Cossack Chorus and the Trapp Family Singers, both on Columbia's roster, bore an aura of exoticism—the one with its repertoire of Orthodox liturgical music, Russian opera excerpts, and folk songs and dances, the other with its quaint Austrian peasant costumes and overtones of sentimental conjugality. The all-Negro De Paur Infantry Chorus was a symbol of American victory in the recent war. The American Male Chorus, which entered the field briefly in 1947 ("Twenty young men from all parts of the country—Protestant, Catholic, Jewish"), was trying to capitalize on the waning doctrine of democracy-in-and-through-music. And who could resist the cherubic charm of the Columbus Boychoir? The Robert Shaw Chorale, with its thirty singers and seven instrumentalists clad in severely formal attire, had nothing to sell but the classics of choral literature.

James A. Davidson was a man with the skill, courage, and flair equal to the requirements of a tough business. He represented Margaret Truman during her brief singing career in the late forties, and through her persuaded President Truman to initiate the FBI investigation of Columbia and NCAC that led to the court case of 1955. He referred to his agency as "the Tiffany's of the concert field," and thus was somewhat nervous about risking a tour by an "ordinary" choral group, and an untried one at that. It was his salesman, Walter Gould, who convinced him that it was worth a try. First, Gould reminded his boss, most of the agency's artists were at or near the peaks of their careers, and it would be wise to nurture some younger talent to take their places in the future. Second, Shaw had begun to accrue considerable popular appeal through his recordings, chiefly the first volume of *Christmas Hymns and Carols* issued in 1946. Third, the radio series Davidson had already secured for Shaw would, he hoped, intensify that appeal.

Tours by the agency's well-known soloists and group attractions could be set up by mail, relying on inquiries prompted by advertisements stressing rave press notices from both respected critics and small-town reporters. To find buyers for the new Robert Shaw Chorale, Gould had to get out and beat the bushes. He sketched out a tentative itinerary and followed it through in person.

Concert booking and management were hard work. An agent had to see that local sponsors maintained a balanced season with well-timed concert dates. Where conflicts were unavoidable, special promotional campaigns had to be designed. Then there was the perennial problem of finding auditoriums in which artists could be presented to the best advantage. Even in the early fifties, cities like Los Angeles, Seattle, Portland, Spokane, Birmingham, and Atlanta lacked adequate facilities. In many towns the only alternative to a high school gymnasium with a crude stage at one end was a movie theater, where half the sound went straight up into the flies and most of the rest was soaked up by the velour drapery. Pianos might be untuned, if not untunable. Lighting equipment? Antiquated, or partly inoperable, or already set up for the cues in the community theater group's next play. Dressing rooms? Crammed with junk.

A manager also had to reckon with the musicians' unions. The oldest and largest, the American Federation of Musicians, dealt with orchestra players; the new American Guild of Musical Artists was expressly concerned with the concert tour industry.

In 1940, the year James Petrillo became its president, the AFM, a branch of the American Federation of Labor formed in 1896, had somewhere between 140,000 and 160,000 members from both the entertainment and symphonic fields. Petrillo set out on a massive campaign to combat the loss of income his musicians were suffering because of the recording industry's growth. He led a two-year strike against the recording companies, which was settled in 1942 when RCA Victor, Columbia, and Decca agreed to pay the union royalties of from a quarter of a cent to five cents on every record sold. The union was to put the money into a welfare fund for unemployed musicians. When the Taft-Hartley Act of 1947 invalidated that arrangement, Petrillo had to begin all over again. The settlement of the 1948 dispute created the Music Performance Trust Fund, which, supported by "contributions" from the record manufacturers, was to be used by MPTF to provide free live performances for charitable and educational purposes.

In 1936 AGMA was organized by a group of solo artists, including Lawrence Tibbett, Jascha Heifetz, and Gladys Swarthout. Their first accomplishment was to persuade the Columbia and NCAC managements to guarantee minimum fees and engagements under exclusive contracts and to limit commissions and promotional charges.

AGMA's membership quickly expanded to embrace choristers, members of corps de ballet, stage directors, and stage managers. Then, in 1939, the claims of Actors Equity and Chorus Equity were arbitrated, leaving to those two the exclusive control of singers and singing actors in the Broadway musical theaters. In 1940 another jurisdictional dispute was settled, this time with Petrillo's union, whereby all instrumental soloists, as well as all accompanists, were to pay dues to the AFM, while AGMA retained control over their contracts with managers.

AGMA introduced group life insurance benefits, negotiated salary scales that almost kept pace with inflation, and tried to encourage union orchestras to use professional choruses. It also protected its members touring with group attractions; in 1948 the Guild's policy limited performances to a maximum of six per week and travel to 300 miles per day.

There is no power whatsoever, though, that can mitigate the daily trials and tribulations of touring, which has always been a kind of life best tolerated by musicians with plenty of youthful stamina.

Hours of immobility in a bus seat someone designed for the "average" human body produces cramps in *your* legs and a crick in *your* neck. If you open a window a crack to dilute the diesel fumes with a dusty breeze, you must put up with a draft around your feet.

Mile after mile of roadside scenery blurs past at seventy, punctuated by the polyrhythms of telephone poles against fenceposts against Burma-Shave signs. You doze until one of the card-players in the rear of the bus signals with an ear-splitting shout or a slam that a winning streak has been capped or a losing one broken.

The remoter the rest stop the more likely there'll be room in the parking lot for a short game of touch football, and the less likely the blacks will be harassed.

A blizzard or a flash flood revives conversation with companions you haven't bothered to talk to for several days. Will we make this evening's concert in time—or at all?

Having lost twenty minutes looking for the concert hall, you waste another twenty waiting for the local contact to let you in. You stifle yawns through a half-hour warmup rehearsal. On to the hotel for a shower and supper, leaving conductor and road-manager to build risers out of locker room benches and lunchroom tables, remove drapes to expose the brick wall (will those radiators bang tonight?), and improvise a sound-shell with pieces of scenery and scrap lumber.

Or postpone supper, for temporary lack of appetite, until after the concert. Chances are you'll go without if the sidewalks are rolled up at sundown. Otherwise you follow the hot-grease smell to the neon sign that flashes "EATS—GAS" in prophetic juxtaposition.

But usually you can count on the post-concert reception with the predictable spread of food and drink. And the pallid rejoinders to pallid openers.

Wait for a taxi or walk in the rain back to every hotel where every jukebox in every bar downstairs gets louder toward 2:00 A.M. And be up at 6:00 for a 7:30 departure. And repeat.

But whenever the curtain rises there is no time before or after, and no space in the dimness beyond the podium. Once again you are totally immersed in the music you are trying to get entirely *right* for once.

Gould offered prospective sponsors their choice of two programs. The heavier one began with Bach's *Jesu, Meine Freude*, followed by five part-songs by Brahms and eight sixteenth-century motets and madrigals; after intermission came Poulenc's Mass in G Major, the *Six Chansons* of Hindemith, and Copland's *In the Beginning*. The other started with Bach's Cantata 131, the eight Renaissance pieces, and eight *Liebeslieder Waltzes* from Brahms's opus 52, while the second half consisted of the Copland work and Hindemith's *Chansons*, four folk song sketches arranged by Gail Kubik, four Negro spirituals (Dawson's "My Lord, what a morning" and "Soon-a will be done," a Kubik arrangement of "Soon one morning," and Shaw's own setting of "If I got my ticket"), and four Broadway show tunes. The second program was the one requested most.

The tour opened in Cleveland on Sunday, October 3, 1948, under the auspices of the Cleveland Civic Concert Association. The reviews were typical of those received all along the way. Herbert Elwell of the *Plain Dealer* was excited by the ensemble's versatility, its tonal beauty and balance, and its clear enunciation. Above all, he attributed to Shaw "a perception of rhythm such as the gods give but rarely, and probably only to young Americans."

The itinerary led the troupe circuitously westward through Chicago and Milwaukee, to Kansas City and Tulsa, then south. On the twenty-third Shaw wrote a newsy letter to the Collegiate Chorale:

Dear you-all—
—which is 'cause where I am. At this moment (the first unhectic one in our three weeks of punt-pass-and-pray) in the Buccaneer Hotel over-looking the surf on the Gulf of Mexico in the great nation of Texas.
The tour has been a "qualified" success: Concerts every night, and sometimes twice a day; programs running as much as two and three-quarters hours with encores, never less than 2 hours 10 minutes; voices tired once or twice at crucial places, and some laryngitis and illness, and at least four concerts bad from performance-standards; and reviews fabulous (even at bad concerts). Sometimes the choir has sounded not less than wonderful—and that helps.

Tonight we sing in Houston. Big football day there today, and circus tonight. So don't know whether we'll have a crowd or not.

I've been traveling with the choir about half the time—and seeing a lot of country. Rest of the time by train and plane to arrive early enough to remake some of the world's worst stages into acoustical "triumphs." —Can't be done a lot of times. —But that is the *big* problem (along with vocal fatigue). If the choir can hear themselves, and warmly—then we have a good concert.

In Valparaiso, Indiana, they couldn't hear themselves clearly, so after the first movement of the Bach cantata Shaw moved the entire ensemble onto the floor in front of the stage.

Audiences, though enthusiastic, were often disappointingly small. "Perhaps there is something wryly wrong with our vaunted taste for music," wrote the *Chicago Tribune*'s usually acerbic Claudia Cassidy. "Some of the more gaudily pretentious frauds perform to packed houses in an atmosphere no less luxurious for being in the worst possible taste. Yet Robert Shaw's Chorale, possibly the finest chorus of its kind in existence, fails to fill Orchestra Hall of a quiet Sunday afternoon." In Houston the large house was dotted with fewer than five hundred people.

Whenever there was time, Shaw visited nearby high school and college choirs and conducted them in a few minutes of rehearsal. Although it invariably gave the students a tremendous boost in morale, now and then it demanded the utmost in tactfulness on Shaw's part. Once, having accepted an invitation to conduct a group of youngsters in his own "Set down, servant," he quit after a few measures and turned the choir back to its director, who proudly led them on through it.

"The choir made a stirring religious paean of it," observed an innocent newspaper reporter. "You could tell Mr. Shaw liked it that way. Then he explained why he himself hadn't gone on through the spiritual with the choir. He sensed that the regular director's interpretation was different than his own. The difference was in the cryptic rhythm.

" 'It's better than my way, too,' he conceded."

The Chorale wended its way along the Gulf Coast to Pensacola, then up to Atlanta (where risers had to be constructed of Coca-Cola crates) and Richmond (there to enjoy its first day off after twenty-six consecutive performances), back down for a loop around the South (in one day alone covering over 600 miles), thence north to New Hampshire, and finally into Pennsylvania. Thirty-eight concerts in forty-three days!

Back in New York after the tour, Shaw juggled an ever-increasing variety of operations—conducting the Juilliard Chorus, keeping the Collegiate Chorale afloat, making plans for two tours in the 1949–50 season, guest conducting here and there, and studying orchestral scores with Herford.

During Lent the Robert Shaw Chorale presented a six-concert series sponsored by the American Broadcasting Company and the Protestant Radio Commission, called "The Music of Penitence." The repertoire consisted of two cantatas and a motet by J. S. Bach, Palestrina's Stabat Mater and other Renaissance classics, some early American anthems, three motets by Poulenc, and the first radio performance of Stravinsky's Mass in C. Shaw wanted to make it an annual, even a year-round, series, in the hope that Americans would "soon judge for themselves how good the best is" and forsake modern church anthems, which he called "popsongs with sacred texts."

The work at Juilliard was frustrating. He expected that the constraints of academic rule and regulation would assure better rehearsal attendance than he had ever been able to get from the Collegiate Chorale, but it wasn't happening. The baffling complexity of Bernard Rogers's new Passion was not exactly endearing to the students, either, and Shaw tried to console them:

> Rehearsal has been like trying to run through some highly intricate football plays with five men and six hypotheses (which change position, too). It's hard to go swimming when there's only a little puddle here and a drop or two over there, and who knows how long it will be before the next rain, and whereinhell's the river? You think you have this little splash staked out, but the next time through you can't find it, and how you gonna get your feet wet?

The Collegiate Chorale, preparing for the premiere of its third major commission, Peter Mennin's symphony *The Cycle*, at its Fourth Annual Sponsor's Concert on March 18, was little better off. Shaw wrote them a pep talk.

Shoulders to the wheel, —all for each, each for all—let us pull together—heads held high—feet on solid ground—marching forward into the sun—bound to win—hearts on fire—noble resolve—arm in arm—.

You know: get yourself off in a corner: grab a holt of your lapels, shake slightly, and address you—"Blank," sternly, "on a week from Friday night you is going to sing in Carnegie Hall. Now, you didn't join no chorus to be no soloist (that's the Clincher)—and dad-burnit, son, if you don't do some mighty tall rehearsin' in the next fortnight you're liable to rate personal critical attention—a callow breed, son.

"Moreover," and the jaw juts a bigger than average trifle out of respect—nay, admiration—for the new strength of purpose which floods the mind. "Moreover," you repeat, trying to think of something to say, "I got just two more weeks to tell that old Servant Of Brotherhood Shaw where he gets off. For 7 years he's been crawlin' down my back with that hysterical hate-filling screaming that's supposed to be 'love of Music.' Well, I been called more unfriendly things in any one night by that one little Serv. of Broth. than I was in 4 years in the Army—and I ain't gonna miss a single minute of any chance to rub his nose in it.

"You can tell that little SOB that I'll see *him* Monday."

B of S

Owing to the demands of nonstop conducting and teaching, not to mention the questions from the more astute interviewers he encountered on the road, Shaw was continually reiterating the articles of his personal credo. He chanted them like mantras, and in the process extruded new and sometimes harsh truths. His persistent feelings of inadequacy in front of an orchestra didn't jibe with his dictum that "music is one art, . . . a single craft." His inability to learn scores easily at the piano prevented him from living faithfully by the doctrine of "conducting as the art of listening." He didn't begrudge himself the effort, but learning a score one note at a time required more hours than he could find free. Moreover, he could never find time to listen to any music but that which he was conducting.

At the Sponsor's Concert Shaw announced he had been granted leaves of absence from Juilliard, Tanglewood, and the Collegiate Chorale until at least the autumn of 1950, and possibly two full years. His intention was to spend the first summer in Paris studying with Nadia Boulanger, attending concerts, and meeting composers. Then, with time out for tours in the fall of 1949 and the spring of 1950, he would study orchestral conducting in San Francisco under Pierre Monteux and his associate, Artur Rodzinski.

A few days later he set out on the 1949 spring tour, a four-week trek through the upper East and Midwest. After that there was a backlog of recordings to catch up on. In mid-June he fled to Europe, alone.

Aboard ship he carried a gift from Thornton Wilder. The two men had become acquainted earlier that year when Shaw, inspired partly by Wilder's device of placing actors in the audience, approached the playwright with an idea he had been mulling over for six or seven years—a new type of operatic work with a libretto by Wilder and a score by Igor Stravinsky.

> I had travelled from NYC to Wooster, Ohio, with him where he was performing the role of the Stage Manager in his *Our Town*, and we spent the hours surrounding rehearsals and performances discussing the possibilities of a musical drama linked somehow to the "meaning" of the volunteer "peoples'" chorus.
>
> My only "plot-idea" was callow and nebulous: What if we began with a bare stage, and gradually assembled a "chorus" from out of the audience?—man in all his diversity joining others equally committed—to what?
>
> We were never able to get beyond Thornton's original practical and experienced objection: "Dreamer, in *Skin of Our Teeth* it took me fifty minutes of playing time to get *one* person out of the audience onto the stage, and now you want me to arrange for one hundred!"

Nevertheless, a cordial friendship developed, and they corresponded off and on for many years.

The gift, entitled "Steamer Thoughts," was a hand-written collection of short pieces containing philosophy from Goethe, epigrams from Pascal and La Rochefoucauld, musical quizzes on Bach and Handel, and character sketches of Shaw. One was entitled "A Bow to the Audience—What Is It?"

> They have come to hear great music. They hope to God it is in good hands. If Robert Shaw is no good why is he there? We hope and can assume that he is modest before the task of unfolding the reaches of the MASS IN B MINOR. [The two had also conferred in May at the Potsdam Festival, where Robert was conducting the

Mass.] But there is a contract in the air: He has given public notice that he does not believe that he will misrepresent or degrade that score. But he is not here to wave his hands in the vacant air. Sixty people are with him, all bent on the same assignment. When his bow is quick and curt it does just what he is trying to prevent: It calls attention to himself. How indicate to them that in acknowledgment of this applause he is not merely one Robert Shaw, but the man, the symbolic man, whom those sixty persons are going to trust, on whom Bach is depending? The man in whom we have placed our own hopes? By a very slow and quiet bow—a lowering of the head which is neither servility nor self-gratulation: Which says: I am here at the service of you all, and of something greater than you all. That inclination of the head you can hold a very long time, —the longer it is the more eloquent it becomes, and the more impersonal it becomes.

Another began:

Robert Shaw stands badly. He walks with a kind of roll, throwing his shoulders from right to left, as much as to say, "I can stand up as straight as anybody. But today's off the record. Let's be informal." This comes from a psychological factor frequent in those who arrive early in life to positions of authority. The director of a chorus must be tyrant and absolute. However persuasively, tactfully, he fills the role, they must efface themselves in obedience. This set up a conflict in the younger Shaw. He did and he did not want to be a tyrant. His modesty shrank from it; his anxiety before the demands of high art shrank from it. So off the podium he adopted, he fell into, this carriage that seemed to say to others: "Look, I'm just a fella. Look, I don't take up much space. Look at my self-effacing slouch—I wouldn't browbeat anybody."

These conflicts—constructions—make for loneliness, for they are a play-acting and cut one's self off from the audience for which they are intended.

As an antidote, Wilder admonished his friend to "carry a princely posture."

Shaw went first to Paris, where he introduced himself to Mlle Boulanger, who had heard much about him. She was characteristically cordial and referred him to one of her associates for the solfege studies he requested.

One evening he met Poulenc and received an invitation to visit the composer a few mornings later in his apartment on Rue de Médicis. Shaw arrived at the appointed hour, but was surprised to find the composer had not yet arisen, and then embarrassed to learn he had come on the wrong day. While waiting for Monsieur Poulenc to shave and dress, he put on the record player a pre-release copy of the Mass in G major that he had brought along. Poulenc rushed back into the room at the sound of the first Kyrie and sat transfixed, shaving lather drying on his face, listening tearfully until the end. Then, as if unburdened of thirty years of reputation as one of the more witty and sophisticated members of *Les Six*, he exclaimed: "At last, the world will now know that I am a *serious* composer!"

Shaw had found enclosed with the "Steamer Thoughts" some letters of introduction to a few of Wilder's acquaintances in the *haut monde* of arts and letters—Sir Laurence Olivier, Madame Marie Bosquet, Lady Colfax, and Alice B. Toklas. He used the one to Miss Toklas, but otherwise found himself uncomfortable in the rarefied atmosphere of the Parisian salons, having no musical motives for being there. Instead he spent most of his time with the only American he knew in the whole city—Bill Brown, a student from Yale. After a few weeks of boozy nights and woozy days—of "running away from home," as he put it—he had had enough. He met Maxine and the children in Shannon, Ireland, and went with them to Switzerland, where eight-year-old Johanna and six-year-old Peter were put in school. But soon he succumbed to the urge to return to Scarsdale to begin preparations for the approaching concert season.

He welcomed the return to the concert stage when the fall tour began on October 2. The program consisted of Bach's Cantata 4, Poulenc's Four Penitential Motets, Debussy's *Trois Chansons*, some Schubert songs for male chorus, three late-Renaissance pieces, a few operatic choruses, and several folk songs arranged by Gail Kubik. This tour, with sixty-one concerts in seventy days, was a little less strenuous than the first two, but it had its quota of bad weather, lost luggage, and illnesses, and Shaw injured his back while moving some scenery. Though houses were not always full, the Chorale never got by with less than six encores, after which Shaw would laughingly beg the cheering crowd, "Please go home." Audiences were invariably charmed by his relaxed, informal manner—his brisk hop-skip-and-a-jump from the wings to the podium, his way of supplementing the printed program notes with enlightening commentaries, and his humorous ad libs in the lighter parts of the program. In one of the encores, as a couple of the men tapped out a rhythmic accompaniment on the lid of the grand piano, Shaw would point to them and shout over his shoulder, "TWO YEARS AT JUILLIARD!"

Above all, it was the ingenuity and eclecticism of his programming that swept listeners along. Most critics approved of the pattern, but some thought the folk songs and similarly ingratiating pieces cheapened the overall effect. "In the background, it seems, always 'a cigarette burns,'" wrote one reviewer, recalling Shaw's association with Waring, and the Chesterfield show's syrupy theme song.

Shaw flew to San Francisco to begin his studies with Monteux and Rodzinski early in January of 1950, still in the throes of a profound slump after the sustained emotional high of nightly performances and the constant pressure of time schedules, interviews, and unforeseen crises. He wrote to Wilder, who, surprised to hear from him, musingly replied: "Something tells me that on the whole you're not a natural letter-writer; so when you do write a letter it means that you are sort of at your wit's end for company and talk and general sociability. Eight hours a day at solfège! Oh my God. I sure hope the Maestro gets there soon and you can start hearing how he blends an oboe into the strings in Debussy.

"Hope your dejection has passed—a *little* misery never hurt anybody. You can't conduct Mozart's G MINOR unless you've had lots."

On March 10 Shaw sped off with the Chorale on tour number four—three weeks in the East, with the same program as the previous one.

The next three tours were the most arduous to date, both physically and musically. From January 7 through March 18, 1951, the Chorale presented sixty-five performances in thirty-six states between the Atlantic Coast and the Rockies. The following autumn, between September 29 and December 16, the seventy-nine-day itinerary began in Aurora, Illinois, extended all the way to Vancouver, B.C., south to San Diego, and back to Pittsburgh, Pennsylvania— sixty-seven opening nights. On February 28, 1952, they returned to the West Coast, this time for only thirty days.

Tour poster, 1950–51 season

The first four Chorale tours, with the Bach cantatas and the motet, had been revolutionary, inasmuch as music as challenging to both performers and listeners had never before been programmed by any professional touring group. For years, artists had played down to small-town audiences on the assumption they were less mature than those in the major cities. But Shaw refused to concede any such difference. For the three tours of 1951–52 he augmented the thirty-member chorus with a twenty-piece orchestra, and devoted the entire first half of the program to Mozart's Requiem in D Minor.

The vagaries of touring made it difficult to keep even the easiest program at peak level, and everyone involved—except Shaw—wondered whether, over the long haul, they would be able to sustain the technical security and emotional vitality the Requiem deserved. And would audiences in the hinterlands sit still for such heady fare?

After a performance in a shabby little industrial town where the local sponsors had warned that the Requiem was "too highbrow," a young woman waited until the last autograph seeker had left, then approached Shaw. "I suppose," she said quietly, "there are two kinds of people who can understand that music—those with a musical education, and those who have known great sorrow. I am no musician. Thank you very much."

Speaking at the commencement ceremony at the College of Wooster, where he received an honorary doctorate in late March of 1951, Shaw reflected on the first tour with the Requiem. "There is no doubt—and it is cause for thanksgiving—that our country is involved in a striking growth of musical activity. Nothing stands between the people—whatever that is—and Great Music—whatever that is—but bad performance, and pedantry, and the narrow mind." The final performance, he recalled, was to be in Boston's Symphony Hall, and it had to be at least as fresh and convincing as the best.

> Music comes hard.
> Sixty-four performances under every conceivable condition of fatigue and tension, a growing technical mastery, a deepening understanding. On the sixty-fifth performance it happens. Now they know—and without notable exception, fifty professional musicians break down and shed tears.

You finally realize that the mind and the spirit are not poles apart, that intelligence and the heart don't cancel each other, that if you finally can comprehend how a work is constructed, it is not proved to be a machine. You scratch and you scramble over intellectual difficulties, and you get mad and curse your own weak little mind and cry and quit daily. But every once in a while running through the bones you see blood, and every once in a while you hear music.

All three Requiem tours were punctuated by unwelcome surprises, as usual. A bus breakdown outside of Manhattan, Kansas, delayed the concert there nearly an hour. At a lunch stop in Lake Charles, Louisiana, two of the men who took a walk to stretch their legs failed to return by departure time. They had been arrested on suspicion of passing bad checks in another town they hadn't even been near. Springing them from jail took precious time, and it was still three hours' drive to Houston. The "auditorium" at the University of Kentucky turned out to be the monstrous 15,000-seat Coliseum, built by and for the school's basketball team, and completely panelled with acoustical tile. Shaw wrote back to the Collegiate Chorale: "One should be able to hear himself think—if he were given to reflection—during a championship game. —But for music, for chamber music like a Mozart Requiem, the Yankee Stadium would be as good a bet. Kyrie eleison!"

On the Wednesday after their appearance in Cullowhee, North Carolina, they battled a snowstorm through the Great Smoky Mountains and across the Cumberland Plateau to Nashville. Thursday morning the highways were absolutely impassable, so Shaw cancelled the next two dates, in Oxford, Mississippi and Monroe, Louisiana, and bought train tickets to Birmingham. There was no concert scheduled there, but it was "south," and that sounded good. On Friday they boarded the night train to Jackson, Mississippi, for their next engagement. All available pullman berths went to the women, while the men took turns napping in the few empty coach seats and standing in the aisles. By curtain time Saturday, four of the troupe were too ill to go onstage.

Some sort of a causal relationship seemed to prevail between weather and music, and Shaw contemplated the mystery in a parody of Frost's "Mending Wall," which he sent to the Collegiate Chorale from eastern Pennsylvania.

February 28, 1952

From the diary of a fallow-traveler—

Today is a fine day in Wilkes-Barre, because last night was a good night in Williamsport. —Nice hall, wonderful audience, and the best *first* concert we've ever had. —More than a trifle Frost-y, this, but—

> Something there is that doesn't like a bad performance,
> That sends the frozen air-swell
> To tremble black and wet, upsetting
> Larynx, bowel and bow-arm—
>
> For the life of me
> I can't see why it should be so.
> Weather is one thing
> And music . . . is another.
> Is it that wrong notes are rain-makers?
> Or that tunes well-played
> Will shift the cold air masses?
> I turn to him again, "But why?
> Surely song cannot prescribe the season."
> He does not even interrupt
> The warming leisure of his walk.
> He only says,
> "Good music makes good weather."
>
> I confess that I am slow
> To find between the two
> The logic in this linking.
> But every year and every tour
> It happens so—good weather
> Follows sure on good performance.
> And I must guess that he has hid
> Some instinct knowledge that to me
> Is comfter-bly obscure,
> "Good music makes good weather."

By the end of 1951 the Collegiate Chorale, founded to test the applicability in an amateur milieu of rehearsal and performance techniques developed in the professional entertainment field, had moved from its initial preoccupation with patriotic, seasonal, and

The Robert Shaw Chorale

popular music to a dominant interest in serious choral compositions by contemporary Americans. Next, under the stimulus of
periodic associations with great conductors and orchestras, and
with the guidance of Julius Herford, it had "discovered" the choral
works of Brahms, Verdi, Beethoven, Mozart, and Bach. From
within the large chorus had emerged a group of about forty singers
who sought to demonstrate the viability of their "amateur's creed"
on a professional level, with special attention to the choral classics
of more modest dimensions. Alumni of the Chorale had meanwhile
been infusing the essentials of the tradition into American musical
life, principally as teachers and conductors, and the Robert Shaw
Chorale had started demonstrating new standards in repertoire and
artistry from coast to coast and border to border.

Shaw's ultimate ambition, the establishment of a permanent
repertory chorus comparable to a symphony orchestra, was yet to
be fulfilled, owing to several obstacles. To begin with, the type of
singers he liked best to work with were "at the perilous period—

of no one knows how long duration—in which they will or won't become notable solo artists." They were upward bound in their careers. Out of the personnel that had toured with him during the 1950–51 season, Shaw told a reporter the following October, four had since received Fulbright Fellowships for study abroad, one had been signed up by the Metropolitan Opera, two more had won prizes in the Blanche Thebom contest for opera singers, and two more had given debut recitals in New York. Several others had found security in college teaching jobs. This meant that a new Robert Shaw Chorale had to be built every September, at least, if not twice a year.

On top of that, there was not enough continuous, high-paying employment in the field to keep a single group intact between tours. The hope of another radio series had not materialized, and recording dates were neither sufficiently numerous nor significantly profitable. From the very first, virtually every radio and recording chorus Shaw conducted had been a prescription group made up for the specific engagement at hand. Finally, it was questionable whether New York audiences were willing to support a full-time professional chorus.

Nevertheless, Shaw firmly believed there was a place in American musical life for the kind of institution he had in mind, and he was determined to take one more step to try to establish it. On January 6, 1952, in Carnegie Hall, he conducted the first of a projected seven Sunday night concerts in his new Choral Masterwork Series.

Nothing comparable had been heard in New York since the days of the old Friends of Music, which from 1913 to 1931 presented an annual series featuring rare or unknown works, mostly orchestral, as well as premieres of compositions by Bloch, Schoenberg, Mahler, Honegger, and others. Shaw's series went like this:

January 6—Mozart, Requiem; Ravel, *Trois Chansons*; Debussy, *Trois Chansons*; Bartók, *Cantata Profana* (American premiere).

January 27—Bach, Mass in B Minor.

February 3—Hindemith, *Apparebit Repentina Dies*; Brahms, *Nänie*; Josquin des Pres, *Miserere*; Dello Joio, *Psalm of David* (New York premiere).

February 17—Beethoven, *Missa Solemnis*.

April 13—Bach, *Christ lag in Todesbanden*; Bernard Rogers, *The Passion.*

April 27—Stravinsky, *Symphony of Psalms*; Schütz, three motets; Poulenc, *Stabat Mater* (American premiere).

May 11—Haydn, *The Creation.*

The Robert Shaw Chorale and the RCA Victor Symphony were to appear in all but the third concert, which was to be performed by the Crane Chorus and Orchestra from Potsdam, New York, with Shaw and the Crane conductor, Helen Hosmer, sharing the podium. The Collegiate Chorale was paid $3,000 to assist in the Beethoven, Rogers, and Haydn works.

The series was planned jointly by Shaw and Herford, but its financial backing was entirely in Shaw's hands, and from that standpoint it was a gamble. Even though the Robert Shaw Chorale was one of the hottest attractions in the concert business, along with Heifetz and Rubinstein, it was impossible to cover expenses with box-office receipts. The *Missa Solemnis* alone would cost nearly twice as much as the hall could return, full, at reasonable ticket prices. Given the greatest possible degree of success, Shaw expected to lose at least $10,000; the maximum deficit could be more than $50,000. In reply to questions from incredulous friends and reporters, he said firmly, "Look, this is the only way I know to make the kind of music I believe in with the kind of people I believe in for the kind of audience I believe in."

Shaw had been absent from the New York concert scene for two years, and people were eager to hear the chorus the rest of the country was raving about. The opening concert was a *succès fou.* Olin Downes of the *New York Times* averred that Shaw's studies had " 'paid off' in depth and understanding, the further development of his conductor's technique, and his capacity to interpret a score."

Yet Downes, like several other critics, regretted the apparent lack of vocal sensuousness and spontaneity in the Chorale's performance. "When Mr. Shaw conducts," said Downes, "one hears an orchestral chorus." *Time* magazine's headline for its review read "Too Much Perfection." Of the soloists, only Florence Kopleff was unanimously lauded. Arthur Berger of the *Herald Tribune* called hers "one of the great, rich voices of our time." The rest of the series was, by and large, a *succès d'estime*. After the sixth concert, Berger remarked, "It is rather a pity that attendance has not equalled the ambitiousness of the project."

That ambitiousness was measurable not only in terms of the breadth, difficulty, and expense of the project, but also in the meticulous care that Shaw lavished upon each score. Poulenc, receiving in Paris a private recording of the performance of his *Stabat Mater*, later remarked to Jay S. Harrison of the *Herald Tribune*: "I can only say that [Shaw] understands me better than I understand myself. Understands me? No. He divines my intentions. It is as though the work were performed fifty years after my death. Never in my lifetime did I expect to hear a composition of mine played with such calm and perfection. You know Shaw? He is, of course, a genius." Poulenc played the tape for Ned Rorem and declared, "He's known how to play my music at the same speed as the blood flows through my veins."

On April 21 Shaw called the Collegiate Chorale's board of governors into special session to announce the cancellation of the seventh concert. The public would be told only that his new translation of *The Creation* would not be ready in time. The other reason was that he could not afford the cost of the performance. He had already lost $40,000 on the Choral Masterwork Series.

At the end of May, Jacob Avshalomov, then conductor of the Columbia University Chorus, whose *Tom O'Bedlam* was to win the 1953 Music Critics Circle Award following its premiere by the Collegiate Chorale, assessed the overall importance of the series in a letter to the *Times*:

> The choral art has been raised to a more dignified level, where skill and devotion are more nearly in balance. This gives courage to those who are composing today as well as to those who make music in the lower reaches of amateur endeavor.
>
> Although it is the mode to be condescending about Mr. Shaw's handling of the orchestra, he has shown a greater development in this regard during the past couple of years than some of our distinguished orchestral conductors have manifested toward the chorus in a decade. Concerning interpretation and music insight, who is without failings and blind spots? But the course of choral practice consistent with our times has been set. Let's hope the resources will be available for another series next year. Dammit Bob, good going!

Shaw was already making plans for a three-concert Choral Masterwork Series in 1953, at a projected personal loss of $25,000:

Sunday, February 15 (Collegiate Chorale, Robert Shaw Chorale, Choir of the School of Sacred Music of Union Theological Seminary, RCA Victor Symphony Orchestra)—Hindemith, *When Lilacs Last in the Dooryard Bloom'd*; Janáček, Festival Mass, *M'sa Glagolskaja* (erroneously announced as an American premiere; the first and only other performance to date had been given by the old Friends of Music in October, 1930).

Sunday, April 12 (Robert Shaw Chorale and Concert Orchestra) —Bach, *Komm, Jesu, Komm*; Schubert, Mass in G; Milhaud, *Six Sonnets of Jean Cassou* (New York premiere); Foss, *A Parable of Death* (New York premiere).

Sunday, May 3 (Collegiate Chorale, RCA Victor Symphony Orchestra)—Haydn, *The Creation.*

Two letters written to the Collegiate Chorale that winter attested that these concerts were not simply artistic rituals.

February 12, 1953

Things which one believes most deeply should be, I suppose, the most clearly defined and capable of expression. —But, somehow, it is not always the case. There seems to be a reservoir of understanding in all people, the transference of which is a fragile, tentative and sometimes painful thing. Thus it is when one speaks as earnestly as he can about such understandings, and does so spontaneously—as I did at the close of Wednesday's rehearsal—when it's over he wonders whether he's said anything at all and the things which he would like to have said, and whether they were said in such disorder or in such a manner as to maim their intent.

That which should be repeated above all is appreciation for the intelligence and devotion which all of you have brought to the study and preparation of these two rather difficult works [Hindemith's *Lilacs* and Janáček's *Glagolskaja*]. No group in my experience has worked with such earnestness nor is more deserving of a sense of accomplishment. Still, no piece of great music ever is performed perfectly, and I see no reason to expect that it should happen on Sunday night.

—But I do believe that—in view of our labor thus far—we have a right to expect and demand of ourselves not flawless performance but humanly great performance. Music has finally to issue in sound; and the sound has no meaning unless it is the voice of the spirit. The only *crescendo* of importance is the crescendo of the human heart. The only song worth singing is the "song of the bleeding throat" (as that of Whitman's gray-brown bird).

Presumably, from the first startled wail of terror or grief which fractured a prehistoric stillness the highly complex abstraction of language has developed. But if the first anguished human cry be lost in the babble and small talk of the cocktail party then our progress has been "toward degeneracy." Music added to speech is a further complexity and an intellectual sophistication—but its purpose is quite the opposite: and that is to seek once again and to magnify the first-hand intensity of original experience.

The grammar of music is essential, and those of us who would be musicians are obligated to become experts in its manipulation; but the meanings of notation, of marks of dynamics and tempo, are not limited to their dictionary equivalents. They are frail and meagre and hopeful suggestions to the human spirit to respond to the "why?" behind the symbol.

We've worked hard on musical disciplines. They aren't good enough. They never are. —But all that we have accomplished is worth nothing at all unless it releases the spirit to sing and shout, to laugh and cry, or pray the primitive prayer. I earnestly believe, too, that the spirit—and only the spirit—can guide us to the sound. If hearts hymn, then the sound is illumined. If the inner necessity is large and compelling then the sound will be more than we need. People are only a little less movable than mountains, and the same thing moves them both.

Someone asked me later Wednesday night what I had meant by saying "music is the most moral of the arts." (I probably did say it.) At least two things come to mind in justification of the instinct. The first is that the making of music is the everlasting and inescapable act of creation. With the visual arts a work is completed. It may be viewed by men of succeeding generations, usually singly. But the life of music is reborn at every singing. It actually doesn't exist on paper, but in time and in sound. It has existed in the composer's spirit—but at each singing it seeks a new life. And the performer, though his craft is that of representation and his proper approach that of humility, cannot escape the responsibilities of creation. —And that has some moral references.

The second thing that comes to mind is that of all the arts music is the most linked with *community* of expression. This meaning of music is somehow most open to the amateur musician, and nowhere does it find its expression so fully as among people who sing together. It rests upon a common devotion to the composer's utterance and a mutual respect for the personal dignity of fellow-workers. —And that has moral references.

The words are hard to find, and they come out colder than they go in—and much too pompously.

Robert

To enhance the "community of expression" inherent in the choral medium, Shaw, with the help of Julius Herford and Alice Parker, devised new translations of the texts of Bartók's *Cantata Profana* for the 1952 Series and Janáček's *M'sa Glagolskaja* and Haydn's *The Creation* for the 1953 Series. It was not a task to be treated casually. The definable, paraphrasable meaning of each line, the metrical patterns of the syllables, and the phonetic quality of every sound had to be matched as closely as possible in English, word for word, phrase for phrase, and above all, spirit for spirit.

The libretto of *The Creation*, originally written in English, was set to music in a free and condensed German translation made by Haydn's friend Baron van Swieten. Before the score was published in 1799 van Swieten retranslated it into English in an often quaint, sometimes virtually unparsable mode of expression, misplacing accented syllables, allowing awkward vowel sounds to occur on crucial notes, and altering the lengths and contours of some melodic lines.

In Gabriel's famous aria, familiarly known in van Swieten's translation as "With verdure clad," the second line in German ends *hier sprosst den Wunden Heil*—literally, "here blooms the healing [herbs] for wounds." Haydn set the word *Heil* (healing) to an elaborate *fioriture* that would be vocalized on *ah*, the initial phoneme of the diphthong (Ex. 1).

Ex. 1

Wun-den Heil,

Van Swieten's English version, "here shoots the healing plant," substituted the broad *a* of "plant" for the more eloquent sound of the final German word. Shaw's solution, "here dwells a healing grace," conveys essentially the same meaning, is much more fluent overall, and provides the felicitous sound of "grace" on the melisma.

Ex. 2 shows Haydn's choral setting of *Stimmt an die Saiten*. Van Swieten's revisions (Ex. 3) weakened the rhythmic momentum of the music. Shaw managed a more satisfactory compromise (Ex. 4). And so on throughout the oratorio. Even the recitatives had to be recast, principally to assure naturalness in declamation.

Ex. 2

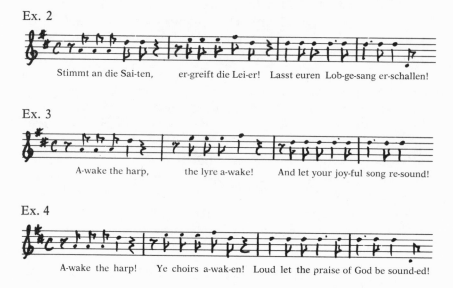

Stimmt an die Sai-ten,   er-greift die Lei-er! Lasst euren Lob-ge-sang er-schallen!

Ex. 3

A-wake the harp,   the lyre a-wake!   And let your joy-ful song re-sound!

Ex. 4

A-wake the harp!   Ye choirs a-wak-en! Loud let the praise of God be sound-ed!

The text of Janáček's *M'sa Glagolskaja* is a translation of the Ordinary of the Latin Mass into a Slavic folk tongue. Janáček, acutely sensitive to the melodies, rhythms, and sonorous flavors of the language, set it in a concise rhetorical tone-speech without lingering over the lyric or dramatic implications of his material, yet infusing it with intense, volcanic emotional urgency.

When the work is sung in the original language only the driving, trochaic *ámin* (amen) betrays its religious purport. Otherwise it sounds like a paean to a people's history—and that is precisely what Janáček, an agnostic, intended, for he composed it in 1926 to commemorate both the millennial of a patron saint, Wenceslas, and the tenth anniversary of the founding of the Czech nation. It is a testament to his deep affection for his national heritage.

At the same time, no matter in what language it is rendered, the Ordinary of the Mass carries the force of associations accumulated through social and institutional traditions belonging to the entire Christian world. It is "centuries full" of meaning. For those to whom it represents a sacred tradition, any translation must be literal, without regard for metrical similitude or the subtleties of vocal coloration. It will not tolerate poetic license. Shaw's reading from the Credo, "I believe in the Holy Spirit, Comforter, Author and Creator, Lifegiver," is metrically and sonorously parallel with the corresponding line in Janáček's text, but it is not semantically identical with the diction of the Book of Common Prayer's "[I believe] in the Holy Ghost, the Lord and giver of life."

The dilemma is unresolvable: To keep faith with the spirit of Janáček's music and at the same time keep the Faith inviolate. Consistent with Shaw's doctrine of the "community of expression," his choruses have sometimes sung the work in English, other times in the "original" language.

Shaw enumerated the "Hazards of Translating Bartók's Cantata" in an article he wrote for the *New York Times* in October of 1951. The text of "The Enchanted Deer," written by Bartók and translated into German by the composer after the work was completed, is based on a Romanian legend of an old man who has raised his nine stalwart and dearly loved sons only to follow the hunt. Wandering in the forest, the young men cross an enchanted bridge and are instantly transformed into stags. Though their father begs them to return home, they cannot, because their antlers could not pass through the doorway. They are doomed to roam the forest for the rest of their lives.

> Ne'er in clothes can wander,
> Only wear the wind and sun. . . .
> And our mouths no longer
> Drink from crystal glasses,
> But only mountain springs.

Shaw and Herford enlisted the aid of Paul Vajda, head of the Hungarian division of Radio Free Europe, who coached them in the phonetics and grammar of the Hungarian language and explained the special qualities of Bartók's story—"its blend of rustic, peasant simplicity and fairy-tale fancy, the awkward, even rough imagery and the ancient pervasive lyricism."

The reconciliation of sense with sound and rhythm was made more difficult by the fact that Hungarian, like German, allows compounded words, which may be run together with only one principal accent. "There are whole lines," said Shaw, "which are formed of a single word. It is not a simple thing to find in the English language six one-syllable words, or three of two syllables, or even two of three syllables which can be run together as smoothly as a single six-syllable Hungarian word—and still make sense."

The problem of supporting the rhythmic freedom of the original text, and thus of the music, was especially perplexing in the fugal writing. "Such is [Bartók's] great mastery—and *economy*—that he will take the first half of a fugue subject, or the last third of it, or the middle two-fifths—or all of them at once—and use them as building materials. And woe to the translator who has not arrived at a text neatly and sensibly divisible by two, three, or five!"

But ultimately, Shaw concluded, the real problem in translating any text "lies in . . . whether one has achieved withal a poetic sensibility and a spiritual quality which grants the music a new life within a new language and another people." On the day after the performance Francis Perkins told readers of the *Herald Tribune* that Shaw's version of Bartók's story "never gave the impression that these were not the original words."

At that time he was reluctant to translate texts originally written in French. "The sound of the language itself," he said, "is as much a part of [the music] as are pitch and rhythm. Debussy in English is like oysters with maple syrup." Nevertheless, in the interest of "community of expression," he has since translated Honegger's *Jeanne d'Arc au Bucher* and Berlioz's *La Damnation de Faust* and *L'Enfance du Christ*.

5.

Back to California

IN THE MIDST of rehearsals for the 1953 Choral Masterwork Series, Shaw was deeply engrossed in preparations for a new enterprise scheduled to begin in mid-July. The preceding August he had announced his acceptance of the conductorship of the San Diego Symphony Orchestra, and he had since been carefully constructing an innovative plan embracing performance, education, and broad community involvement.

At the turn of the present century only about sixteen symphony orchestras were known to exist in the United States. Each had arisen not, like most European orchestras, as an adjunct of an established and preferred operatic tradition, but out of the social, economic, and musical conditions unique to a new nation striving mightily to accelerate the processes of its own cultural evolution. Several had originated in the early 1800s as cooperative ventures in which the members shared the modest proceeds from their occasional concerts. Some were the creations of wealthy philanthropists who implanted them, whole and hearty, into the cultural wilderness. Others began as accompanying ensembles for choral festivals. Still others were germinated on college campuses.

A half-century later, despite the Depression and two world wars, there were said to be around five hundred orchestras in a more or less salutary state of health. About thirty described themselves as "professional," meaning that all their members were paid, though not necessarily a living wage, and in no instance on a year-round basis. Another small group was "semiprofessional," with stipends paid to all, or at least to a few key members. Thirteen orchestras were receiving financial support from city, county, or state governments. The vast majority were made up chiefly or entirely of amateurs who played merely for the satisfaction of it.

By 1966 there were more than a thousand orchestras reportedly active in America, variously described as "major," "metropolitan," "urban," and "community" types.

It is impossible to generalize about the causes of this phenomenal growth. Nomenclature was vague, classifications arbitrary, and statistics—of questionable accuracy at best—were changing so rapidly that chroniclers could hardly keep abreast of the tide. The Baltimore orchestra got under way with the security of a municipal appropriation; the one in Rochester, New York, stepped out of the pit of a motion-picture house. In the twenties the popularity of high school orchestras may have been a contributing factor. In the thirties the influence of good music on radio and recordings may have helped, and the Federal Music Project obviously played a constructive role. No doubt the spread of interest in live music reflected in the success of the organized audience plan had something to do with it, although Civic and Community allegedly tried to discourage such competition. Post–World War II prosperity and the expansion of many cities provided fertile ground for the crop, as did the growth of college and university music departments. The AFM's Music Performance Trust Fund and the music industry's American Music Conference liked to claim a share of the credit. The American Symphony Orchestra League, founded in 1942 to "improve the standards of civic symphony orchestras," incidentally brought to light the identities of many that had long been in existence.

Most important of all, there was, beginning in the late thirties, a sizeable group of experienced and gifted American conductors in the field, most of whom were born between 1890 and 1915. In 1953 a good many of the major orchestras were still under the control of distinguished Europeans, but many of the others, more or less newly arrived in the ranks of professionalism, were being conducted by Americans. Howard Barlow was in Baltimore, Victor Alessandro in San Antonio, Alfred Wallenstein in Los Angeles, Howard Mitchell in Washington, D.C., Walter Hendl in Dallas, Thor Johnson in Cincinnati, Milton Katims in Seattle, and Izler Solomon in Buffalo. In North Carolina, Benjamin Swalin had built one of the first regional orchestras, and in Atlanta, Henry Sopkin, starting with a youth orchestra, had developed a promising semi-professional organization in only nine years.

Some of these men had served their apprenticeships in radio studios or theaters, in WPA projects, with amateur and college groups, or as teachers in public schools. Most were string players, and several had learned their craft at the feet of giants like Toscanini and Koussevitzky. Each brought to his job not only broad musical training and technical know-how but also personal qualities that could be developed only through experience: leadership, a power to communicate with players and audiences, musical integrity, ambition, showmanship, intense and endless industry, a fierce desire always to learn and improve, and the courage to survive adversity and criticism—in short, the ability to galvanize an American city into *wanting* to have a good symphony orchestra.

With models like these to inspire them, more and more younger men—and even a few women—began to entertain the possibility of becoming conductors, even though their number exceeded the availability of orchestras. For many of them, the solution was a typically American one. In 1952 a survey of one hundred thirteen conductors in twenty-eight states revealed that nearly half had founded their own orchestras.

Shaw was aware that the orchestral tradition in San Diego had survived a mercurial history since its tentative beginning in 1910. During the twenties a high-school music teacher named Nino Marcelli had managed, by relentless cultivation of young local talent and assiduous stimulation of civic support, to erect a semiprofessional orchestra of about seventy musicians. In 1927 Marcelli initiated a series of summer concerts in the "organ pavilion" at Balboa Park. After eight immensely successful seasons the orchestra moved to Ford Bowl, which had been donated to the city by Henry Ford after the close of the California-Pacific International Exposi-

tion of 1935–36. The Bowl lay directly beneath the landing approach to the municipal airport, but that was deemed insignificant
in those days.

Attempts to develop a year-round symphony season encountered
first one frustration and then another. For some years patrons
were amply content with the outdoor summer concerts and it was
not until 1938 that conditions appeared to warrant plans for a
short winter series. Unfortunately, the impact of the Depression
caused the project to be abandoned before the first concert. The
recently formed San Diego Symphony Association, with the col-
laboration of the Federal Music Project, was able to make it
through the next few summers. Nikolai Sokoloff, founding conductor of the Cleveland Orchestra and national director of the FMP,
conducted for a while, remaining on for a year after the WPA was
shut down in 1940.

Following a wartime hiatus of six years, Marcelli began all over
again. At last, in the summer of 1950, the San Diego Symphony of
sixty-five musicians was reactivated on a semiprofessional basis
under the direction of Fabien Sevitsky, nephew of Serge Koussevitzky and then conductor of the Indianapolis Symphony. That
same year the San Diego Philharmonic was founded to present concerts in the winter season, but despite the efforts of experienced
conductors like Werner Janssen, a variety of problems plagued the
organization, and it failed to gain ground. At the time the city had
a population of about 322,000, but nearly one-third were transients
stationed at the large naval base, and there was barely enough
support for one orchestra, let alone two. While the Philharmonic
Society struggled vainly for existence, the Symphony Association,
abetted by the new Women's Committee under the leadership of
Mrs. Fred G. Goss, wife of the Symphony's manager, garnered the
available financial resources. In 1953 the Symphony's players were
being contracted at the prevailing scale of fifty dollars per week for
four rehearsals and one concert.

Even though the two organizations combined their forces in
1955, two years later the Association could afford no more than a
seven-concert summer season plus four children's concerts and
some chamber music events during the winter.

Shaw's performance schedule for 1953 consisted of six consecutive Tuesday evening symphony concerts in Ford Bowl and, within

the same period, three Friday evening "Inside Concerts" of chamber music at Hoover High School sponsored jointly by the Symphony Association and San Diego State College. Instead of the
frothy trivia usually served up to hot-weather audiences, Shaw's
programming focused upon works of major dimension and import.
"Only the music of the highest intellectual and emotional quality
is worth the time, money, and effort of presentation," he explained
to the press. "Actually, only music of this quality is of interest;
only this music makes any contribution to community and individual life. It is possible, and *only* possible, within a framework of
excellence to find variety. There is no variety in mediocrity."

The first season's repertoire included symphonies by Brahms
and Schubert, piano concertos by Mozart and Mendelssohn, Beethoven's violin concerto, Honegger's *King David*, and the *Missa
Solemnis*. The lightest pieces on the list were Falla's *El Amor Brujo*
and Ravel's *Bolero*, with dancing by Antonia and Luisa Triana and
Company, and Prokofieff's *Peter and the Wolf*, narrated by actress
Maureen O'Sullivan.

The chamber music concerts offered two of Bach's solo cantatas;
string quartets by Beethoven, Schubert and Bartók; Brahms's
Liebeslieder Wälzer, op. 52, and Bach's double concerto in C major
(with Lukas Foss and Julius Herford as soloists). Foss conducted
his own cantata, *A Parable of Death*, and U.S.C. composer Leon
Kirchner was pianist in his *Sonata Concertante*.

The same uncompromising adherence to principles prevailed in
subsequent seasons. Even Shaw's concessions to popular taste reflected his commitment to quality—stars like the Dave Brubeck
Quartet, and the Hi-Lo's, a virtuoso vocal jazz ensemble (whose hot
licks were said to have ignited the fire in the lighting system that
threatened to interrupt their performance).

Shaw's faith in the aesthetic capacities of his audience was vindicated by annual increases in attendance. Receipts the first year
were 60 percent above the previous summer, and the figure continued to rise each season. Major events such as the *Missa Solemnis*
and the Berlioz Requiem (complete with *general-pausen* for passing aircraft) drew near-capacity crowds to the 4,200-seat Bowl. The
inadequacy of 1936-vintage parking facilities became a serious
problem for the management.

At first the weighty repertoire pressed the seventy-piece orchestra to the limits of its abilities, but Shaw patiently and cheerfully urged his musicians on, accepting each crisis as a personal challenge. In the fall of 1953 he reviewed his initial season in San Diego for the enlightenment of his friends in the Collegiate Chorale:

> Working with the San Diego Orchestra was one of the happiest experiences of my life. For the most part it is an orchestra of professional—but occasionally professional—musicians. That is to say, at this time, there is not sufficient year-'round activity to support an orchestra on that basis. Most of the members (some of those of top quality) therefore find regular employment in the aircraft industries or the education fields. They love music, and they play well.

Shaw might have chosen to further his career as an orchestral conductor primarily on the strength of guest engagements. In the summer of 1953 he was invited to conduct both the San Francisco and Los Angeles orchestras. But conducting someone else's orchestra was not the same to him as the satisfaction of building his own. He was determined to learn his craft from the ground up, and San Diego was as good a place as any to begin—a place to refine his technique on the podium, to study the psychology of handling musicians beholden to no higher authority, to learn to deal with a board of directors and a women's committee, and to experiment with his own ways of attracting and holding audiences.

He was an apt and eager student. As he told *Time*'s correspondent, "The ages 45 to 65 are a man's most productive years, and I'm just ten months short of 40—so I haven't any time to lose."

The "curriculum" was rigorous, demanding the utmost tact and diplomacy. At the end of the 1955 season *Time* reported that during his first two seasons, the musicians treated the new conductor as a kind of musical Boy Scout, frequently were noisy in rehearsals and harried him with unimportant questions. "But this year they defer to his authority with respectful silence, and pass their questions up through the concert-master. Shaw, at home with the instruments as never before, is using a baton for the first time. 'I'm beginning to feel the orchestra in my fingers now,' he said last week. 'My fingers taste the sound, my ears taste the sound. I can't explain it—I just am closer.' "

Shaw accepted the invitation to conduct the San Diego Symphony on the condition that he could establish an educational program in connection with it. In January of 1953 he outlined the philosophy underlying his plan, in a letter to the Collegiate Chorale.

Dear People—

With Julius Herford I did some writing this past week incidental to the Workshop in The Choral Arts we plan this summer for San Diego, California. I wanted to read some of it to you Monday evening at rehearsal, because some of the thinking has grown out of the work with the Collegiate Chorale over the past ten years, and because it seems also to glove with our present endeavor. But Monday night the necessity seemed to be for work; and maybe it's just as well to save our "ponders" for the middle of the week. At any rate I'd like to write some of it to you now.

Mr. Herford and I had arrived at a schedule of courses which laid heaviest emphasis upon score-study (as opposed for instance to techniques of "directing") and also upon the close relationship of this score-study to actual rehearsals and performances. That is, almost every score to be analyzed was also to be rehearsed and performed. And the "Statement of Purpose" continued—

The thinking which has led to this organization of the study of musical performance certainly is not unique to us. [In some ways it was similar to the programs he had been a part of at Juilliard and the Berkshire Music Center.] With others we have felt the necessity of a wholeness—an integrity—among the separations and specializations which in our time too frequently have fractioned music as an art and man as an artist.

It is the general practice of our time, for instance, to segregate the choral literature (and its practice) from that of the symphony from that of the solo artist from that of chamber music; but it would seem to us that in the Missa Solemnis and the late quartets the same spirit motivates the same language; and we find it necessary that practicing choral musicians should have the opportunity to study the scores of symphonic and chamber music.

We are similarly aware of the thinking which sets score analysis, theory, musicology and history on the impractical side of music in opposition to technique and performance on the practical side; but it seems to us that it is at least our duty as performing musicians to know about the score that which can be known and, at the same time, that such knowledge is without essential meaning until it is illuminated by the "miracle of sound."

That composers and performers—creators and interpreters, thinkers and feelers—should find themselves antagonists in the community of music, and that a "star system" should exalt the latter and dismiss the former is a lamentable schizophrenia of our time; for it seems imperative to us that, as performers, our objective studies are to the end that we may widen our understanding by the greatness of the music, rather than limit the flow thereof by the breadth of our ignorance, or dim its light by bushels of self-revelation.

The performer ought not to establish the kingdom of himself, but may, by the most strenuous training of his mind and senses, find a way into the broad and timeless stream of the creative spirit. The artistry of performance is not a technique which can be bestowed or acquired by imitation, but an occasional resultant of insistent, pervasive and humble musical thinking. The composer who knows best what a Bach fugue is, is never in danger of copying the external appearance of a form; and the performer who knows best the substance of a score, or a composer's language, will at least be in a position to invite the possibility of illumination. "He who neglects the visible will not find revealed to him the invisible."

It was Schoenberg's modest hope that a man "who has attempted all his life to train his mind and senses—so that nothing which might happen in his art would be wholly accidental—, at the moment when the impact of inspiration was overwhelming, could count that his mind and senses would function as they *had to*."

That which most stands between great music and the people is bad performance; and that which stands between the performer and great performance is the fractional nature of his musicianship and his incomplete humanity. Music is a single art, and the artist is a whole man. In a world where subdivision and specialization are a way of living, the integrity of the knowable and the intuitive offer a way of life.

We do not imagine that perfection is possible, nor are we interested in its cult, surmising with Artur Schnabel that the proper faith is not "in perfectionism as an end in itself, but an idealism which is endless." In this respect [Dr. Herford and I] are happy to be students together—as indeed we have been for the past seven years, but now with others—in the varied knowledges and performance qualities of great music, knowing that eventually we shall come a few steps closer, and occasionally, the "miracle of the sound will reveal itself."

Eighty men and women from thirty-eight states and Hawaii enrolled in the first workshop. Herford's classes occupied twenty to twenty-five hours per week, and Shaw's rehearsals consumed another ten to fifteen. It was a grueling six weeks. "Hours of abstraction—of theory, history, evaluation—but not one moment which does not move directly into the sweat and know-how of rehearsal and performance," recalled Shaw. The benefits were directly proportional to a student's musical maturity, intellectual acuity, and physical endurance.

Shaw was perfectly willing to pay the tuition for his own education. Each season he put his own salary and several thousand dollars more back into the venture in order to assure conditions under which he could operate most efficiently. From New York he brought contralto Florence Kopleff and baritone Benjamin DeLoache, who also taught vocal repertoire and pedagogy in the workshop. He brought John Wustman, who had been assistant conductor and pianist with the Robert Shaw Chorale, and Tom Pyle, the Chorale's road manager and a baritone chorister, and later praised their work in a letter to the Collegiate Chorale:

> Nobody—but nobody—is better than J. W. as a rehearsal accompanist. His fine musicianship and intelligence, and his human decency and spirit of cooperation time after time doubled rehearsal progress. —And nothing like the work T. P. did has ever been done by a single human being. He was the trouble shooter, art director, public relations man, stage manager, narrator, baritone soloist, auditioner, ghost writer, secretary, general manager—he ran the works, coordinating symphony, college, guest artists, rehearsals, board meetings. That's all.

In 1954 he invited Alice Parker to teach choral arranging in the workshop, and at the close of the session she and Tom Pyle were married in a ceremony at the Shaws' summer home. In 1955 Clayton Krehbiel, a veteran Shaw associate, came along as administrative assistant.

For the first few years both the chorus and the orchestra had to be reinforced in various sections. Shaw helped pay expenses to enable Shigeru Hotoke, a music teacher at Kailua High School in Hawaii, to attend the workshop. When the tenor originally scheduled to sing in the quartet for the Brahms *Liebeslieder* cancelled two weeks before the performance. Shaw hired an instructor to teach Shigeru the German phonetics, and put him in the ensemble. Another year he brought in as concertmaster a young Italian-born Hungarian violinist, Robert Gerle, who had already won prizes in Paris, Geneva, and at Tanglewood. In a gesture of confidence, Shaw persuaded a group of local benefactors to loan Gerle $15,000 to buy a Stradivarius, starting the fund with a thousand dollars of his own. A few years later, though Gerle was conscientiously repaying them, they cancelled the balance of the debt.

Shaw continued to invite soloists like Blake Stern, a Juilliard graduate, charter member of the Robert Shaw Chorale, and the Evangelist in the Chorale's recording of the *St. John Passion*. At the same time, the roster of guest artists was enhanced with names of international renown, such as that of Mack Harrell, who came in 1954 to sing and to conduct seminars in vocal technique and repertoire. Shaw made a point of featuring them not only in the repertoire on which they had built their reputations, but also to encourage them to perform works of their own selection. As he remarked to a newspaper reporter at the beginning of the 1955 season, "Infrequently does Rudolf Serkin have the opportunity to play Bach and Mozart along with his Beethoven. Infrequently does Margaret Harshaw have the opportunity to match her Wagnerian fame with a portrayal of Dido. Seldom does one hear Benny Goodman in that fantastically beautiful clarinet concerto of Mozart's."

One of the main attractions of the San Diego situation was the opportunity it provided for Shaw to test his belief in the doctrine of music as a "community of expression" in the broadest sense. He premiered works by area composers and commissioned new ones from Howard Brubeck of Palomar Junior College, Robert Heninger of Point Loma High School, and summer San Diegan Robert Kurka. In 1955 he named as his assistant conductor Daniel Lewis, chairman of the music department at Helix High School in San Diego and a member of the orchestra since its reorganization. The soprano soloist in four of the nine concerts in the summer of 1953 —and on many other occasions during the next four seasons—was Shaw's younger sister, Anne Shaw Price.

Anne's career intersected with her brother's several times. After graduating from Pomona College in 1943, she was hired by Fred Waring as a member of the female trio that sang the obbligatos and "punctuation" in the Glee Club's arrangements. While in New York she also sang in several of Robert's early RCA Victor Chorale recordings. In 1944 she married Harrison Price, a Cal Tech engineer, and in 1946 they moved to Lima, Peru, where for several years she took active part in that city's musical scene—which Robert was to enter briefly as a visitor in 1964 and 1965. Upon moving to Los Angeles in 1951 she joined Roger Wagner's professional Chorale and soon began soloing with orchestras such as those at Pasadena and San Diego. In 1952 she became a lecturer in vocal repertoire at U.C.L.A. When Robert invited her to take part in his first San Diego season she was already well known among West Coast audiences.

To supplement the workshop chorus Shaw recruited two hundred singers from the military base, from church choirs, and high school choirs. He used college groups such as the Women's Alumni Choir from Occidental College, prepared by Howard Swan. He brought in half a dozen high school string quartets and several groups of brass and woodwind players. These ensembles were coached by orchestra members and allowed, with special approval of the musicians' union, to play in one or two of the concerts each season. To cultivate a corps of knowledgeable listeners, he asked Julius Herford to teach a course for laymen in which the highlights of the season's repertoire were explained.

Shaw seized every opportunity to preach the tenets of his faith in the viability of art at the grass roots. In the daily *San Diegan* he wrote:

> I strenuously believe that those elements which we call culture in a society—art, education, and religion—must not be considered the monopoly of the society page or the prerogative of women's world, but are the equally necessary concern of the marketplace and the city hall.
>
> The general illness of our civilization is the divorce of its art from everyday community and economic life, and its gradual restrictive association with in-growing groups of particularized and precious esthetes, or its ultimate sponsorship for purposes other than enjoyment—as though the ability to appreciate art were the solid gold Cadillac of class distinction.
>
> We cannot import creativity—we cannot buy the produce of the human spirit, nor can we exchange it for political, social or economic advancement—without selling it into slavery or stunting its growth. It is not a question of whether we shall have "culture." Every community has its culture. Culture is not an ivory towered cult, but the total spiritual environment and produce of community life. And in this area none of us can perform by proxy.

When he returned to New York in the fall of 1953 he expounded on the same theme at greater length, in a letter to the Collegiate Chorale.

November 5, 1953

I tried for three hours last night to get some of this down on paper, but finally had to give up when the paper was full of half sentences and half paragraphs. I'm not at all sure that morning light will guide me past more of the same, but I'll try again.

One of the primary assumptions of music is that human beings can and should understand each other with reference to that whole produce of the human mind, heart and will which we call art— matter which seems to us to possess *esthetic* and *spiritual* value, even though it be not infrequent to see that value measured in terms of dollars. There must be in this regard a very close connection between that which we call integrity in art and simple basic good-will towards men. A less than saintly every-day life on the part of the artist, or preoccupation of his produce with man's degeneracy, does not finally contradict this relationship. Even were its subject matter the imminent and desirable dissolution of the human species, just at that point at which the creative understanding acts to produce a work of art, it affirms that man does not live by bread alone, and that he is one of a community of men upon whose understanding—of himself and his ideas—the meaning of his own existence is predicated. Art is at once exhaustively personal and inescapably social.

At this moment I am not sure that I can state precisely what constitutes an *amateur standing* in art, for I know a number of professional musicians who are incurably amateur in their attitude toward music. The fact of compensation or the amount therof is neither proof nor inverse sliding scale of amateur standing. To be an amateur artist means, I suppose, to be unwilling or unable to set a price upon the effort and love which attends the creation of beauty. When you get right down to it, to be an artist *is* to be an amateur. One can no more think of being a professional musician than he can of being a professional person. To be an artist is to arrive at some sort of resolution of the mind and matter struggle. It's a yea to the proposition that there are ideal human values lasting beyond one's own mortal limits, and that it is a necessary part of being human to seek, enjoy and transmit these values. To be an artist is not the privilege of a few but the necessity of us all.

The wonderful thing about the amateur chorus is that nobody can buy its attendance at rehearsals, or the sweat, eyestrain and fatigue that go along with the glow; and nobody but the most purposive and creative of musical minds—from Bach in both directions—can invite and sustain its devotion.

Good-day,
R

Shaw withdrew from touring for the 1953–54 season in order to devote full time to the study of orchestral repertoire, keeping only a skeleton schedule of performances. In December he conducted sixteen Robert Shaw Chorale members on NBC-TV's Martha Raye Show, and in January prepared a somewhat larger professional group for a concert version of Verdi's *Un Ballo in Maschera* under eighty-seven-year-old Toscanini. For the eighth consecutive year he conducted the Crane Chorus and Orchestra in the festival at Potsdam, New York, this time leading a company of some seven hundred student and amateur musicians in the Berlioz Requiem. In the meantime he acquainted himself with nearly two hundred orchestral works.

That season was his last with the Collegiate Chorale. He relied much on the assistance of Margaret Hillis and Ralph Hunter, who had frequently taken over for him during his recent absences on tour. He conducted the group in its tenth appearance on the *Herald Tribune*'s yearly Forum, and in its eighth annual Christmas Festival concert. The final engagement of the season was a Brahms Requiem at the Cathedral Church of St. John the Divine in New York. At that time it was announced that the new permanent conductor of the Collegiate Chorale was to be Ralph Hunter.

The Robert Shaw Chorale resumed touring in 1954–55, presenting sixty-three concerts on the fall itinerary and thirty more in the spring. The program was a varied one, with Bach's *Jesu, Meine Freude* and Avshalomov's *Tom O'Bedlam* attracting the most attention from the critics. The fee for the attraction was $3,000, and it took full houses in large auditoriums for sponsors to break even. But the Chorale's—and Shaw's—popularity had grown to the point where there was no problem in that respect. Crowds were tremendous—4,500 in Milwaukee, Wisconsin; 5,000 in Moscow, Idaho; 9,000 in Lexington, Kentucky. Appropriately, in June Shaw received the Alice M. Ditson Award from Columbia University for having brought "a new vitality to choral music in the United States."

His schedule increased in a steady crescendo. In the fall of 1955 he toured seventy days with Honegger's *King David* and Bach's *Magnificat*. In the spring of 1956 he took the Chorale on a ten-week tour to Europe and the Middle East. After a week of recording for RCA he raced to San Diego to begin his fourth season, then to

Anchorage, Alaska, to inaugurate a new music festival there, and finally to Cleveland to assume the post of associate conductor to George Szell. The Cleveland job consumed all his energies, and there was no time for touring until the fall of 1958.

Meanwhile, the San Diego Symphony's season had expanded to seven orchestra concerts, and the association was ready to try again for a winter season. They wanted Shaw to take the helm, or at least to return as a guest conductor, but late in the winter of 1958 he warned them that he would not be available for a winter season until at least 1961, and he asked for a leave of absence in the summer of 1959. Contractually, he explained, he was five years behind in recording, and two years behind in touring. In mid-April he asked to be relieved of responsibilities for the coming summer. More than sixty concerts in Cleveland, three guest appearances with the Boston Symphony, and three more with the New York Philharmonic had left him physically and emotionally exhausted.

Roger Wagner, Maurice Abravanel, and Daniel Lewis substituted for him that summer. The symphony's first full winter season, in 1959–60, was conducted by Earl Bernard Murray, associate conductor of the San Francisco Orchestra.

The tour of Europe and the Middle East in 1956, part of the cultural exchange program sponsored by the Department of State and the American National Theatre and Academy, took thirty singers and twenty instrumentalists to nineteen countries in ten weeks. It was one of the longest and most difficult overseas tours ever attempted by so large a group. A European road manager was to have met them in Cairo, Egypt, but when he saw the final itinerary he decided not to show up—sixty concerts in seventy days was unheard of, and therefore impossible.

Florence Kopleff, who had been with Shaw since the early days of the Collegiate Chorale and had sung on every tour and many recordings, frequently as a soloist, took over the payroll duties. Tom Pyle made all the transportation arrangements. Maxine, whom Shaw had invited along on the tour, handled the public relations, running interference for her husband with stubborn stage hands and haughty concierges.

European audiences and critics were skeptical of a chorus that would presume to sing both classics and folk songs on the same

RSC departure for Europe, 1956. At Shaw's left: Maxine, Tom Pyle, Walter Brown of Columbia Artists
Management, and Walter Gould

program, but their skepticism was quickly dispelled, and nearly
every concert had to be extended by from seven to ten encores.
One German critic noted that Shaw—"obsessed with music"—and
his group had demonstrated that "choral singing, which we preferably exercise as a community performance of enthusiastic laymen, may be placed under the law of perfection." Financially,
however, the entire tour was much less satisfactory than had been
hoped. The company was seldom in one vicinity long enough for
favorable reviews to affect box office receipts, and language barriers prevented the good news from preceding them to other
countries.

The tour was a financial hardship for the singers because the
AGMA pay scale was so low it barely covered expenses. On the
other hand, each country limited the amount of U.S. currency that

could be taken out, in some cases to less than the orchestra members were entitled to, so Shaw made up the difference out of his
own pocket. He and the singers made the sacrifice, he told one
reluctant trouper, "because we believe the cultural, social and political implications warrant it."

The troupe bounded across the continent, from Spain and Portu-
gal to Greece and Turkey, to Scandinavia and Iceland. They even
penetrated the Iron Curtain as far as Belgrade, Yugoslavia.

The Middle Eastern segment of the tour was the most memorable. Tension was mounting between Israel and her Arab neighbors,
and the United States, as counterprotagonist with Russia in that
arena of the escalating Cold War, was in a precarious position.
Shaw and his musicians did their best to improve America's image.
In Beirut he announced that all proceeds from their concert would
be donated to the relief fund for Lebanon's recent earthquake victims, and he was quickly awarded a medal of honor for his gesture.
He was surprised and disappointed, though, to find that the audiences there, and those in Syria and Egypt as well, consisted largely
of Europeans and Americans.

The Chorale's longest and most satisfying sojourn in any one
country was in Israel, where they sang eleven concerts in ten days.
Within range of Arab guns, in a tent at the Ein Gev Festival on the
shore of Lake Tiberias, they presented Mozart's Requiem and "A
Gallery of American Choral Art" to an overflow crowd. They took
part in the traditional Passover-eve celebration in the communal
settlement of Givat Brenner, and sang Bach's *Christ lag in Todesbanden* and Schubert's Mass in G at the Y.M.C.A. in Jerusalem on
Easter Sunday.

They arrived in Tel Aviv just before curtain time and rushed on
stage prepared to sing the Requiem, only to discover the orchestra
parts had been left behind in Haifa. Luckily, there were enough
music students in the audience with their own study scores that an
appeal from Shaw enabled the performance to proceed on schedule
as the players read from piano-vocal and miniature scores.

Among the students at the San Diego Workshop in 1955 was
Mary Hale, conductor of the Community Chorus in Anchorage,
Alaska. Mary was instantly impressed by Shaw's integration of

study, performance, and community involvement, and was positive that a similar festival would work as well in Anchorage, provided the same people were running it. She discussed the possibility with Shaw, Herford, and others on Shaw's staff, and easily convinced them of the attractiveness of the locale. They in turn were politely interested in the idea of a festival in a town up there on "the last frontier," but privately skeptical of its practicality. They underestimated the determination of Mary Hale and her fellow Alaskans.

When Mary returned home she quickly aroused the enthusiasm of her chorus members and the players in the Anchorage Symphony, as well as the support of a number of other citizens. A few weeks later she announced her audacious plan in the town's two newspapers, sent clippings of the articles to Shaw, and confidently awaited his reaction. Shaw, amazed and intrigued, replied that he and Herford would come if the others would, and if the Anchorage musicians would prepare the Mozart Requiem. Mary phoned John Wustman, Robert Gerle, and Blake Stern. They would come if Shaw would. The first Alaska Festival of Music was on the way, under the banner of Mary's motto, "Music to Match Our Mountains!"

From conception to consummation, the first Alaska Festival of Music was a model of the type of community involvement Robert Shaw admired and encouraged. Mary Hale set up a board of directors representing the chorus and orchestra, plus seven "business advisors" and the president of the community college. Together they recruited hundreds of volunteers to help with the menial chores. Cub Scouts distributed brochures and posters; other civic organizations took responsibility for moving pianos, ushering, manning the parking lots, and hosting the guest musicians. By opening day, Monday, August 27, observers had gotten the impression the entire city of Anchorage was taking part.

All the guest artists, including Shaw, had agreed to come to the eight-day festival for expenses only—a sizeable sum, considering distances and the high cost of living in Alaska. In lieu of fees they were extended a generous measure of frontier hospitality. They were supplied with automobiles by various dealers, and their hotel rooms were decorated with flower arrangements by the Garden Club. There were informal parties nightly, and sightseeing trips

and salmon-fishing excursions as time permitted. Within minutes
of their arrival, the guests and their hosts were on a first-name
basis with one another.

Most days the schedule began at 1:00 P.M. A series of classes and
lectures was offered for credit through the college. Herford gave
talks on music appreciation and the music of Mozart. Master
classes were given by Wustman in the art of accompanying, by
Stern in vocal literature, and by Gerle in violin and chamber music.
All four men presented solo recitals; Herford's was a lecture-recital
on Book Two of Bach's *Well-Tempered Clavier*. Shaw conducted
open rehearsals of the chorus and orchestra, and a Friday evening
students' concert. The final concert on Tuesday, September 4,
opened with Bach's double concerto in C major with Wustman and
Herford as soloists, and a Mozart violin concerto featuring Gerle.
The Requiem employed three separate quartets of soloists chosen
by Shaw from the chorus, with Stern the tenor in each.

Ticket sales easily covered the artists' expenses. Total attendance
for the five performances exceeded 7,000. Trappers, construction
workers, fishermen, and Matanuska Valley homesteaders came to
see what Mary Hale and Robert Shaw had wrought. Traffic jams
were the worst in the city's history. A new gold strike or an oil discovery couldn't have caused more excitement.

The next year the festival was headed by the same teams, and
Shaw persuaded five more of his friends to come along to assist
with performances of *King David* and the *St. John Passion*. Herford's "Lectures for Laymen" were televised, to create a larger
nucleus of informed listeners. In 1958 the board of directors commissioned a new work by Jacob Avshalomov, then conductor of
the Portland, Oregon, Youth Symphony.

Shaw had to cancel his appearance in the summer of 1958 for
the same reason he withdrew from his San Diego post, but the
festival went on anyway. A few years later he officially assumed
the responsibilities of musical director, and in that capacity continued to take a personal interest in the management of the festival, intermittently serving as guest conductor until 1973.

Year by year the scope of activity was expanded to include art
exhibits, poetry readings, and seminars on Eskimo, Aleut, and In-
dian music. Chamber music and church music workshops were
added. The budget increased proportionately as more musicians

were imported to supplement the amateur orchestra, whose members also eventually received a small stipend. Soloists were flown from Japan, Norway, and France free of charge by cooperating airlines, adding an international flavor. The festival soon became a major Alaskan tourist attraction. Through it all, community participation continued undiminished. Even the devastating earthquake of March 27, 1964, failed to quell the typical Alaskan "do-it-yourself" spirit.

6.

Cleveland's Orchestra
and Chorus

IN THE SPRING of 1956 Shaw gave notice there would be no Robert Shaw Chorale tour the following season and announced his acceptance of George Szell's invitation to move to Cleveland. "Some people seem to regard this as the big switch," he said to a reporter, "but I'm not one of them. There's a great opportunity out there to work with a fine orchestra and a master conductor like Szell. I expect to learn a lot."

As Szell's associate, Shaw's assignments were varied. He was to build a community chorus and prepare it for performances of up to six major choral works per season, and conduct at least four pairs of concerts in the regular symphony series (including some of the choral performances), several of the Sunday afternoon "Twilight Concerts," and a few performances on the orchestra's annual tour. He was expected to attend all of Szell's rehearsals and performances and be prepared to mount the podium at a moment's notice. Finally, he was to plan the orchestra's educational series and share the conducting of it with Szell's other associate, pianist Louis Lane.

Cleveland had had a varied and active musical life throughout the nineteenth century. There were choral societies, chamber music ensembles, and music clubs within the communities of European immigrants who had come to work in its refineries and factories, and there was also enough wealth there to bring touring virtuosos, opera companies, and orchestras to the city. But failure to establish a resident symphony orchestra left Cleveland conspicuously behind many smaller cities, such as Cincinnati and Minneapolis.

In 1915 an energetic and iron-willed devotee of the arts, Adella Prentiss Hughes, organized a group of affluent patrons into a Musical Arts Association to expand and stabilize the season of visiting attractions. Mrs. Hughes soon realized that perpetuating the tradition over the long run would require the cultivation of interest and support in a way that would cut across ethnic and social barriers. At her insistence the association, with the help of a $6,000 gift from John L. Severance, eventually engaged Nikolai Sokoloff to undertake a yearlong study of music education in the Cleveland public schools and recommend a new program of instruction in instrumental music.

Thirty-one-year-old Sokoloff, who had been appearing as guest conductor with the Cincinnati Symphony, was also asked to organize an orchestra of local theater musicians and amateurs to present a few concerts in local schools and community centers, and on December 18, 1918, "Cleveland's Symphony Orchestra," as it was called at the time, presented its first concert. Two years later Arthur Shepherd, a gifted and prolific composer born in Paris, Idaho, in 1880, was named associate conductor to Sokoloff and placed in charge of all concerts in the orchestra's expanding educational program.

That an orchestra should serve an educational as well as an artistic function—an idea that evidently had arisen in the United States around the middle of the nineteenth century—raised several serious procedural questions: At what age should exposure to symphonic music begin? Should it be voluntary or compulsory? Should all children be educated in its mysteries, or only a select few? Should concerts be free, or should children be taught that music, like most other pleasures, must be paid for? Would it be best for performances to take place on the schools' premises, or should the audience be brought into the concert hall? Should the repertoire focus on story and musical characterization or on exploratory sound and structure? Some of the most successful and widely imitated answers to these questions came to be known collectively as "The Cleveland Plan."

In 1930 Mrs. Hughes, then manager of the orchestra, and Russell Morgan, supervisor of music in the Cleveland schools, concurred that to realize fully the objectives of the educational program, something more than enthusiasm, good intentions, and good music was needed. Together they persuaded the Symphony's board of directors to commission the Cleveland schools' assistant supervisor of music appreciation, Lillian Baldwin, to develop a program that would utilize the resources of the school system.

Miss Baldwin initiated three distinct series of educational concerts—a "Little Folks'" program for grades three and four, the "Childrens' Concerts" for grades five and six, and the "Young People's Concerts" for junior and senior high school students. With the capacities and interests of each age level in mind, repertoire was chosen by Shepherd's successor, Rudolph Ringwall. Miss Baldwin wrote study guides for each series, containing simple explanations of forms and styles, illustrations of themes, and brief biographies of the composers. There were even instructions on how one should act at a concert. The study guides were distributed to classroom teachers and music specialists—along with suggestions for their use and lists of reference recordings—to be integrated into the regular music appreciation curriculum. At least ten study periods were to be devoted to each program, in advance of the concert. All children in the third through the fifth grades and all junior and senior high school students enrolled in music classes received the preparatory instruction. Concert attendance was optional for all.

In keeping with the educational purpose of the entire program, concerts were scheduled on weekdays during school hours. To make each concert as "normal" as possible in all other respects, students who elected to attend were bussed to Severance Hall, and were expected to pay for their transportation as well as a nominal admission fee.

Shortly after Shaw's accession to Ringwall's job was announced, Lillian Baldwin resigned, expressing doubts about the new conductor's qualifications and motives. After all, he was inexperienced in what had by then become a very specialized kind of musical direction, and since he had self-admittedly come to Cleveland "to learn," it was evident that he was bent on finding an orchestra of his own sooner or later.

Shaw felt his way through his first two seasons of educational concerts, studying the musical thrust of the tradition, the intricacies of the administrative setup, the attitudes of the audiences, and the predispositions of the school teachers. One fourth-grade teacher objected that Falla's "Spanish Dance" and the "Hoe Down" from Copland's *Rodeo* were too "far afield," too modern, and that the children should first be introduced to "the familiar standard music." Prokofieff's *Peter and the Wolf*, she advised, was a little long for a nine-year-old's attention span. Shaw replied tactfully: "To one who has heard substantially no music at all, the sounds of his own time may be more interesting and meaningful than those same sounds are to one raised in a particular orthodoxy, or, as Charles Ives has it, the grooved and well-oiled permutations in expediency."

In 1958 Shaw infused his own idea into the Cleveland Plan—a four-year cycle of programs designed to make the series more interesting to the teachers and the orchestra members, as well as to lead the young audiences progressively through a broad range of musical types and styles. He prepared four different programs to be played in four consecutive years for the fourth-grade students, eight for the fifth and sixth graders who attended two concerts per year, and eight more for the junior and senior high classes. In the fifth year the cycle began again with the same programs. Klaus George Roy, a Viennese-American composer and musicologist who was assistant manager of the orchestra and editor of its program book, was hired to write new study guides.

For the younger children especially, Shaw devised clever demonstrations of the instruments of the orchestra, musical themes, and structural devices, which were calculated to extend and enhance Roy's study guides. He maintained a cordial yet fast-paced and entertaining manner of address while carefully gauging the students' reactions and continually revising his apparently spontaneous commentaries.

The children's comments were genuinely spontaneous: "I'm sorry you played *Peter and the Wolf*," wrote one concertgoer, "because I've heard it a million times and I'm sick of it."

"Do you ever," another wondered, "get lonely when you are conducting?"

Shaw might have replied that that was the only time when he was *not* lonely, for in a sense, he never truly lived and breathed anywhere but onstage. His marriage had been a succession of separations almost from the first, until it seemed that he and Maxine shared their happiest moments over the telephone when Robert called from some distant city. When he went to Cleveland, she remained in Scarsdale with the children, Johanna, Peter, and John Thaddeus (born in 1957).

In 1961 they bought "Sevendoors," an ivy-covered, arched and carved house with a widow's walk overlooking the entrance to the harbor on Nantucket Island, where, he wrote in a letter to the Cleveland Orchestra Chorus,

> . . . houses crowd cobbled lanes
> in seldom relieved—nor wanting it—
> soft and weathered, feathered
> shingled shades of gray.

Robert loved it more than any place they had ever lived, but he seldom found time to spend there.

George Szell, born in Budapest in 1897 and trained in Vienna, had been a prodigy as a pianist and composer, and had served apprenticeships as a conductor in half a dozen European opera houses. He had taken over the Cleveland Orchestra from Erich Leinsdorf in 1946, the same year he became a naturalized American citizen, and in less than ten years had shaped it into one of the foremost symphonic instruments in the world.

Szell's forte was the music of the Austro-German school—Haydn, Mozart, Beethoven, Schubert, Schumann, and Brahms—about which Shaw was especially eager to learn more. Also, Szell was a meticulous technician, and in that respect had been compared with Toscanini, although Shaw viewed the two men differently. "The chief thing Toscanini communicated," Shaw once recalled, "was a vitality of forward motion and a zest for singing that's almost happy, even under sad circumstances. It's just a song of the bleeding throat: Burst a blood vessel and yell. And so you get the vast go-for-broke all the time, no matter what the risks. If it's a little rough here, you continue to fly." With Szell it was quite the opposite. He developed the whole out of the microcosm. Somehow, each little drop of tone was responsible for the whole piece, and nothing could be out of place. And if one little thing *was* out of place, then it was "impossible for the flower to happen." To make it happen, Szell demanded that his players listen closely and constantly to one another. Playing, like conducting, was for him "the art of listening."

Szell did resemble Toscanini, though, in that he was a literalist. "So far as I can tell," Shaw said in his tribute to his Cleveland mentor at the latter's death in 1970, "he never put his own image ahead of that of the composer—though he was not at all embarrassed to put his concept of the composer's image ahead of someone else's."

Finally, Szell was a compulsive student. "He was," said Shaw, "an incredible craftsman—rich in skills that had to be learned and practiced—and so far as I can tell he never allowed himself to stop learning. His was as far from 'lazy' as a man's mind can get. He practiced music as a great doctor practices medicine. Completely devoted and unexceptionally responsible."

There were frictions, however, that made Shaw's Cleveland years the most trying he ever experienced. He was perennially on the point of resigning. Gifted, intractable, and sometimes inexplicably defensive, Szell was notoriously hard to get along with. He had strewn enemies from the Metropolitan Opera House to San Francisco and back. Many of the players in the Cleveland Orchestra let it be known they felt happier working under Shaw. Yet Shaw himself eulogized that "in a world accustomed to prefabricated arts and disposable ethics I surmise that people like George Szell are impossible to get along without."

Once when Szell was vacationing in Vienna, Shaw wrote to him:

> It's an overwhelming responsibility to follow you and to deal with an instrument you have built to such virtuosity. The sense of inadequacy—of having begun with too little too late—is an almost constant companion. It occasionally vanishes during performances, but my-oh-my the study and the rehearsals! My respect for your knowledge and craft *burgeons* in your absence.
>
> The major frustration continues to be the inability to "auralize" the score prior to rehearsal, and then to hear into the texture of

the orchestra during rehearsals. I wonder, really, whether a person, no matter how rare or earnest his general aesthetic intuition and desire, can hope to overcome the lack of basic musical grammar. The poet has to be someone for whom spelling, punctuation, grammar and the problems of vocabulary do not exist. It's a terrible thing to be continually writing X because one can't spell his name.

Inevitably, whenever Shaw conducted an entirely instrumental program, he was compared with the maestro in all quarters, with little hope of completely objective treatment from the critics. On the other hand, when he conducted a choral work such as the B Minor Mass, everyone conceded that this was truly his *métier*. Louis Biancolli, the discriminating New York critic, dubbed the Cleveland Orchestra Chorus "the first chorus of the land."

"It is astonishing—like some sort of magic," Szell once said to Shaw. "Simply by the quality of the beat one can make an instant change in tone, tempo, balance or color. This chorus is simply more responsive than an orchestra."

Shaw has always found it necessary to audition from five hundred to seven hundred singers in order to produce a good volunteer chorus of, say, two hundred voices—thirty-five first sopranos, thirty-five second sopranos, forty altos, forty tenors, and fifty basses. The secret of the sound of a chorus is in the audition. Even former members of a Shaw chorus must reaudition each year.

Preliminary auditions last for ten days or more, from noon until around 10:00 P.M., with somewhere between fifty and seventy persons heard daily. To alleviate nervousness, one or two minutes are spent in greeting and conversation with every person; then tests of the singer's tone quality, control, range, and musicianship are given. As many as four-fifths of the initial number of applicants may be summoned to one of the four sectional auditions, where Shaw listens again to individual voices, then to each voice in combination with several others, and lastly in the total sectional ensemble, until the desired sound is achieved. The actual size of a chorus will depend on the number of tenors found acceptable.

From beginning to end it is a tedious and time-consuming task for Shaw and his staff, and a traumatic experience for most of the applicants. One year, Shaw made light of the entire process.

Dear Friends:

It is my unpleasant duty to inform you that your reaudition for the Cleveland Orchestra Chorus has been successful and that you may expect to resume orbit sometime between 7:30 and 7:45 P.M. next Monday, September 26.

You may wish to know some of the considerations which have guided our evaluations and qualified you for readmission. Believe me, it ain't been easy.

Number One: Any good-looking woman was admitted, ipso facto and sans souci. This might sound to you like a pretty personal way to go about this sort of thing, but I assure you that George [George Silfies, COC accompanist] and I had either (1) to agree, or (2) to voluntarily disqualify ourselves before a decision was reached, and, as George says, a chorus is a pretty personal sort of instrument; let's keep it that way.

Number Two: Anybody who was really scared made it. I mean *really* scared. George and I got a big kick out of seeing some of you who really suffer. You know, clammy hands, all choked up in the voice, stomach muscles shaking like crazy. Stumble up the steps or trip over the electric fan. Start sight-reading from right to left and all that. Anybody who gave old George and me a sort of pin-the-butterfly chuckle had it made.

Number Three: Anybody who had a cold got in. Almost all the great singers we know are hypochondriacs, and we didn't feel we could afford to pass anybody up here. I remember one person who's had throat trouble at every audition since 1956, and that's the kind of sensitive person we like to have around.

Number Four: There are always a few special rules for tenors. For instance, their reading test would be a little more accurately described as sight-improvising. I ask them to make up a note and hum it, and if George can find it on the piano they're in.

I try not to look when these things are going on, because I don't want to be influenced by appearances or things like that, and George says three tenors made it this year just by blowing their noses.

Number Five: Husband and wife teams stood a good chance this year, particularly when one partner to the marriage (and here we accept their word completely) was a bass or a tenor. This is a sort of insurance policy. Remember last year when the churches got mad because we had scheduled the *St. Matthew Passion* for Easter Sunday? Well, suppose one of our concerts happens to fall on Mother's Day. From here on we have our own built-in mothers and fathers and anyway, like George says, you can't win 'em all.

These things, plus little things like giving preference to people who are studying medicine or engineering or math, because they have lots of free time and could make extra rehearsals, or to folks who live fifty or one hundred miles from Cleveland, so that their families could learn independence. These are the things, my friends and fellow Americans, which lead me to believe that this year's chorus will be the chorus of 1960–61, and I'm sure we all know how we all feel about all that. Pax nobiscum.

Robert

Most of Shaw's letters to the Cleveland Orchestra Chorus, like those to the Collegiate Chorale, dealt with fundamentals—rhythm, phrasing, diction, and the like.

As regards the complexities which choral musicians face, I will illustrate them with reference to Movement VII of Britten's *Cantata Academica*, "ut ad longaeva. . . ."

A metronomic marking of 144 to the dotted quarter (m.m. = 144) means that there are to be 144 pulse units to the minute. This means that each pulse unit is to receive 416/1000's of a second, or a little over 4/10's of a second. During that time the word "floreat" is to be sung—to be phonated on pitch. There are the following distinct sounds in "floreat": f-uh-l-aw-rrr-eh-ah-t. That is to say, even if we count the burred "r" as a single sound—which it isn't, and if we allow the neutral vowel between "f" and "l"—which we need, we are obliged to deliver eight different sounds in 4/10's of a second. If this time were divided equally—which we can't do because some of the sounds are incapable of pitch—this would give us about 5/100's of a second per sound.

Now, take just the last part of that word, ". . . reat," which is supposed to occur on an eighth note. At a tempo of m.m. 144 to the dotted quarter the eighth-note receives 138/1000's of a second. Each sound, then, in "rrr-eh-ah-t" might expect a little less than 35/100's of a second. If one counts "rrr" as a multiple sound, then figure on 23/100's of a second. (Not a heluva a long time.)

If, on the other hand, we were to take the final syllable of the word "sanitati," which also occupies an eighth-note, one is instantly aware that the "t" consonant takes almost no time and can move immediately into the "ee" vowel, and might conceivably leave almost the whole 138/1000's of a second for the pitched vowel. In the one instance we have 23/1000's of a second per sound, and in the other perhaps five times that much, and yet both are supposed to be capable of sustaining the same pulse and rhythmic feeling.

Go one step further: Note that in the 21 words of the text of this movement there are approximately 60 syllables comprised of 135 successive sounds—multiplied by any textural repetitions. Note, also, that in spite of the use of rhyme and alliteration—and the resultant economy of the sounds of speech, and in spite of the basic simplicity of Italianized Latin (only five vowels, for instance, versus three or four times that many in English) there still are some twenty distinct and different sounds to be phonated, all in a very rapid sequence totalling 135.

Note, also, that of these sounds only 8 are capable of sustained pitch (vowels, l, m and n), 6 of them are capable only of a sub-vocal fragmentary pitch prior to the consonantal explosion (b, d, j and the like) and 6 of them are capable of no pitch at all (t, k, s and the like)—and the picture grows a little more complex.

Suppose you were the most facile of instrumentalists and had to produce this variety and complexity of tone factors (any given four within 35/1000's of a second) at any given dynamic level, within a given general color range of bright to sombre, and suppose you had no manipulative, habitual method of controlling the pitch except by "thinking" and "willing" it ahead and hoping that the proper neural sequence had been set up and that the larynx would respond—this could give even instrumentalists fits.

RS

Sometimes he reserved space for acknowledging the work of those responsible for keeping the Cleveland Orchestra Chorus going while he was on tour with the Chorale. In 1959 it fell to the COC's assistant conductor, Wynn Morris, and Szell's associate and staff pianist, Louis Lane, to prepare the chorus for a performance of Berlioz's Requiem. Upon returning to Cleveland in early April, Shaw rhymed an appreciation.

> OWED to every quatrain-lickin'
> Long-ungone but not forgotten,
> Double-quickin', thin and thickin'
>   Son of Berlioz:

> Had not you all been, in my absence,
> So stewardy and stewardessy—
> (And fonder now—which absence accents)
> The Requiem had been *so* messy.

> So hail! thou peerless-split-conductor!
> Vale! Wynn, and Vale! Louis!
> Should the Szell be hard or softer
> We will do the way you do us!

> Epilogue: Or, An apprentice-,
>   assistant-, associate-conductor's
>   lot is not a happy one:

Since all we knows of Berlioz
We really owes
To Loo's and Morris—

Ah! Mer-de-mal!
Should Szell in-stall
Another col-
'r of a horris!

While Shaw was away in the winter of 1961, Margaret Hillis—
who commuted regularly from her various occupations in New
York to Chicago, where she conducted the Chicago Symphony
Orchestra Chorus—was asked to stop in Cleveland en route and
conduct his COC rehearsals. Frank Barr was his chorus accompanist that year. Together with Edna Lea Burrus, Shaw's loyal and
invaluable personal secretary, they were eulogized in a verse letter
that began: "Hillis and Burrus and Barr / Were a trio unique—and
still are."

He seldom complimented the chorus as a whole, but when he
did, it was with care and unmistakable sincerity—and a touch of
humor.

> I've been wanting to write a fan letter for some time (into every
> life the little acids of appreciation must fall—overdew, and seldom
> unrestrained)—but it's hard to get the pencil out of my cheek.
>
> There are two things about this chorus which delight its con-
> ductor, which seem "special" in his experience, which make for
> unusual accomplishment, and to which he most frequently refers
> when speaking to outsiders about the chorus.
>
> Number One is the unusually high level of intelligence of this
> group of people. I'm not writing of musical talent, but of general
> intelligence.
>
> (You're bright! See if you can get that through your thick
> skulls!)
>
> The second pleasure and undoubted source of accomplishment
> is allied to the fact that most of you are non-professional in music
> and, in any event, join this endeavor for honors heavily fraught
> with no profit. I am not speaking of amateurism itself. We have
> talked much of its values in times past. What I have in mind at
> this moment is one of the extra boni (bonuses?) of a society like
> ours. It is the very diversity of professional interest and accom-
> plishment of its members.
>
> To be sure, music is its own very complex science; but it is also
> wind, sand and stars in the eyes, love-nest and blast-off, itch to the
> initiate and poetry to the peasant.

And thus, while no amount of know-less can add to our enjoyment of music, the variety of our intellectual occupational backgrounds sweeps through our musical recreation, enlivens and enhances music's allegory, secularizes, sanctifies, inspirits and (praise Ford) *outbreeds*.

Suffice it to be advised that when you are bullied hence for non-sense, you've had its retraction before the fact—in writing.

R

When the occasion demanded it, he could chastise the chorus with such finesse that they felt enlightened rather than intimidated. But once he was so angered by the singers' lack of preparation for a rehearsal that he wrote them a scathing letter and lined it out in the shape of a dagger.

When rehearsing an orchestra or a professional chorus, Shaw's communication is concise and matter-of-fact; all that professionals want to know is "what to wham and when." His manner before an amateur chorus is less formal. Amateurs are as susceptible to suggestion as to command, and often a jest can achieve results more quickly than a technical explanation. One COC member made note of a few of Shaw's one-liners:

"Sing those staccatos like a judge on a pogo stick."

"You've got to sing it like you mean it, not like a plastic Jesus in the windshield."

"That's right, the notes go up and they go down. You go up and you go down. Now, shall we learn the notes, and go up and down together?"

"You tenors will have to sing sharp on that note. Pretend that your hand is in a trap."

"Your *sforzando* shouldn't sound as if you were in a crowded elevator and it suddenly stopped."

"You basses sound like you've been rammed from the rear."

"You altos sound like an anteater in heat."

Mr. Szell to Mr. Shaw: "When you beat they follow you. How can I get them to follow me?" Mr. Shaw to Mr. Szell: "I follow them."

During his first two seasons in Cleveland Shaw's time and attention were devoted to his duties with the orchestra and chorus, except for conducting in Anchorage the summer of 1957 and recording some albums for RCA Victor. But by the fall of 1958 he was back in his usual stride, his contract allowing extensive leaves of absence so that he could meet his obligations to Columbia Artists Management and also accept some engagements at festivals and workshops.

The Robert Shaw Chorale toured for eight weeks in February–April 1959, with a varied program that included the Fauré Requiem and Brahms's *Alto Rhapsody*. The next year Shaw realized a long-held ambition by taking Bach's B Minor Mass to thirty-five cities and campuses—against the advice of his best counselors, and at a net loss to himself of about $20,000. In the introductory notes for the tour program-book he explained why he had insisted on presenting such esoteric fare to provincial audiences:

> . . . Like the reply of those who scaled Mount Everest to those similar questions—because it is there. It is undoubtedly one of the very few very great achievements of the human mind and heart. —And this is reason enough to take it on tour. It always seemed to me to be an unreasonable crystallization of disdain, indifference and acquisitiveness to offer less than this "best" to American audiences. I can sometimes sense in audiences outside of the metropolitan areas this gradation of sophistication and experience but I have never felt that this represented also gradations of intelligence, sensitivity or desire.

That his faith was fully justified was amply evident all along the way, but the most moving testimony occurred at the University of Wisconsin in Madison. There, he recalls, after the final chord was sounded, he "shuffled off stage in silence, waited, waited, waited, —then peered around the curtain to discover that the audience had risen and was simply standing there facing the performers—who were also standing—in absolute silence." (Shaw had a similar experience one other time—at the close of the Cherubini Requiem for an audience of students, faculty, and townspeople at Kent State University, one month following the massacre of May 4, 1970.)

Instances of such transcendent empathy are rare in any case. It is perhaps impossible for a layman to understand the intensity of a musician's emotional involvement in a performance, and particularly in one of such magnitude as the B Minor Mass. Seldom is the subject even discussed, for it is much too personal to be exposed to public diagnosis. Shaw once expressed his own feelings in a letter to the host and hostess whom he had offended by failing to extend his appreciation and greeting to them upon leaving their postconcert reception.

Over the past dozen years of concert touring through the United States I suppose I have been "received" as frequently as the "next fellow"—meaning, in my instance, five to seven receptions per week for as many as sixteen consecutive weeks or a total of twenty-five to thirty weeks per season. —And I can manage most of the time to chit an appropriate chat, though it seldom has been a relaxed and pleasant experience. I realize that these parties have been undertaken—in most instances—to show the performers an appreciation more personal than applause. (On tours I employ a manager whose principal post-concert duties are to see that I meet and thank the responsible hosts and hostesses.)

—But frankly, I would rather be off in some dark corner with two or three people—as opposed to sixty or eighty. One may talk with the few, but must *address* the many, whether they be met serially or simultaneously.

Actually, I, for one, would be *most* comfortable in the company of the few folk who had most exhaustively and intimately shared the responsibility of the performance.

Most performances are failures: and accepting graciously endless patterns of congratulations is not only embarrassing but, probably, ultimately ulcerous.

Even worse are those rare occasions when flesh and spirit have conspired, when the right and real thing has happened. Almost anything anyone says then is already too much.

Beyond this I have to admit to a rather special sort of dementia attendant upon performances of two works in the choral-orchestral repertoire:

For whatever complex of reasons—dimension, duration, intellectual tension, religious symbolism, ecstasy—for whatever complex of reasons, whenever I have been involved in a performance of the *B Minor Mass* or the *St. Matthew Passion* I simply have not operated humanly or socially with much charm or productivity for some hours afterwards and, on occasion when the luxury of leisure was available, for two or three days thereafter.

Somehow, to me, these are "shocking" works: works capable—together, perhaps, with the abrupt cessation of weeks of intense effort—of leaving one in a state approaching some sort of emotional "shock."

On the seventy-one–day tour to the West Coast in the late winter of 1961, Shaw had intended to present Handel's *Messiah*, but he gave in to the urging of Frederick Schang, head of Columbia Artists, and postponed that plan for a few years in favor of Bach's motet *Singet dem Herrn*, Haydn's *Seven Last Words*, Carissimi's *Jephte*, and Britten's *Ceremony of Carols*, plus the usual encores. The responses of audiences and critics were typically enthusiastic, except that Alfred Frankenstein of the *San Francisco Chronicle* had one reservation: "A program as beautifully chosen as this is seldom to be found on the circuit of commercial concert-giving. The payoff came with the encores, a considerable number of them, mostly Negro spirituals and other folk songs sung in arrangements of unrelieved vulgarity. They drew lots of applause mingled with the soft plash of the cognoscenti being quietly sick in their hats."

The sting of Frankenstein's insult was forgotten when, a few days later, the most dreaded mishap of all struck the troupe. Tom Pyle, riding in the small van that carried the portative organ, harp, and two cellos, was grievously injured in an accident near Vancouver, Washington.

In 1962 the Chorale toured with the *St. John Passion* for forty-nine days, from January 29 through March 18. Late in the tour they appeared in Carnegie Hall, and Paul Henry Lang chastised Shaw in the *New York Times* for what he considered to be an unsuitably subjective, introspective interpretation of the Baroque masterpiece: "Our choirmasters who preach instead of conducting are remiss in their sworn duties and are invading the province of the pastor." If anything, Shaw was flattered, for he had abjured the coldly objective musicological approach as much as the inflated romantic one, in favor of an intensely personal but humanely credible invocation of one of Christianity's most dramatic moments.

In June he took 120 members of the Cleveland Orchestra Chorus on the first of three annual trips to San Juan, Puerto Rico, to participate in the Festival Casals. Under Shaw's direction the chorus sang four chorales from the *St. John Passion*, Schubert's Mass in G, and Bach's Cantata 82 with William Warfield as soloist. As an *hommage* to Pablo Casals they surprised the eighty-five-year-old master with a rendition of his motet, "O vos omnes," which he had never before heard sung. The climax of the twelve-day festival was the performance of Casals' oratorio, *El Pesebre* ("The Manger"), inaugurating the venerable cellist-composer's personal "crusade for peace," which was to last for more than ten years. At the

With Pablo Casals in Puerto Rico. Photograph cour-
tesy of the Ohio Bell Telephone Co.

close of the festival, the chorus flew to New York to present the
oratorio in Carnegie Hall.

Shaw also carried out a rigorous schedule of guest appearances
—a Verdi Requiem at the College of Wooster in April; a *Missa
Solemnis* at the University of Kansas in May and another at the
University of Minnesota Choral Arts Workshop in July. Later in
July he conducted Bach's *Magnificat*, Schubert's Mass in G, and
Stravinsky's *Symphony of Psalms* at Michigan State University. In

early August he conducted a week-long Sacred Music Workshop for Fred Waring using music from the COC's album, *Great Sacred Choruses*, which had been recorded for RCA Victor in the fall of 1961. In mid-August he made his second visit to the Marlboro Music Festival in Vermont, where a community of professional musicians from all over the world had assembled every summer since 1950 to play chamber music; he conducted Beethoven's Fantasy in C Minor, op. 80 (with the festival's founder, Rudolph Serkin, as pianist) and the Schubert Mass.

On September 26 he conducted the Robert Shaw Chorale in a performance in Springfield, Massachusetts, for the opening of the Junior League's annual concert series. The next day he began rehearsals with the Chorale in preparation for their tour to West Berlin, Yugoslavia, and the Soviet Union, which had been set up under the State Department's Cultural Exchange Program.

7.

The RSC in Russia and South America

THE COLD WAR between the United States and the U.S.S.R. was waged not only in the political sphere but in every area that afforded competitive opportunities: science, medicine, space technology, the arts. On the cultural front, hostilities were opened by the Soviets in 1946 when Andrei Zhdanov, chairman of the Central Committee of the Communist Party, launched an ideological campaign to reinforce certain policies originally established in the 1930s. In a series of "resolutions" Zhdanov purged the Party's literature, drama, film, and music of all traces of Western "formalism" and affirmed the principles of Socialist Realism. Nothing was permitted thenceforth that was alien to "the aesthetic needs of the people." Choral music was deemed one of the most viable mediums for the furtherance of the Party's objectives.

Following Zhdanov's decree on music in February of 1948, Soviet musical life was totally isolated from that of the West, and its official spokesmen expressed attitudes clearly reflecting Premiere Stalin's own xenophobia. As a Russian critic wrote in the June 1949 issue of *Sovyetskaya Musica*: "In fighting for peace and democracy, in defending the genuinely great culture of humanity, we must unceasingly unmask the poisonous propaganda of reactionary bourgeois individualism [and] the misanthropic, cosmopolitan art of decadence and degeneration."

149

Meanwhile the Russians energetically propagandized musically in behalf of their own cause in every part of the globe. Having signed a fishing treaty with Iceland shortly after World War II, they moved in with a cultural campaign that all but engulfed the island. Russian musicians, including the great violinist David Oistrakh, visited every village, playing not only for but *with* the people.

Reaction in the West to such forays was halfhearted at first. In 1949 the International Music Council was set up under the auspices of the United Nations Educational, Scientific and Cultural Organization, with headquarters at the UNESCO House in Paris. One of the IMC's purposes was to foster the exchange of music and musicians among the nations of the world. Four years later, however, the council's entire budget was still a paltry $26,000, and its usefulness as a weapon in the cold war was correspondingly insignificant.

In 1952, sensing the import of the Communist bloc's initiative on the cultural front, the U.S. Department of State made a feeble gesture of retaliation. Blanche Thebom, the Metropolitan Opera's great mezzo-soprano, was asked to give a concert or two in Iceland on her way to Europe. In the next two years a few more American artists made similarly unofficial, incidental side-trips to the same locale. There was no money available for an all-out countercampaign; it was self-evident to most American strategists that bombs were more potent than Bach.

In 1954 President Eisenhower's strategies to combat the ideological, economic, and military expansion of the communist system prompted his requesting Congress to fund a continuing Program for Cultural Presentations to *assist* artists to tour abroad for the purpose of demonstrating that "America, too, can lay claim to high cultural and artistic accomplishments." Congress appropriated $5.9 million, to be administered by the State Department's Bureau of Educational and Cultural Affairs and the United States Information Agency. Setting aside overhead costs, about half of the remainder was earmarked for supporting American industries' participation in foreign trade fairs, and $2.5 million was allocated to the fields of "education and entertainment." Within a few months the federal government cautiously exported José Limon's dance company to Brazil and Uruguay, a team of duo-pianists to Italy, and Isaac Stern to Iceland. A production of *Porgy and Bess* was dispatched to Spain, Italy, Israel, Greece, Egypt, and Yugoslavia.

When the Iron Curtain itself was finally parted in 1955, it was not by government forces after all. Robert Breen, producer of the Gershwin opera, made arrangements directly with Nikolai Bulganin, chairman of the Soviet Union's council of ministers. Breen's success called attention to the atmosphere of liberalization that had been building in Russia since Stalin's death in 1953, and that was heightened when Premier Nikita Khrushchev renounced Stalinism once and for all at the Twentieth Party Conference in 1956.

Two years later, in January of 1958, the ambassadors of the United States and the Soviet Union opened a new era of "cultural diplomacy" with the signing of the first of a series of two-year cultural exchange agreements. The term "culture" was used in a broad sense, embracing industry, agriculture, and commerce as well as the arts. In music, the exchange was to cover performers, composers, and musicologists.

The two countries entered into the agreement with identical motives. Each hoped to pick up technical information for updating its own cold war tactics. At the same time, each desired to soften public opinion in the other country, and thus perhaps to modify its adversary's defense economy. Finally, each aimed to correct the worldwide image it had acquired from the other's propaganda and from its own past deeds—Russia as a backward country in which culture withered under a heartless dictatorship, America as a people driven by materialistic greed and wholly indifferent to the higher life of the mind and the spirit.

Nevertheless, it was an uneven contest. Russian artists were servants of the state, so their tours were completely and generously subsidized. American artists were welcome to tour abroad if their patriotism prompted them to do so, and if their schedules permitted it, but they received far less money than they might have earned on a domestic tour. Their expenses were covered only in part by government funds; the rest had to be made up from private contributions and box office receipts. Also, the differential between the dollar and the ruble allowed Russian artists to reap extra bonuses in America, while American stars lost money in Russia.

Moreover, while the Russian part of the program was immune to criticism from within the state, American procedures were regularly monitored by vote-conscious congressmen and concerned citizens. Representatives William B. Widnall of New Jersey and John J. Rooney of New York complained that our performers were being overpaid. Actress Helen Hayes, head of the Theater Guild American Repertory Company, whose tour had consumed about half of one year's allocation in that category, was criticized for taking a weekly salary of $1,500—roughly half of what she would have made on Broadway.

Soviet artists were obliged to go wherever and whenever they were ordered, but Americans were chosen on the basis of recommendations, reputations, or competitive applications. In 1956, in order to minimize political pressures, the State Department's Bureau of Educational and Cultural Affairs relinquished responsibility for the selection of talent to the American National Theater and Academy, a federally chartered (1935) but privately funded agency. The move was unsuccessful. After the application of a chorus from the University of Arkansas was rejected by ANTA, the same organization went off on its own and proceeded to win an international choral competition in Italy. Quite naturally, Senator J. W. Fulbright of Arkansas questioned ANTA's judgment.

Actually, in some respects the college choruses, bands, and orchestras constituted one of America's most effective cadres on the cultural front. Since their members required no salaries, they did not have to depend on box office income as much as the professional groups did, and thus could perform in small towns as well as in major cities. Since their members went mainly for the educational value of foreign travel, they eagerly made friends with college-age youth in the host countries. Above all, since such groups consisted not only of music students but also of musical amateurs from other academic disciplines, they represented a cross-section of American life and convincingly demonstrated that music is not an exotic but an integral element in American society. The Soviets had nothing comparable to offer.

By the fall of 1962 the controversy over ANTA's qualifications to screen anything other than theatrical talent reached the point where Lucius D. Battle, Assistant Secretary of State for Educational and Cultural Affairs, was constrained to launch an investigation, and all overseas bookings beyond those already planned or under way were temporarily suspended.

Only a few months before, the United States and Russia had signed their third two-year cultural exchange agreement. In return for the Bolshoi Theater Ballet, the Leningrad Philharmonic Symphony Orchestra with David Oistrakh as soloist, and the Ukrainian Dance Ensemble, the Soviets were to receive Benny Goodman's orchestra, the New York City Ballet, and the Robert Shaw Chorale and Orchestra. For Shaw's group, the State Department set up four concerts in Yugoslavia and six in West Berlin, in addition to six weeks in Russia with thirty concerts in eleven cities.

As usual, Shaw held auditions and scheduled two weeks of rehearsals, at twenty to thirty hours per week, just prior to the departure date. The problem was that no one yet knew precisely what was to be rehearsed. Some weeks in advance, Shaw had submitted to ANTA and the State Department nine or ten tentative programs, with the understanding that the foreign concert managers would come back with counterproposals—some of this, some of that. Replies were slow, however, and it was not until a week of rehearsals had passed that the repertoire was finally settled.

When he left New York, Shaw and the troupe were in a state of shock. The European tour of 1956 had followed directly upon a good many weeks of concertizing in the United States. This time they were to open cold at the Berlin Festival with three mixed programs. The Russians had also requested the B Minor Mass.

Soviet cultural officials had at first been only mildly interested in the Chorale, and even less in the Mass. They doubted that Shaw's group could stack up to their own country's resplendent choral tradition, and they were not favorably disposed toward religious music of any kind. Reluctantly, their U.S. delegation attended one of the final rehearsals of the Bach and went away deeply impressed. Unfortunately, there wasn't enough time to mount the kind of publicity fanfare that had preceded the arrivals of Goodman and the New York City Ballet.

The first two concerts in Moscow consisted of some sixteenth-century motets and madrigals, pieces by Debussy, Ravel, Ives, and various contemporary American composers, plus the *Friede auf*

Erden of Schoenberg, whose music had been interdicted long ago by the Communists. For encores there were spirituals, hymns, and a few Russian folk songs.

Opening night was a veritable triumph, according to *Newsweek*'s correspondent: "As the last refrain of the old Negro spiritual, 'Dry Bones,' thundered into the ornate marble tiers of [the Moscow Conservatory Hall], the first nighters began the insistent rhythmic clapping that signals a demand for an encore. Suddenly the Robert Shaw Chorale, a 'sleeper' in the Russian-American cultural exchange program, had turned into a smash hit." The news spread via the grapevine well in advance of the official press. Just before a concert in another city some days later, a student hastily penned a note in his best English: "Dear Mr. Shou. Very ask you perform Negro sperichuelle 'Decay bone.' Very ask you please."

Long before the third concert—the B Minor Mass—all seats and standing room had been sold. One embassy employee was offered sixty rubles (about $66) for a ticket, although the top box office price was only 3½ rubles. Militia were stationed at ten-foot intervals behind iron pipe barricades twenty-four hours before the concert to keep hysterical Muscovites from breaking into the hall. The Mass was presented nine more times in other Russian cities, with similar success. In Lvov the concert had to be stopped when the crowd outside rioted, broke open the doors, and stormed into the already packed hall.

The Mass was also broadcast in its entirety, including applause and intermissions, throughout all the Iron Curtain countries over the state radio network. "For three hours," Shaw recalled, "the only fare available to this 'materialistic,' 'atheistic,' 'eye to the future' audience was an ageless monument of Christian creed, philosophy and art."

Several months after returning to Cleveland, Shaw recounted some of his experiences to the congregation of the First Unitarian Church:

> A wonderfully kind and wise old man travelled with us constantly as our impresario. A representative of Goskoncert—the State Bureau—he and his staff arranged meals, travel, hotel accommodations, stage preparations and entertainment. He became extraordinarily beloved by all of us. At our last conversation during

the 2:00 A.M. ride to the airport in Moscow I asked him if he could explain the tumultuous response of the Russian audiences. He replied—through an interpreter—"First, it's possible, you know, that you may have underestimated the Russian people—mind and heart. And on the other hand—we assumed that you wanted to do the Bach Mass to show off—that Americans could produce this difficult and complex thing. I was with you in every audience, you know. And it never failed; within three minutes after you had begun to sing, people forgot that you were Americans or performers, and that they were in a concert hall. They were simply hearing *Kyrie eleison*, "Lord our God have Mercy," or *Dona nobis pacem*, "Give us Peace." It was like one heart talking to another heart—or more like Bach's heart was talking to all of us."

He went on, "Do you remember the first time I saw you?" I said, "Yes, at the airport," "No," he said, "after that. Our first concert was at the Conservatory Hall. The hall was on the third floor. You had a rehearsal the afternoon of the first concert, and the elevators were not working. All the risers and stage equipment were on the ground floor. —Some tons. And when we came to visit the rehearsal we found the conductor and four of his singers in work clothes carrying all this equipment up six flights of stairs to the stage level. It took about an hour and a half, as I recall, and I said to the officials with me, 'If this man cares as much about music as he does his risers, this will be different.'" We never had to carry risers again.

Late in the tour, when we were pretty exhausted, in one of the smaller cities we came upon a multi-purpose stage presided over by a theatre manager who has his counterpart in almost every concert association in the United States' touring circuit. All for sight—not one percent for sound. Drapes stage level to grid. No ceiling. 'Like giving a concert in a dirty clothes hamper—or under water. What made it so discouraging was that the stage had a back brick wall that had been calcimined an attractive off-white grey-blue and which would give us some reverberation for our tired voices. Mr. Petrov did all he could to convince the theatre manager that velour drapes would eat up half of the sound, but he was not of their official family and was running into local autonomy.

At which point the conductor converted his impatience into a mash of sadness and said gloomily, "Gentlemen—No Concert"—and walked out of the building, slowly, so as to be overtaken. It's a walk he's taken out of almost every high school auditorium in Grand Junction, U.S.A. —Sure enough, the interpreter caught up with him. "It's okay. They'll do anything you want." I wish it had been Petrov who said it (it would have been quite like him)—but it was an embassy escort who said, "Robert, you've just had your first Soviet-American diplomatic conference."

There were, of course, a few reminders of the cold war combat. One of the singers was accosted by the police while he was strolling the streets of a northern city, and was unceremoniously ushered straight back to his hotel room. Just before concert time he reported the incident to Petrov, who questioned the hotel management and other officials. The incident simply had not occurred.

Our first concert in Leningrad [where several hundred people stood in line all night to get coupons from a government bureau that would entitle them to stand in line all the following day just to *try* to get standing-room tickets] coincided with the Cuban crisis. At 4:30 in the afternoon, prior to a five o'clock rehearsal in the fabulously beautiful concert hall, our embassy escort called my room, saying he had to talk to me before rehearsal. After a day of attempting to communicate with the Embassy in Moscow he had succeeded and had been informed of President Kennedy's action. So far as could be ascertained the news had had some coverage in the Soviet Union by radio—but not yet by press. Under the circumstances, we should of course go ahead with the concert, but be prepared for possible anti-American demonstrations either inside or outside the hall. The company was so advised. —And it was a grim moment.

Absolutely nothing happened, of course. The audience could not have been more lavish in its cadenced applause. It easily surpassed the Moscow demonstration of our opening week. The public outside the theatre was friendly and smiling—filling the boulevard between the concert hall and the hotel.

I suspect these are the three answers. In the first place their information was not as complete or as frightening as ours.

In the second place, if there is a great "Russian Soul" or psyche or attitude or something like that, I suspect that among its major characteristics is a compartmentalism—an isolation of the philosophic from the factual, art from hunger, music from war. The diplomat at the concert hall and the conference table are not frequently recognizable as the same person.

In the third place, I suspect that the great central block of the Russian common people are even more desperate for peace than their American counterparts. I never saw a hint of evidence that they could out-produce the United States. There was still every evidence that they could out-starve us.

—And so I imagine that in a situation so characterized by cross mis-informations, where the American people are at least generally suspected of being over-riding imperialist aggressors, that any offering of what can be tasted as unalloyed good-will, must bring tears of relief and thanks to the heart.

I am dismayed and embarrassed by the glib "togetherness" boys who intone that music will bring the world together. Singing together has some grand and glorious and salutary results, but among them are not the settling of economic or political or military problems. These problems have to be settled economically and politically. What cultural exchange *can* do is act as a lubricant and a delay-before-harsh-measure-any-old-decision factors. It can gain us time. And it can make us aware of the possibility of getting along with these or other people.

And even with the phenomenon of apparent mutually exclusive compartmentalization of art and politics—if a deputy minister of foreign affairs comes to 7 out of 9 Moscow performances, including 3 performances of the Mass, several in attendance with our ambassador, and if he says in a private manner in a public reception, "All this makes our work somewhat easier, Mr. Ambassador," there is every reason to believe that it isn't more difficult.

Shortly after the Chorale left the Soviet Union, Khrushchev's government cracked down on experimentation and abstraction in all the arts, and reaffirmed the Stalinist doctrine of Socialist Realism. To the surprise of Western observers, a number of prominent citizens openly protested the move; there was even talk within the Ministry of Culture of reviving some of the great Russian liturgical music for concert purposes. In the opinion of at least one embassy official, the outburst of liberal sentiment was inspired largely by the Americans' visit. He wrote to Shaw, "The blow you and your people struck for freedom is, believe me, a great one."

On January 3, 1963, the Chorale set out on a twenty-five-day tour of the eastern United States with Bach's *Jesu, Meine Freude*, Mozart's *Psalms*, Schoenberg's *Friede auf Erden*, Ives's *Harvest Home Chorales*, Ravel's *Trois Chansons*, and a few excerpts from *Porgy and Bess*. The following year's tour, lasting from January 13 until March 23, took them as far west as Kansas and Nebraska with a program consisting of Carissimi's oratorio, *Jephte*, Britten's *Rejoice in the Lamb*, Haydn's Mass in D Minor, and some of Brahms's *Liebeslieder*.

A month and a half later, on May 15, 1964, the Robert Shaw Chorale and Orchestra embarked on their third mission for the State Department, this time to South America—Colombia, Ecuador, Peru, Chile, Uruguay, Paraguay, Brazil, and Argentina—with two eclectic programs and the B Minor Mass.

The responsibility for cementing relations between the Americas was great, for once again the times were perilous and our country's image was steadily worsening.

At home, the blacks' struggle for equality, which had flared into open conflict and tragedy with increasing frequency since the early fifties, was about to burst into conflagrations even more devastating than those of the "Negro revolt" of 1963. Ruthless measures by police and white bigots to suppress civil rights demonstrations marshalled by black leaders such as the Rev. Martin Luther King, Jr., had already aroused indignation among the people of foreign countries otherwise friendly to the United States. On July 2 the Civil Rights Act was to be signed into law by Lyndon Johnson, but as of mid-May the "long, hot summer" of 1964 was still ahead, to be punctuated by violence in Mississippi and rioting in several Northern cities.

Tensions between the United States and Russia had become somewhat relaxed since the resolution of the Cuban crisis. In early August a nuclear test ban treaty was signed. At the same time, the People's Republic of China was swiftly rising to status as a world power, and was soon to enter the arms race by detonating its first nuclear bomb. Despite a widening ideological rift between Moscow and Peking, however, all members of the communist bloc continued to vie with the United States for the allegiances of the new nations that were struggling from beneath the old yokes of imperialism in Africa and Southeast Asia. In 1962 the United States had begun supplementing its economic aid and military advisorship to South Vietnam by sending troops there—an act that was to lead to overt though unofficial warfare by August of 1964. The rest of the "free world" looked on uneasily.

In every South American city where they appeared, the Robert Shaw Chorale and Orchestra, heralded by publicity emphasizing the success of their previous overseas tours, was received with exceptional cordiality and without the slightest hint of animosity. On the day of their appearance in Concepción, Chile, a torrential rain inundated the city's streets and washed out many roads elsewhere in the province, yet that night the auditorium was filled to capacity. Shaw recounted some of their other experiences the next October in a letter to the Cleveland Orchestra Chorus:

There is a very strong interest in the choral art in all South American republics, but of those visited (all but Bolivia and Venezuela) the choral movement in Chile is most remarkable.

Our schedule in Santiago, after a noon-time arrival, briefings and a press conference, began with an evening reception for the entire company (thirty-six vocalists, twenty-four instrumentalists) given by the Federation of Choruses of Chile in a high school gymnasium. I had been asked to arrive a few minutes after our group, which, as guests of honor, were placed in the front and center of a large expanse of tiered seats flanking one side of the basketball court. As I stepped through the door onto the basketball floor I was sure I had been ushered into the wrong arena. Here were some four to five thousand yelling, shouting, banner-waving "fans"—obviously here to greet the Beatles, Mickey Mouse or Liz and Richard.

It was a fantastic evening. Having first been greeted by songs of friendship and welcome—which these thousands had rehearsed for weeks ahead—we then were treated to an amazing staged full-hour revue of folk music and dance—lighted, costumed and choreographed with full professional competence but with amateur, native and animal vitality. Following this each of the choruses there represented filed by with gifts and souvenirs—pottery, metal work, sculpture, pictures or pennants. —And after we had "improvised" our scoreless hymn of thanks and murmured some words of appreciation—with unpremeditated but fortuitous references to how a young late great North American [John F. Kennedy] would have enjoyed being there (which references occasioned the evening's only moment of silence and tears: this man was *really* loved down there), after, also, an hour of auto- and photo-graphs, we were ushered into what must have been a combination locker room and cold storage for informal mingling, snacking and wining.

For the next three days, in addition to our rehearsals and performances, I met every morning with nearly one hundred choral conductors, assembled from Chile's interior—of which there's very little—and from her extremities—which are about twenty-five hundred miles distant from each other. We rehearsed and rehashed, paneled and seminared, traded literature, techniques and compliments.

We learned that there were more choruses in Santiago than at which one might shake a single stick. In addition to choirs associated with schools and religious institutions, every factory, bank, department store, insurance company or agency of public service or government seems to sprout some sort of choral activity. Frequently these were also coordinated with groups of dancers and strummed strings. —The point was that music was not a spectator sport but daily do-it-yourself bread, wine and TV.

On the fourth day we were invited to a twi-night reception-dinner afforded by the chorus of the General Tire Company of Chile. The factory was located about an hour's ride out of Santiago, and we reported first to a quonset qubhouse built by the members of the chorus with materials donated by the Company. Here we were wined, canapéed and sung to by a charming motley of executives, workers, wives and children. —For this chorus not only crosses management-labor lines, but also those which separate the generations. The youngest members would surely be no more than six years old, and the eldest, retired grandparents.

Following this there was a gargantuan barbecue dinner at a public park pubhouse which began with Chilean wines and bouillabaisse, continued with Chilean wines and great joints of braised meat, Chilean wines and salad, and ended with Chilean wines and dancing. It was at this point in the evening that I won my spurs. Rowels rampant on my corrugated rubber-soled seven-leg boots, I was led by a lamb to her daughter and allowed the first dance. That is, it was the first dance for me. *Every* dance is a first dance for me. For them it was fun time—like turning a turtle upside down. —There's not a lot to this dance: just feet, hands, hips, eyes, spurs and handkerchiefs. The only trouble is that everything is supposed to move at once. I didn't seem to be able to figure out how to keep my poncho out of my spurs. Every time I'd step on it, it'd jerk my chin down on my knees. (I remember thinking it wasn't quite fair: two against one. The chin was bound to lose.) This was supposed to have been an ancient gaucho dance of courtship. Courtship! Rape would have been less risky. Ah, art, Ah, diplomacy.

To return to this letter's matter. The manager-director of the factory, a North American from Akron who'd been handed this job about wartime drove me from the reception to the dinner. It was one of those "Now, I don't know anything about music, but . . ." beginnings, but what followed was extraordinary: ". . . what is there about this singing in choruses that gets to people and gets to the best in them? I've been here for more than twenty years. We always had all sorts of labor-management problems and trouble. A few years ago some workers came to me to ask if they could start a chorus. Why not? Pretty soon I noticed that the chorus included people from all levels and elements in our factory. . . . I've never seen anything work like this. When some problem comes up these guys sit down together like they could stand each other and it's all settled. Nothing has been so important in this big company as that little chorus."

All this—and Mozart too.

                                                           R

Latin Americans were surprised, almost as much as the Russians had been, at the presence of two blacks in the troupe—tenor soloist Seth McCoy and soprano chorister Diane White—and even more so to learn that there had been blacks in nearly every Robert Shaw Chorale since 1948. Shaw had never made a crusade of civil rights; he had always considered any applicant, regardless of race or religion, who showed suitable talent and ability in open competition. On the other hand, he did not shrink from the obligations of human rights. Although in southern communities there was seldom any alternative but to accept hospitality for black singers from private individuals, on tours through the northern states Shaw simply refused to patronize any hotel that would not house the entire troupe. The members of the Chorale overcame the ignominy of discrimination in southern restaurants by purchasing groceries at a market and eating a picnic lunch on the bus.

That same spirit of solidarity was noticed by a critic in Rio de Janeiro. "The chorus and orchestra of Robert Shaw," he noted approvingly, "through the universal power of music, supersedes all barriers (as it proved in the Soviet Union), including this one of color prejudice, against which is enjoined the most terrible of struggles within the North American democracy."

Shaw returned to South America in June of 1965, under an American Specialist grant from the U.S. Bureau of Educational and Cultural Affairs, to conduct choral and orchestral performances and workshops in Santiago, Montevideo, Buenos Aires, and Concepción. Clayton Krehbiel flew down in advance to lead preliminary rehearsals of the Requiems of Mozart and Brahms, Britten's *Ceremony of Carols*, Bach's *Christ lag in Todesbanden*, and several shorter contemporary American choral works. That same summer was Shaw's first as director of the Choral and Orchestral Institutes at Oakland University's Meadow Brook Summer School of Music in Rochester, Michigan. The two following summers, with the cooperation of the State Department and the Rockefeller Foundation, he invited eleven choral conductors from Argentina, Brazil, Peru, Venezuela, and Mexico to study at the school. In August of 1966 he travelled to the Southern Hemisphere once again to conduct—for "expenses only"—the *Missa Solemnis* in Lima, Peru.

It was at Meadow Brook that Shaw briefly entertained the hope of at last establishing a resident professional chorus. The time was ripe, since colleges and universities were then scanning the horizon for innovative educational schemes, so he and Walter Collins, dean of Oakland University's school of music, and Walter Gould, wrote up a detailed proposal, but neither government agencies nor private foundations were interested in underwriting the additional cost of the project. In 1969 the school was reorganized, and Shaw terminated his association with it.

There was no tour by the Robert Shaw Chorale in 1965, but in the spring of 1966 Shaw took a full-length *Messiah* on the road for six weeks, including a turn through the South.

The Civil Rights Act of 1964 had prohibited discrimination or segregation in voting, education, and the use of public facilities or accommodations, but for many months there were repeated acts of resistance from whites. It required surpassing courage for a black to assume a seat in the front of a bus—or the front of an auditorium.

The Chorale's buses were stopped at the outskirts of Birmingham, Alabama, by police who, seeing blacks aboard, surmised they carried a contingent of "freedom riders" bent on testing the progress of desegregation thereabouts. Not satisfied with the explanation that the travellers were there to present a concert, the officers escorted the buses into the city where the drivers were compelled to maneuver their vehicles through an obstacle course designed to separate professionals from ringers. Later the troupe was insidiously harried in the neighborhood restaurants. Hooded members of the Klu Klux Klan stalked back and forth in front of the hotel entrance. The word was out that Shaw had refused to perform if audiences were not integrated.

The concert took place in Birmingham's Municipal Auditorium at 3:30 P.M. on Easter Sunday. As the singers filed onto the risers the applause mounted with an unusual crescendo, and when each one turned to face the audience it was discovered that Negroes, who normally would have been expected to sit at the rear of the auditorium, filled the first ten rows of seats. With the opening notes of "Comfort ye, my people," sung by Seth McCoy, those black faces began to glisten with tears. The orchestra musicians, caught up in the emotion-charged atmosphere, were playing blind. The music before them literally swam. By the time McCoy began his aria, "Thou shalt smite them with rods of iron," it seemed as though the very earth beneath them was atremble.

When they returned to New York in June the same troupe—except for those instrumentalists who were not members of the union's Local—made an epochal recording of the work for RCA Victor.

The 1967 tour began on April 3 in Red Bank, New Jersey, extended south into the Carolinas and Georgia, then west to Kansas City, Missouri, northeast to Chicago, and back through Washington and Philadelphia, ending in Flushing, New York. The program, one of the most esoteric to date, consisted of Poulenc's Mass in G Major, Hindemith's *Six Chansons*, Schoenberg's *Friede auf Erden*, the *Psalm 90* of Charles Ives, Webern's *Entflieht auf leichten Kähnen*, the *Trois Chansons* of Debussy, and Alberto Ginastera's *Lamentations of Jeremiah*. As with previous RSC tours, the thrust of it all permeated the American choral tradition. Choral conductors in colleges and universities—and even in a few high schools—began jotting down those same titles on their repertoire lists for "next year."

Although no formal announcement had been made, it was widely rumored that this, the twenty-first tour in fifteen seasons over a period of twenty years, was to be the Chorale's valedictory. After the performance in Chicago the *Tribune*'s critic, Thomas Willis, regretfully mused:

> What would it be like not to have the Robert Shaw Chorale coming around? . . . Not to have the courtesy of courtly bows or the immaculate taste to make platform manners more than perfunctory exercise. Not to hear those Shaw rhythms which start from deep within where each of us has an unconscious timekeeper. Not to experience the deep regard for the evocative and imaginative power of words which makes this conductor's recitation of a song translation a memorable experience in its own right.
>
> If yesterday afternoon did indeed turn out to be the Chorale's farewell Orchestra Hall appearance, about the only happy note to be sounded is that it was quitting when it was on top. Otherwise it would be a sad day to be chronicling.

As if to confirm the rumor, the final encore was a repetition of the middle section of Ives's *Psalm 90*—"Teach us to number our days."

8.

Recordings and Arrangements

A FEW WEEKS AFTER returning from the final Robert Shaw Chorale tour, Shaw conducted his last recording for RCA Victor. As with most of the steps in his career, he had been virtually thrust into the role of a Red Seal artist.

Among the many visitors to the early Collegiate Chorale rehearsals were some RCA Victor executives who recognized the group's potential commercial appeal. In the fall of 1944, twenty singers from the "small choir" prepared an audition recording of Shaw's own exciting arrangement of "Set down, servant," which had become a kind of theme song of the Chorale and a trademark of Shaw's style. Early in 1945 the contract was signed.

During the next few years one of his major responsibilities was to prepare choruses for other conductors who were recording complete major works such as *Boris Godunov* and *Carmen* (the third and fourth issues in Victor's series of monumental and elaborately packaged "Recordramas"), Bernstein's *On the Town*, Blitzstein's *Airborne Symphony*, and the ten recorded performances with Toscanini. Shaw's reputation benefited from all these associations, and especially from Toscanini's commercial popularity—nearly 150,000 copies of the Ninth were sold within two years of its release in 1952 —but he was also doing significant things on his own.

In quick succession came a series of premiere recordings, starting modestly with the *Six Chansons* of Hindemith in the spring of 1945 and continuing with Bach's *Magnificat, Jesu, Meine Freude,* several cantatas, the *St. John Passion*, and Poulenc's *Petites Voix* and Mass in G. Two of the most important and long-awaited firsts, however, were Bach's B Minor Mass and Brahms's *German Requiem*, both recorded in 1947.

To the detriment of the inherent buoyancy and transparency of the intricate score, the Mass had long been a vehicle for large amateur choruses. Nearly twenty years earlier it had even been recorded by the huge Royal Choral Society and the London Symphony Orchestra under Albert Coates. (Only one excerpt had been recorded in the United States—the *Laudamus te*, sung by Dorothy Maynor and conducted by Sylvan Levin.)

Shaw, however, prompted by Julius Herford, and in the interest of historical verity, chose to employ a relatively small ensemble of professionals—sixty singers and thirty-five players, the same ones he had used for the performances at Hunter College on January 28 and 29, 1947. It was a prodigious undertaking. The best available recording site with a pipe organ was Town Hall, but the audibility of street noises made it unsuitable during the daytime, so the job had to be done between midnight and four in the morning. It took a total of five nights' work.

The two-volume album of seventeen twelve-inch, 78 rpm records attracted considerable attention. Many reviewers deemed it a technical and an artistic triumph, but there were divergences of opinion, which might have been traceable to variances in the pre–high fidelity quality of their playback equipment. *The Nation* complained that the recording was "mostly on one high level of volume," while Harold Schonberg, writing in the *Musical Digest*, found it "prevailingly quiet and lyric." In any case, it immediately won a citation from the *Review of Recorded Music*, "In Recognition of Recorded Music as a Cultural Influence."

The Requiem of Brahms, also traditionally a *tour de force* for choruses of festival dimensions, had not yet been recorded in its entirety. Again following Herford's advice, Shaw selected forty-one singers and fifty-eight players for his recording (December 3–6, 1947), this time to achieve contrapuntal clarity and precision. Royalties from the album's sales were signed over to the Collegiate Chorale, with which he had first performed the work.

The album's release in the summer of 1948 coincided with the appearance of another complete recording by the Vienna Philharmonic and the Gesellschaft der Musikfreunde under Herbert von Karajan. Irving Kolodin, in his *New Guide to Recorded Music,* favored the European recording because of the "richness of texture lacking in the cleaner, drier sound" of Shaw's version. He opined that

> Shaw, the musical man of tomorrow, hasn't the culture—perhaps the desired word is merely "experience"—to match what today's Karajan produces in sorrowing compassion, resurgent faith, and human wisdom from this wonderful work of Brahms. . . . One may note the difference of treatment visually, for the more measured pace preferred by Karajan in the opening and closing sections requires three sides for each, against two for Shaw. . . . From Shaw we have an accomplishment that adds considerably to his stature; from Karajan, the performance of Brahms's *Requiem* for which we have been waiting.

Similar coincidences were to occur later on. His second recording of the B Minor Mass, issued in 1961, was met by Deutsche Grammophon's release of Karl Richter's version with the Munich Bach Choir and Orchestra. His 1966 recording of Handel's *Messiah* joined two other releases the same year. Both of his recordings won Grammy awards from the National Academy of Recording Arts and Sciences.

Shaw's twenty-two years with RCA encompassed an era of sweeping changes in recording technology and marketing. Until the advent of magnetic tape early in 1949, the recording process was a tense, uncertain, start-and-stop affair. A "master" had to be cut directly on a wax or acetate disc in segments of no more than four minutes' duration, corresponding to the capacity of one side of a 78 rpm record. Since the master could not be played back without risking damage to its delicate surface, a performer's selection of the "take" for reproduction had to be based solely on what he heard in the studio, rather than over a loudspeaker as the record listener would hear it. By recording on tape, however, thirty or more minutes of music could be performed without interruption, and the tape could be played back immediately for evaluation. A taped performance could also be artificially enhanced with reverberation to present the illusion of concert-hall resonance and

Recording session, 1948

spaciousness. Moreover, errors could easily be edited out of one take and replaced with corrections from another.

All this definitely relieved some of the tension of the recording process, but it also meant that more than ever the recording engineer was the performer's partner in establishing the artistic quality of a recording. In August of 1964 Shaw recorded Stravinsky's *Symphony of Psalms* and Poulenc's *Gloria*. Finding a slight flaw near the beginning of the best overall take of the *Psalms*, Shaw instructed the recording engineer to replace measures two, three, and four with the same measures from a different take. The engineer accidentally dubbed in measures five through eight, which resemble the other three. Shaw hastily approved the master tape, overlooking the mistake, and the album was issued with what to a knowledgeable listener is an obvious fault. The more astute critics considerately ignored the blunder; a less attentive one merely heard "too much bass!" Nevertheless, RCA Victor's LM/LSC 2822, reissued in a corrected version, won a Grammy in 1965, partly because of the *Gloria* which was a premiere recording.

In June of 1948 Columbia fired the first salvo in the industry's "battle of the speeds" by unveiling its 33⅓ rpm Long Playing microgroove record. Columbia magnanimously offered to share rights to the process with all other companies, but the following February RCA returned fire: the seven-inch, 45 rpm Extended Play microgroove record, with many previous releases—including some of Shaw's—reprocessed into the new format. Unfortunately, the EP, though it had some compensating attributes, was grossly misnamed; it could hold no more music than a 78 rpm record. In contrast, the LP offered up to twenty-six uninterrupted minutes of listening per side.

Record buyers' reactions to the LP were immediately favorable, and within ten months all the other major American recording companies had fallen into line behind Columbia. Finally, in January of 1950, while insisting that the EP was still the best for popular music, RCA bowed to necessity and solemnly announced that it would make available its "great artists and unsurpassed classical library" on LP records, and belatedly began again to reprocess many of its old releases.

Almost instantly the entire economic structure of the industry was changed. First, the market expanded explosively. The retail purchaser paid about a third less for one twelve-inch LP containing the same amount of music as a five-record 78 rpm album. Furthermore, the tape recorder had already freed artists and engineers from the confines of the studio with its cumbersome, expensive, precision equipment, and the pressing of LP discs in vinyl plastic had proven to be much simpler and cheaper than in wax or shellac. Anyone with enough ambition and a few thousand dollars of capital could get into the business. By early 1952, LPs were being produced under 120 different labels. Nearly 70 of these were devoted partly or wholly to classical music, and their combined output in just forty-five months was more than double the entire repertoire produced on 78s throughout the preceding fifty years. Small retailers, who could not afford to keep up with the growth of the LP catalog, gave way to cut-rate dealers with huge inventories and to record clubs offering irresistible discounts. To encourage their own regional distributors and independent dealers, RCA initiated a price war in 1955, reducing the cost of Red Seal records by two dollars and of popular records by one. Other measures to meet the competition followed in due course. RCA started its own record club, and also began marketing budget-priced records on its new Camden label.

Meanwhile, for at least a few years, RCA's original stand on the EP record had been vindicated. Through its intensive promotional campaign, RCA had convinced buyers of nonclassical records of the convenience and economy of the smaller record, and soon all the other companies, Columbia included, were compelled to put most of their popular titles, and a few classical ones as well, on 45s.

The flexibility and wide frequency range of magnetic tape, combined with continuous improvements in LP manufacture and audio technology in general, created two more shock-waves in the industry during the fifties—a fanatic pursuit of "high fidelity" and a fascination with stereophonic recording.

The concept of binaural, or stereophonic, recording had been germinating since the early thirties, and in 1954 RCA had begun taping many sessions with the probability of its eventual perfection in view. Masters were recorded on three-track tape containing mikings of the right, left, and middle dimensions of the acoustic perspective, and the three tracks could then be combined into either a single track for monophonic discs or a dual track for stereo tapes.

RCA released a short list of orchestral titles on stereo tape in 1956. The tapes, like the equipment to play them on, were inordinately expensive, and the market was slow. But by the time the stereo disc and playback cartridge were perfected in 1958, the company had a sizeable backlog of stereo master tapes to meet initial demands.

Shaw's first stereo disc, *Deep River and Other Spirituals*, was released in October of 1958; the first half of it had been taped in June of 1956. In it, the intermingling of choral parts was even more evident than it had been on monophonic discs. The integrated texture was simply spread out farther from left to right and at some distance, in a kind of wrap-around effect, while soloists always emerged front and center. The same characteristics could be heard in the album of *Stephen Foster Favorites* recorded in May of 1958. With *A Chorus of Love*, recorded in August of 1959, the voices were arranged more conventionally, in deference to the new medium, producing a distinct separation between high voices on one side and low voices on the other.

When he signed his first contract with RCA Victor, Shaw looked forward to recording the works of Bach, Beethoven, Brahms, and the like, but the agreement was that he would also do two or three albums a year containing music with a broader appeal. RCA's first suggestion was an album of Christmas carols, a genre for which Shaw has had a lifelong affection.

> To "go caroling" in my youth meant a Christmas Eve caravan to the cottages of the elderly or ill—obviously those, it occurs to me now, who would benefit more from rest than a shivaree. We would stand outside the bedroom window, on what was usually a clear Southern California night, harmonize tentatively two or three of the familiar Christmas hymns, shout a loud "Merry Christmas," and noisily push off to the next unsuspecting shut-in. We never did accept what they might have wanted to tender, which Mr. Scholes [Percy Scholes, in the *Oxford Companion to Music*] so nicely designated as "hush money."

In the early forties he had in turn earned the affection of millions of radio listeners for his coast-to-coast Christmas eve radio broadcasts. A group of "semipros" from the Collegiate Chorale would "herald the angels with an hour's uninterrupted montage-medley of familiar and unfamiliar appropriate and festive fragments—a sort of musical opening of presents." Shaw himself would read verses from the Scriptures, and the music would be programmed so as to emphasize the story or the spirit of each passage.

The two volumes of *Christmas Hymns and Carols* made Shaw's name a household word throughout America, and the income from their sales provided Shaw with the means to underwrite some of his other enterprises. The first volume of familiar carols, sung directly from the *Oxford Book of Carols*, was released on 78s in December of 1946 (in both manual and automatic sequence, the automatic record changer having been introduced that year), and was

reissued on LP in December of 1950. In 1952, Volume II was recorded and immediately issued, introducing twenty-six additional
hymns and carols in arrangements by Shaw and Alice Parker. Portions of Volume I were issued on 45s in 1953, and reprocessed
with "enhanced sound" in the same format in 1954; parts of Volume II also appeared on 45s in 1954. In 1957 Volume I was rerecorded with new Shaw-Parker arrangements and issued on monophonic LP; the following year it appeared on stereo LP, and subsequently on 45s, stereo tape, and four-track cartridge. In 1964, Volume I of *Christmas Hymns and Carols* achieved the distinction of
becoming Victor's first Red Seal Gold Record, with total sales in
excess of one million dollars.

On the assumption that the larger public tended to associate
choral singing with religious music, RCA persuaded Shaw to record
Malotte's "The Lord's Prayer" in 1945. ("The Bells of St. Mary's"
was on the other side of the single-disc 78 rpm release.) He did it
under protest, however, for he had already made up his mind to
uphold more dignified standards in church music. For the next
two years he concentrated on recording the music of Bach and
Brahms. When the 1948 moratorium on recording was lifted, he
was ready with a compromise, and in March of 1949 taped *Onward,
Christian Soldiers*, his first album of classic Protestant hymns.

Only since arriving in New York had he become acquainted with
hymns like "O God, our help in ages past" and "All creatures of
our God and King." He performed some of them with Waring's
Glee Club, and learned others through his associations with various church musicians. He developed a profound respect for their
musical and poetic qualities, because, in contrast to the hymns he
had grown up with, they satisfied his desire for a less sentimental
mode of religious expression.

For purposes of recording, Waring's versions were too glittery
and overblown for Shaw's taste, while the strict strophic settings
were not performable except in the context of a religious ritual. So
he arranged them himself in a simple, expressive manner in keeping with the philosophy of congregational music he had expressed
in a sermon delivered at All Angels' Episcopal Church back in
1942. "The moods of the verses of our hymns are not the same—
and they ought to be sung as though they made sense—not as exer-

cises. I believe that joy should sound like JOY and pain should sound like PAIN. I don't want to hear voices—I want to hear souls."

Although he later consented to record "The Rosary" and Schubert's *Ave Maria* with Perry Como, he always preferred the more conservative and durable style of Christian song. In 1950 he arranged and recorded eight hymns and a spiritual for *Hymns of Thanksgiving*, and seven years afterward catalogued sixteen of his favorite hymns in *A Mighty Fortress*. To further satisfy the terms of his contract, he presented a collection of familiar oratorio excerpts in *Great Sacred Choruses* (1950).

Shaw was never at a loss for things *he* wanted to record— Haydn's *Creation*, or shorter works by Palestrina, Purcell, Carissimi, Mozart, Delius, Hindemith, and Ives—but increasing competition and rising production costs throughout the fifties and into the sixties made RCA officials hesitant to spend money on anything they didn't feel would make a sizeable splash in the marketplace. The *Creation*, for instance, would have required twelve recording sessions at a minimum cost of $30,000, and would have been much riskier than a *Messiah*, a B Minor Mass, or a *Symphony of Psalms*. At the same time, RCA kept enlarging their list of albums they thought would successfully compete with those of Columbia's choral star, Roger Wagner. Shaw was open to suggestion, but by no means uncritical. He tactfully postponed a proposed recording of Stainer's *Crucifixion*, and on occasion was bluntly outspoken about the company's suggestions. Richard Mohr, Recording Director for RCA, came up with an idea for an album of Civil War songs in commemoration of the attack on Fort Sumter in 1861. Shaw replied with exceptional haste:

October 3, 1958

Dear Richard:

Your projected album "The War Between the States" must be equally as couth as a belch during communion. I understand the necessity of keeping up with Columbia, and I have nothing against the repertoire, but there certainly must be a less grotesque way to market such a commodity. One might, for instance, call it "Our Own 100 Years War."

All good wishes,

Robert Shaw

P.S. Other titles which suggest themselves are "Prelude to an Aftermath," or "Quemoy or Bust."

Most of the repertoire Mohr had in mind appeared in *This is My Country* (1962; reissued two years later under the title *America the Beautiful*), one of seven collaborations between Shaw and Robert Russell Bennett. Bennett liked to think of himself primarily as a composer of serious music. Born in 1894 in Kansas City, Missouri, he studied with Nadia Boulanger in Paris, held two consecutive Guggenheim Fellowships, and composed operas, symphonies, concertos, and chamber music. It was in more popular idioms, however, that he won his place in American history as a peerless musical craftsman. He wrote numerous film scores, such as Universal Pictures' *Show Boat* (1936), and composed thirteen hours' worth of music for the classic television documentary series "Victory at Sea" (1952–53). Starting at the age of sixteen, he arranged and orchestrated the music for some 250 productions in the popular musical theater, including *Carmen Jones*—for which Shaw had prepared the chorus back in 1943. Together they recorded four albums of operetta and musical comedy tunes and one each of patriotic, religious, and Christmas music. Thanks to Bennett's great dignity, charm, and taste, Shaw recalls, those recording sessions were "very warm and happy" times.

The first album, *On Stage with Robert Shaw*, contained four numbers with band: "Buckle Down, Winsocki," "Wunderbar," "Oklahoma," and "Wintergreen for President"; four with large orchestra: "Gone, Gone, Gone," from *Porgy and Bess*, "Dancing in the Dark," "Romany Life," and "Hallelujah"; and four ("the cream") with strings and a few solo woodwinds: "All the Things You Are," "September Song," "Yesterdays," and "Through the Years." This was the album that elicited Shaw's all-time favorite fan letter:

Dear Mr. Shaw,

My husband and I are great admirers of your choral music and have many sacred recordings which bring us inspiration such as no others can.

Yesterday I purchased your "On Stage" record for a Valentine present for my husband. Because he has a heavy schedule of singing and directing this weekend and next week, I gave him the gift last evening.

I was very anxious to please him with it and hoped it would be something we could enjoy in romantic moods. It was the most *disillusioning* choice I could have made.

The numbers were well done and the selections were good but why did you have to arrange them in such a helter-skelter order. Just about the time a fairly romantic mood can be achieved, the chorus breaks into some rouser like "Wintergreen for President."

And the "piece de resistance" is your following the beautiful "Through the Years" (which my husband sang most beautifully at our marriage ceremony thirteen years ago) with a football song, "Buckle Down, Winsocki." We have to jump up and turn it off before the last number.

PLEASE see if a recording can be made from this one with one side romantic and the other varied in content.

Sharing the above with the Cleveland Orchestra Chorus in one of his periodic communications, he remarked: "—Now, what could ever destroy a marriage like that? I suppose I've read the letter twenty-five times—and it gets sweeter and funnier every time. By now I even laugh at the date!"

A number of other persons have collaborated with Shaw at one time or another, but the longest and most productive association has been with Alice Parker—Mrs. Thomas Pyle—a composer, arranger, conductor, and teacher who has assisted him in the preparation of eighteen recordings, and whose name has appeared along with his on 216 choral arrangements, most of them originally published by Lawson-Gould Music Publishers, Inc., and G. Schirmer, Inc.

Alice Parker first met Shaw in 1947 at Tanglewood, where she spent the summer following her graduation from Smith College. That fall she was admitted to Juilliard for further study in composition and conducting. She also auditioned for the Collegiate Chorale, but although her sight-reading was faultless, her voice didn't quite measure up to the auditioning committee's standards. At her plea, Shaw consented to listen to her himself.

"He sat there with his head down," she recalls, "almost between his knees—trying to keep from laughing, I guess—and when I was through he said quietly, 'If you want to be a choral conductor you've got to learn to sing better than that.' He let me in anyway, on the condition I always sit in the back row and never let him hear me."

She was a hard-working student, observing every rehearsal of the Collegiate Chorale, the "small choir," and the Juilliard Chorus, and taking meticulous notes of everything that went on, right down to the number of minutes Shaw devoted to each step in a rehearsal.

Shaw was impressed by her musicality and industry and one day asked her to try writing an arrangement for him. He was urgently in need of materials for broadcasts and recordings. As she remembers it, she "brought him what must have been the world's worst arrangement. In one place there was a very florid sixteenth-note contrapuntal line with no words to it. He said, 'What do they sing there?' I replied, 'Oh, you put that in later.' And he said, 'Oh no you don't!' I was thoroughly insulted, but it didn't take me long to catch on that you've got to begin with words."

She goes on to explain how the two of them worked together from then on:

> Usually the beginning thing was RCA saying, "we need an album of Christmas carols," or "we need an album of love songs." I would go to the public library with a stack of five-by-eight cards with staves printed on one side, and they'd bring me a whole trolley full of books of folk songs, or carols, or whatever. I'd go through them page by page and copy down the tunes and the words to maybe three hundred of the ones that seemed like they might work for us.
>
> Then Bob and I would go through them together and form three piles—one tiny little one of "this has to be in," a medium-sized one of "no use," and a great big one of "maybes." He would judge way too quickly, I thought, and then realized one of his big concerns was the first verse of the text. If there was anything in it that caught his ear as unsatisfactory, no matter how good the tune was, he wouldn't use it. Because if it itched you a little bit at first it would itch you just terribly the longer you stayed with it. You had to have an affection for the tune *and* the words. If you didn't, that would be the first thing that would come out in the arrangement.
>
> And then I would take the whole stack of necessaries and maybes and I would just flip through those and live with them for a few months, while he was on tour or something, and then we would have a couple of weeks to work strenuously together—frequently here at Singing Brook Farm. At that time I would have arrangements of twenty-five or thirty of these, not because I had chosen them, but because they were the ones that haunted me, that I couldn't get out of my head.
>
> He'd have me sit at the piano and play my arrangements for him—maybe twelve hours at a time, till the pads of my fingers hurt when I touched the keys. The first thing he would want to hear

was the shape of the whole thing. I'd have to play it through without stopping, and he'd stand beside me, and every time he heard something he didn't like his arm would come over my shoulder with a pencil and there'd be a little "x" on the music. At first I'd want to stop and explain why I did that, but he wouldn't let me. So after enough years of doing it I could feel the pencil approaching and I'd look and say, "how on earth could I have done that!" Sometimes I'd play one all the way through and he'd point to the little tag line underneath the final phrase and say, "That's the first idea you've had."

He has an enormous love for and respect for and instinct about anything that works vocally. His own voice is true and clear, and he's incapable of singing something unmusical—uninflected. He simply would never accept anything that wasn't conceived as a vocal sound, or a line which was not complete in itself. When he was working with his glee club back at Pomona and was doing arrangements for them, he was doing it not a bit from theory, but from sound. He was always acutely aware of the sound. Of sound in any form, for that matter. A marvelous ear for pitch, and a sense of rhythm, and tuning, and balance. And I'm sure that when he picked up somebody else's arrangement of a college song and tried to teach it, that ear would tell him right away, "There's something wrong with that phrase, because I can't get them to sing it right." And then, by just endless hard work, he could turn out a new arrangement.

He can recognize a great song in seconds. It has exactly the same quality as any music that survives, which is that there's a right relationship between the tune and the text, and there's a satisfactory relationship—a balancing of parts in the melody itself—that makes it feel alive. There's not a note too many or one too few. And all of those great old songs have either a humor, or a kind of a bounce which is built in, or a soaring kind of melody that is very. . . .

It's just—listen to that sound, and listen to the sound of your own voice singing it when you sing it just as well as you can, which has nothing to do with vocal quality in terms of professional singing, but has everything to do with inflection, the way you breathe, how you accentuate the words, how the text and the tune fit together—so that you're really getting down to the most elementary musical materials. It's very aural, and what you begin to do with it is very improvisational.

Whenever I had trouble with an arrangement he could immediately spot the problem and know what to do. Sometimes he would simply take over and do it pretty much himself. He'd chip it out as if it were solid granite. He'd sit at the piano and play one little phrase over and over until I'd be ready to run screaming out of the room. But in the end it was exactly right. Sometimes what he did, as in the Spanish Christmas carols, was just to change the way one or two syllables fell rhythmically in a line, lending the piece incomparably more richness or finesse—an awful lot of little things all the way through that made the difference between a perfectly good basic idea and a beautiful thing to listen to and sing.

That Negro spiritual "Calvary"—a gorgeous, rangy, modal tune. I tried to do a four-part setting of it, but that kind of tune just does not four-part-set. There's no way you can do a chorale-type harmonization of a melody that moves like that. He saw that I was absolutely stymied by it, so he took it off to the back porch, and sat there for about eight hours working on that one tune. Instead of any attempt to harmonize at all, he started with the text, and came up with that marvelously simple, rhythmic-harmonic bass chant—"Think *about* it, . . . think *about* it. . . ." And this whole arrangement—that's exactly what it means. It's that one idea—the spirit of the tune *and* the text.

And the *sounds* of words. The rhythms and the sounds of the words that make up the accompaniment for "I got shoes" almost make you laugh for sheer joy! And in "Sometimes I feel" the pedal point on the gentle rhythm and sound of "moanin' dove" and the plaintive imitations are the most poignant. . . .

The Stephen Foster album was the hardest one we ever did. The melodic material is so trivial, and all the harmonic schemes are practically the same. About all you can do with "Swanee River" is harmonize it and let it go at that. But the rhythmic ones. . . . One that I've always enjoyed was "Ring, ring the banjo." I remember working out with him that little ostinato figure—"O *rinngg*, O ring-O-*rinngg*-O. . . ." And I remember coming into the next session that we had and saying, "I've just looked at what we wrote, and do you realize that we could use that with *nine* of the sixteen songs in this album?" And "Thou art the queen of my song" *should* be an absolutely beautiful melody, but there's one really wrong note in it that cheapens the whole thing and doesn't allow it to soar.

Generally, the kinds of things we did were different from what he'd conducted for Waring. Waring's arrangers started with the idea of a four-part harmonized setting in the first verse, so the only way to go was up. Open out to eight parts, and if it's a really big piece, open out to twelve. Add a solo, add instruments, and just keep adding. Bob would start with the unison melody, so that it was, what is the simplest way to start this piece, and how long can it be sustained, and where must something else come in? So that you end up with the four-part harmonized setting for your *last* verse. And the texture suggests itself. "Ride on, King Jesus" starts in that powerful unison, and the climaxes are built up with simple canonic imitations of the melody itself. "If I got my ticket" goes the same way. He arranged that one for the radio show in the summer of '48.

He has an incredible sensitivity to the way the people have come to know a tune, too. He'd never let me change a harmonization of a familiar tune. Used to drive me nuts. He'd say, "No, that's what people hear, and that's what's right for it."

Well, then I'd have to prepare the copy that would go to Arnold Arnstein to be copied again and then duplicated for the recording session. After the recording was over I would go through everybody's copy of each arrangement, collating markings—breathing places or places where the singers had had difficulty. But there were very, very few changes made in the recording sessions from what we had outlined, precisely because Bob heard so clearly what he wanted beforehand.

Then I would have to write out the "fair copy" for publication, and read proof, and agonize over the mistakes that inevitably crept in.

In 1953 Shaw and Walter Gould founded the Lawson-Gould Publishing Company, a subsidiary of G. Schirmer, Inc., as an outlet for the Shaw-Parker arrangements and others by Leonard de Paur and Roger Wagner. They also intended to publish new editions of choral masterworks and to encourage young composers. Gould was to be business manager and his partner was to be editor, but Shaw's interests lay more in the area of performance, so aside from the arrangements his principal contribution has been his middle name.

> Eventually he got awfully tired of arranging and recording all those things. The first album we did together—that was *A Treasury of Easter Songs*—was, I would say, ninety-eight percent Shaw and two percent Parker. In the last two albums—the second set of early American hymns and the Irish songs—he didn't change a note of mine. I did everything—the selection of the pieces, the arrangements themselves, the putting of them in order for the recordings. In the years between it averaged out to about fifty-fifty, I suppose.

Alice Parker even conducted part of the very last album recorded by the Robert Shaw Chorale. Halfway through the session Shaw abruptly left the studio, went straight to the airport, and boarded a plane bound for Chicago. "It wasn't that he didn't like the music itself. It was just that he had other things he wanted to do by then. When we recorded the Irish album in August of '67 he had nothing on his mind but the new job in Atlanta."

For Shaw, explained a one-time RSC member, the two decades since the first tour had been white-hot years. "They were white-hot in the way he functioned as an individual, as a conductor, and as a person; white-hot in terms of the musicians he had available to him; and white-hot in the results that accrued."

Shaw reserved a special fondness for spirituals and early American hymns, and he once delivered a sermon about his feelings toward them from Robert Killam's pulpit in the First Unitarian Church of Cleveland. He had intended, he said,

> to present for your entertainment and contemplation an hour of Christian evangelical folk-music—of which we have had some rather sophisticated examples today—whose musical expression was of such purity that it seemed to me to point "Ecce homo"— "behold the Man"—essentially if not finally. I had hoped to have with us at least two and possibly three singers: Clayton Krehbiel, a University of Kansas director of choral music, thoroughbred by Mennonite Stock out of Kansas Wheatfield, whose singing of "Amazing Grace" would convict Santa Claus of sin; Florence Kopleff, who sings from an accountable Semitic Fatherhood of God and an unaccountable motherhood of Man; and a certain Thomas Pyle, bred and born in our fragmented South, the color of whose skin, by freak of percentage white, has never washed the color of his singing.
>
> What wondrous love is this?
> O My Soul
> O My Soul
>
> Amazing Grace
> How sweet the Sound
> That sav'd a wretch like me.
>
> Sometimes I feel like a Motherless child
> A long way from home.

These words are magic to me, and their melodies, shaped and worn by Niagaras and years of tears, are as perfect as anything I know in music.

This is not simple nostalgia; such saintliness is the acquaintance of my latter days. In my youth I was used to thinner, rancid fare: to—

Softly and tenderly Jesus is calling

O there's power—power—
Wondrous working power
In the blood
(In the blood)
Of the Lamb
(Of the Lamb!)

On a hill far away stands an old
rugged cross
The emblem of suffering and shame

I was sinking deep in sin
Far from the peaceful shore
Very deeply stained within
Sinking to rise no more.

Just as I am without one plea
Leaning on the everlasting arms
Lord Jesus Christ—I come, I come.

Strangely even these (as I recount them), can they be viewed
from an historical distance of two or three generations, rather
than through today's TV screening of an evangelistic circus at
Madison Square Garden; Easter Sunrise in the Hollywood-Rose-
Sugar-Cotton Bowl; Forest Lawn Cemetery—Memorial Coliseum;
or the Southern Baptist Longhorn Band blowing a rodeo of Salva-
tion through Buddha-Shinto-stricken Japan—even these songs my
mother taught me—from a distance, stand a strong first in poetic
plausibility to Edgar (Second) Guest.
  —But in the *great* folk-hymns and spirituals—black and white—
of the late eighteenth and early nineteenth century of our country
there is a directness and dignity, and a fervor of utterance which
seems to me to call to and qualify our humanity.

Deep river, my home is over Jordan

Swing low, sweet chariot

His voice, as the sound of the dulcimer sweet
is heard through the shadow of death.

O tell me where the dove has flown,
and where he builds his nest . . .
In sweet religion's humble cote
the pensive dove is found.

Every time I feel the spirit movin'
in my heart I will pray

There is a balm in Gilead to
make the wounded whole

Let heaven and earth and seas and skies
in one melodious concert rise.

I think it is true that these songs and these words call to me in spite of their theology and Christology—not because of it. I recall a line from Lin Yutang in *My Country and My People*:

"Christian optimism kills all poetry. A pagan, who has not these ready-made answers to his problems and whose sense of mystery is forever unquenched and whose craving for security is forever unanswered and unanswerable, is driven inevitably to a kind of pantheistic poetry."

But these songs, I think, contradict for a moment his point of view. There *is* a poetry here—and a humanity. If there is a literature of philosophy and drama—a point of view known as *Existentialism*, it seems to me that this musical literature also proposes and qualifies what man is, an *isness* of the man-kind. And all of us would agree, I think, that this *isness* almost certainly lies in the field of man's feelings, aspirations and intentions, the subjectivity which we call—(however unscientifically) —"emotional."

Robert Killam, minister of the First Unitarian (Universalist-Unitarian) Church of Cleveland for nearly twenty years, viewed his parish as a rallying place for "the man who is discontented and dissatisfied with himself, his community, his world, and religion as he has known it." In one of his sermons, "The Mission of the Liberal Church," he asserted that "there is no distinction or difference between reason and revelation, but . . . they are one and the same." He warned that one who is casting off from old religious moorings must possess "certain tough qualities . . . that are not encouraged by entrenched power and authority: *doubt* and *skepticism* for theologies, *distrust* for external authority and respect for his own reason and conscience, *hatred* for every form of injustice and oppression, *scorn* for falsehood, wherever he finds it, and a passionate and indomitable *love for truth*." Killam also preached of his belief in the essential goodness of man: "His weaknesses and failings are over-matched by his noble qualities if they are given a fair chance. His greatness is to be seen in so many ways .

—in his finer arts, in his thoughts of things invisible, in his work with a world far subtler than the world of science, in his achievements of imagination by which he creates worlds of his own."

In Robert Killam, Robert Shaw found a kindred spirit, and in Robert Killam's church, a spiritual home. Here at last was the place to implement a reconciliation of art and religion, which had become separated, Shaw once said, "at the moment when religion and the church were no longer large enough to contain man's spirit." Here was the laboratory suited to the exploration of the same principles he had outlined to the people of All Angels' Church nearly twenty years before—that a service of worship should be an integrated entity with all its elements revolving around a central mood or idea, and in which the music would become "terribly alive because it was terribly pertinent."

To the appropriate church committees he proposed that he and Killam create just such a service—"a wholeness of Beauty and Truth, an integrity of sound and sight and reason; a religious accreditation of intelligence, taste, and senses."

With unanimous approval, and on the premise that "nothing but the best is good enough," they proceeded to assemble their musical forces. Aided by a $30,000 donation from Thomas F. Peterson, a Cleveland manufacturer, they purchased the requisite instruments: a "hand-shaped, heart-voiced" pipe organ built by Walter Holtkamp, a harpsichord crafted by William Dowd, and a nine-foot Steinway concert grand piano. They hired a string quartet of players from the Cleveland Orchestra and a quartet of professional vocalists. Shaw auditioned singers, mostly members of the parish, for a thirty-five-voice volunteer choir. Grigg Fountain was engaged as organist and associate director of the choir. In September of 1960 Shaw was officially installed as Minister of Music—at no salary.

His inaugural sermon, "Music and Worship in the Liberal Church," occupied him intermittently for nearly nine months, yet it showed the same spontaneity as his letters to his choruses, alternating humor—

> It has been somewhat more than twenty-cne years since last I donned this sort of vesture in this sort of situation, and I was then but somewhat more than twenty-one years of age. By theory and arithmetic this moment should amount to a sort of double major-

ity—or a three-and-one-half bar mitzvah with a full twist. But I more than a little fear that two times some things may be too many and too late, that with the fruits of the mind, maturity is but momentary, ripeness but a day and softness a long, long time. And it might have been better had I been plucked and frozen at the fleeting moment of flavor. . . .

—with his penchant for "thinking with words"—

Etymology has some of the delights and intuitions of great poetry: the wisdom of origins, the association of words not in terms of their local and daily commerce but in terms of ancient and inherent vitalities—which spark them across space, arc time to their axis, and multiply sense by sound. . . .

—leading not so much to definitions as to revelations—

Liberalism is that set of attitudes and conditions which allows and encourages a *free people to grow up.* The liberal church is that institution whose instruction and ceremony encourages a free people to grow up, as Luke writes of Jesus, "in wisdom and in stature and in favor with God and man."

There were seminal insights—

Now, each of us owns to himself moments of reverence, intimations of worth, intuitions of value, instants of worship wherein no other human being walked, nor could have entered.

—persuasion—

Assume with me two things: first that form in art is also a factor of value and meaning. That is to say: if one has exactly so much Space to shape—as in painting or sculpture, or if he has so much Time to inform—as with poetry or music, the achieved proportions of that Space and Time, the relations of line, color and texture, of rhythm, tonality and tempo, of expectation, continuation, recurrence and closure, the matters of proportion are not the eboned and polished hall-tree, hollow-capped and slack-coated, dunced in its corner while love is made in the parlor—but they are root, trunk, branch and leaf, seed, sap and substance of meaning.

Assume with me also that worship is an art, or a confluence of the arts, or at least similar to the arts in that it has a certain amount of corporate time in which to consider matters of worth, in which to propose and to proportion Beauty and Truth.

—and poetry—

>
> Music is Order.
>   Out of the void
>   Out of chaos
>   the creative spirit
>   moving over the face
>   of the waters.
> Out of the random a rule
> Out of darkness a light
> Out of multitude and muchness
>   integrity, the one entire whole and holy.

"Music and Worship in the Liberal Church" was widely quoted in both the general and the musical press, and was reprinted in full in several newspapers and magazines. Portions of it were also used by Shaw in the scripts for an NBC series of four radio programs on "New Directions in Music for Worship," which he narrated in 1962.

"It was our idea," he explained some years later,

> that nothing which man had created that was of quality should be foreign to a service of worship. So we would do Hindu chants, Buddhist or Jewish religious music. We went through the complete Bach Resurrection cantatas in a mental ambience of a congregation that didn't believe the Resurrection story at all. Nobody in the congregation believed in the physical resurrection, or the Immaculate Conception, or the Virgin Birth, but it was possible to do these cantatas because Bach believed them. It was an expression of the nobility of man in his religious convictions. And we'd have Beethoven string quartets as part of the service.
>
> So this was for five years a very warming experience to me. And the minister, a fabulous, wonderful man, would give a series of sermons on the ethical and moral situation in Shakespearean drama, or a series on great American poets. I used to preach there occasionally too. I did a couple in that series on Emily Dickinson and Robinson Jeffers.

He also renewed his acquaintance with other authors whose works he had studied in college—Hartley Burr Alexander and Lin Yutang, Carl Sandburg, Edgar Lee Masters, Robert Bridges. He expanded his theological and philosophical horizons, digesting Martin Buber's *I and Thou* and *Between Man and Man* and Rollo May's *Love and Will*.

Sometimes he drew upon his "only speech," which he had been rewriting and redelivering for some years, called "The Conservative Arts": "What of course I meant by it was the liberal arts, because they are the things that really 'conserve' man."

III.

Phoenix in Atlanta

9.

Atlanta and the Cultural Explosion

IN JUNE OF 1864, Robert Lawson Shaw's great-grandfather, George C. Lawson, an immigrant bricklayer from Yorkshire and still a British subject, enlisted in the Union Army. With the 45th Illinois Volunteers he steamed down the Mississippi, up the Ohio and Tennessee rivers to the vicinity of Shiloh, then travelled overland toward Georgia with General McPherson's Army of the Tennessee to join in Sherman's siege of Atlanta, the principal supply depot for the Confederate Army.

The campaign began on May 7. Throughout the spring and summer the battle raged back and forth among the foothills of the Blue Ridge Mountains, from Allatoona and Acworth to Marietta and Kennesaw Mountain and into Atlanta, until, on September 1, General Hood and his Confederate forces fled from the city. Five days later Lawson wrote to his wife and children: "I saw the cannon belch forth at Allatoona. I saw the whole line of the Rebs and the three long lines of our army, . . . the two armies and thousands of army wagons, with their white covers, stretching away for miles; also hundreds of cannon and over 100,000 men on the move. And it could all be seen with the human eye from the top of Kennesaw."

Lawson's eloquent letters and detailed daily journal show him to have been a practical, industrious, and resourceful man. At every pause en route he foraged for blackberries or apples, bought flour and shortening from the sutlers, and baked pies to sell to his compatriots, sending his earnings home to his family in Galena, Illinois. His stamina was legendary among his comrades: "Hundreds of men fell out and went to the rear or had to be taken in ambulances. . . . I travelled like a brick."

Lawson bore hardships with indomitable humor: "We have nothing to cheer us but the sweet songs of the mosquitos and frogs, and the pleasant sensations caused by scratching those places where the snipe-like insect has inserted its poisonous dart. It may be said of them 'Ten thousand thousands are their songs, but all their joys are one.'" In the face of danger he was stalwartly fatalistic: "The bullets of the sharpshooters whistled all around us and one brushed my hair. It might as well have been a mile away."

His belief in the Union's cause was unswerving, but he felt profound compassion for the victims of war: "It is not possible to tell one half of the destruction wrought in this beautiful city. . . . Sherman has ordered [its 15,000 inhabitants] to leave . . . and go either North or South. . . . The poor women and children have my deepest sympathy."

On November 15, 1864, Sherman and his troops, having set fire to more than ninety percent of Atlanta's vacant buildings, started their historic March to the Sea. It is reported that as Sherman looked back upon the smoldering ruins, no less in pity than in triumph, he asked his band to play the "Miserere" from Verdi's *Il Trovatore.*

If the story is true, then that performance was ironically one of the high points of Atlanta's musical history up to that time, at least in terms of repertoire, for concert life in the young and boisterous city had rarely risen above the level of popular entertainments by blackface minstrel troupes, Swiss bell ringers, or the prodigious blind Negro pianist, Tom Bethune. Serious artists avoided the town because self-styled critics were likely to pelt them with vegetables. The celebrated English soprano Madame Anna Bishop courageously appeared there in February of 1860 with a program that probably consisted of a few tuneful operatic arias and some simple songs on the order of her husband's universally popular "Home, Sweet Home."

There were numerous local amateurs whose endeavors were considered "respectable" by the elite class. The Atlanta Mozart Club, which enjoyed a superior reputation, presented a benefit concert for the First Georgia Regulars early in 1861, but it is not known whether the quality of their repertoire exceeded that of the twenty-three men and five women calling themselves the Atlanta Amateurs, who in May of the same year provided a program of poetry, wit, and patriotism for the benefit of the Soldiers' Relief Fund.

Even in the midst of the occupation, amateurs were called upon to help bolster morale, and on September 24, 1864, only a few weeks before the city was to be razed, Colonel W. G. LeDuc, the Union officer in charge of evacuating the city, organized two charity concerts for a Southern widow.

Within less than two years after the holocaust, Atlanta's musical life was under way with more vigor and variety than ever before. Violinist Barrett Isaac Poznanski, a native of Charleston, South Carolina, who had been studying in Europe with the renowned Henri Vieuxtemps, appeared in Atlanta in April of 1866. Six months later Bell and Johnson's New Opera Hall was suitably inaugurated with performances of *Il Trovatore*, *Faust*, *Norma*, and *The Barber of Seville* by Max Strakosch's Italian opera company. One of the prima donnas was Strakosch's wife, Amalia Patti, sister of the immortal coloratura Adelina Patti, who delighted the less sophisticated ladies and the bored husbands in the audience by practicing "Kathleen Mavourneen," "Within a Mile of Edinboro Town," and "Comin' Thro' the Rye" in the lesson scene of Rossini's opera.

Throughout the last three decades of the century other professional opera troupes, such as those of Maurice Grau, Isabella McCulloch, Walter Damrosch, and Minnie Hauk, visited Atlanta with growing frequency and success. Amateur musical activity increased also, though seldom with much continuity, and usually with emphasis on opera. The Rossini Club, organized in 1876, presented two or three entire operas on the order of Balfe's *Bohemian Girl*, while the short-lived Beethoven Society of the late seventies, Giuseppe Randegger's Atlanta Musical Club (1893–97), and the Symphony Club, formed in 1899, presented scenes from operas and occasionally some excerpts from oratorios. Orchestral music was strictly incidental until 1911, when Mortimer Wilson, a composer and teacher at the Atlanta Conservatory, organized an Atlanta Symphony Orchestra—which endured shakily for four short seasons. Naturally, music in the popular idioms outdrew even operatic programs. While touring professionals brought in ballad concerts of the prevaudeville type, or burlesque opera patterned after Offenbach's racy *opéra bouffe*, amateurs organized brass bands and mandolin clubs. Local amateurs and touring professionals shared the stage at the Cotton States and International Exposition held in Atlanta in 1895, but the principal attraction was John Philip Sousa, who composed his "King Cotton" march for the event.

The population increased to about 90,000 by the turn of the century, and as the city prospered its capacity and willingness to import bigger and better musical attractions expanded commensurately. In October of 1901 the Metropolitan Opera Company complimented Atlantans by including them in its four-city tour of the east, presenting *Lohengrin, Romeo and Juliet,* and *The Barber of Seville.* Its visit became an annual spring event—actually a ritual, almost a cultural fixation—beginning in May of 1910 when Enrico Caruso starred as Radames in *Aïda* before an ecstatic mob of 7,000 opera-lovers.

By the end of the First World War Atlanta's population exceeded 150,000 citizens, justly proud that their city was the "pivot point, think bank, money drop, and motive force" of the New South, and inclined to boast of their ability to import the most worthwhile of the Western world's cultural benefits. Of home-grown claims to fame they could only think of the Uncle Remus stories by newspaperman Joel Chandler Harris, or the Coca-Cola Company, founded in 1892 by Asa G. Candler.

In 1917 H. L. Mencken chided the South abrasively in his essay "The Sahara of the Bozart," which was first published in the New York *Evening Mail* and reprinted in *Prejudices: Second Series* in 1920:

> Down there, a poet is now almost as rare as an oboe-player. . . . For all its size and all its wealth and all the "progress" it babbles of, it is almost as sterile, artistically, intellectually, and culturally, as the Sahara Desert.
>
> In all that gargantuan paradise of the fourth-rate there is not a single picture gallery worth going into, or a single orchestra capable of playing the nine symphonies of Beethoven, or a single opera-house, or a single theater devoted to decent plays, or a single public monument that is worth looking at, or a single workshop devoted to the making of beautiful things. . . . When you come to

critics, musical composers, painters, sculptors, architects and the like, . . . there is not even a bad one between the Potomac mud-flats and the Gulf.

One would find it difficult to unearth a second-rate city between the Ohio and the Pacific that isn't struggling to establish an orchestra, or setting up a little theater, or going in for an art gallery, or making some other effort to get in touch with civilization. These efforts often fail, and sometimes they succeed rather absurdly, but under them there is at least an impulse that deserves respect, and that is the impulse to seek beauty and to experiment with ideas, and so to give the life of every day a certain dignity and purpose. You will find no such impulse in the South. There are no committees down there cadging subscriptions for orchestras; if a string quartet is ever heard there, the news of it has never come out; an opera troupe, when it roves the land, is a nine days' wonder.

The arts, save in the lower reaches of the gospel hymn, the phonograph and the political harangue, are all held in suspicion.

Atlanta's musical leaders were jolted into action. In 1921 the Atlanta Music Club was organized for the express purpose of bringing more and bigger stars to the city's concert halls, but one of its charter members, Mrs. George Walker, perceived that the resources for a promising orchestral tradition were readily at hand: considerable wealth and civic pride among the city's 200,000 souls; several dozen capable musicians employed in the larger movie theaters; and the dashing young Enrico Leide, native of Turin, Italy, who had recently been summoned to conduct the orchestra at the Howard Theater.

With adamantine will Mrs. Walker badgered two hundred affluent Atlantans—a mere twenty percent of her actual goal—into joining the new Atlanta Symphony Orchestra Association, and then hired Leide to assemble and conduct an orchestra. In the fall of 1923 Leide initiated a series of twelve free concerts by his forty-five-member ensemble. The plan was eventually to double the number of players and concerts, but with the advent of sound movies in the late twenties the better professional musicians moved away, and amateurs were recruited to take their places. Leide, who later married Asa Candler's daughter, stayed on, but the orchestra could not survive the onset of military conscription in 1939 and thereupon collapsed.

Coincidentally, that same year a plan for an In-and-About-Atlanta High School Orchestra was set in motion by Anne Grace O'Calla-

ghan, supervisor of music in the public schools, with the cooperation of school officials and the aid of a few interested citizens. Students from nearby communities were invited to take part, and
some came from as far away as Chattanooga, Tennessee. The guest
conductor for the first four annual spring concerts was Joseph
Maddy, founder of the National High School Music Camp at Inter-
lochen, Michigan, who repeatedly pointed out the importance of
providing a chance for orchestra players to continue participation
after graduation from high school.

At the meeting of the Southern Division of the Music Educators
National Conference in Atlanta in 1943, Miss O'Callaghan heard an
address by Henry Sopkin in which the same idea as Maddy's was
persuasively expressed. Sopkin, Brooklyn-born and Chicago-bred,
was a musician of broad experience and a teacher of exceptional
ability, who had gained a fine reputation as a conductor and clinician with school orchestras. Miss O'Callaghan immediately invited
him to conduct the In-and-About Atlanta orchestra in its 1944
spring concert.

Once again the confluence of idea, circumstance, and determination bore fruit. Mrs. James O'Hear Sanders, president of the Atlanta Music Club, attended Sopkin's concert and resolved to carry
Atlanta's orchestra tradition not one but *two* steps further. First,
she persuaded several members of the club to erect an independent organization for the support of an Atlanta Youth Symphony
Orchestra. Second, she engaged Henry Sopkin to conduct its first
two concerts—on February 5 and April 15, 1945. To assure broad
community involvement she named a committee to raise $3,000 to
cover expenses for the opening season. An aggressive publicity
campaign, calculated to counteract Atlantans' preference for imported musical attractions, emphasized the constructive value of a
youth-oriented activity in the face of rising juvenile delinquency.
Ability was the principal criterion for membership in the orchestra; the one hundred players who were chosen ranged in age from
eleven to twenty-five.

Immediately following the April 15 concert Sopkin was asked if
he would consider moving to Atlanta to develop a professional
symphony orchestra. Although at forty-two he was in the prime of
his career as a college teacher and an editor for the music publishing firm of Carl Fischer, Inc., and was earning a fairly comfortable

income of $9,000 a year, he was excited by the challenge and accepted without hesitation—for a mere $3,000 a year.

The Atlanta Youth Symphony Guild and its auxiliary, the Junior Committee, were incorporated in the fall of 1945, and soon raised $5,000 to provide three free public concerts and one young people's matinee. The budget was tripled in the second season so that fifteen "professionals" could be hired at up to $800 each to fill first-chair positions; the orchestra played five free concerts for adults and two for children, and made one "run-out" to Athens, sixty miles away. In mid-season the Atlanta Youth Symphony began calling itself the Atlanta Symphony Orchestra.

By 1950–51 all the musicians were paid, the budget topped $100,000, and the ASO thus entered the ranks of the American Symphony Orchestra League's twenty-five major orchestras. The story of its meteoric rise to majority, as recounted in *Etude* magazine, was so impressive that the U.S. State Department used it as cold war propaganda in seventy-five foreign countries to illustrate what could be accomplished under "the American way of life."

In another four years operating expenses reached $200,000, covering an eleven-concert series (including a "ballet special" and two performances with the new Atlanta Symphony Chorus), four free Sunday afternoon "family concerts," and twelve youth concerts in the schools. The season was further enhanced by appearances of the Atlanta Little Symphony of thirty players, the Atlanta Symphony String Quartet, the Atlanta Symphony Woodwind Quintet, and the twelve-member Atlanta String Ensemble.

By 1965 the budget was up to $330,000 for a twenty-two-week season of twelve subscription concerts, nineteen youth concerts, and two run-outs. In *Gone With the Wind* Scarlett O'Hara had called Atlantans "a bunch of pushy people," and that is precisely what it had taken to increase the orchestra's financial base by 660 percent in just twenty years. The feat was all the more remarkable in view of the fact that during that time Atlantans were also struggling to establish other performing arts locally—opera, ballet, chamber music, and theater—while maintaining an expensive program of visiting artists.

In 1950, for instance, the Atlanta Music Club sponsored three separate series: the Salon Series of morning and evening lecture-recitals devoted to twentieth-century composers; the Concert Artists Series, which offered seven stellar attractions including the London String Quartet and Eileen Farrell; and the All Star Concert Series of twelve events, such as the Sadler's Wells Ballet, the Royal Philharmonic, the Houston Symphony, Artur Rubinstein, James Melton, and the Robert Shaw Chorale. The Junior Service League of suburban Decatur sponsored two concerts, and the Georgia Chapter of the American Guild of Organists three more. The Atlanta Division of the University of Georgia (soon to become Georgia State University), Emory University, and various other local schools also contributed events to the musical season. The climax of the season was the visit of the Metropolitan Opera Company.

From an economic standpoint, and for the good of community relations, it was logical for the ASO to feature local soloists as much as possible, but in order to meet the competition it was compelled almost from the start to rely on big-name stars to attract subscribers. One artist who occupied both roles was Beverly Wolff, a native Atlantan who had played trumpet with the In-and-About Atlanta High School Orchestra and the Atlanta Youth Symphony, left home to study voice, and returned on several occasions as one of the nation's leading mezzo-sopranos. International figures like Stravinsky, Monteux, Barbirolli, and Fiedler were brought to the podium, as well as Americans like Morton Gould, David Van Vactor, Thor Johnson and, in 1965, conducting Mozart's Requiem, Robert Shaw.

Considering that conflicts between artistic standards and fiscal necessities are endemic to the American symphony orchestra, and that the relations between a conductor and his board of directors are inherently strife-ridden, it is amazing that the ASO's first twenty years were marred by only one untoward episode. At the outset of the 1948–49 season the chairman of the board invited Enrico Leide to return as guest conductor, over Sopkin's strenuous objection. The fifty-member board immediately split into two factions, one upholding the conductor's prerogatives in all musical matters, the other openly questioning his right to such authority. The controversy weakened the dedication of some supporters, and by February the orchestra was $18,000 in debt. Although Sopkin's critics were thus temporarily vindicated, the other side eventually won out and, after a strenuous summer-long campaign to "Save the Atlanta Symphony Orchestra," succeeded in tripling ticket sales and raising $22,000 more than in the previous year. An anonymous benefactor cleared the debt from the books.

Some persons had complained that Sopkin's programming was too cerebral; at least one dissident demanded to hear the more tuneful music of Friml, Herbert, and Gershwin. Others deemed his choices unduly conservative. Actually, Sopkin's policy was to educate both the orchestra and the audience to the values of the standard eighteenth- and nineteenth-century symphonic repertoire. Between 1945 and 1965 he served them a generous diet of Bach, all the Beethoven symphonies except the Ninth, five symphonies and nine concertos by Mozart, eight symphonies by Haydn, and two each by Mendelssohn and Schumann. Tchaikovsky's Fourth, Fifth, and Sixth Symphonies were programmed a total of seventeen times. American music was represented by works of Copland, Cowell, Barber, Thomson, Harris, Creston, two or three black composers, several women—and Gershwin. Altogether, Atlantans heard nothing more avant-garde than Ralph Vaughan Williams's *London Symphony*, Hindemith's *Mathis der Maler*, and Stravinsky's *Symphony of Psalms*. The most audacious excursion into modernity was a performance in 1960 of Ives's comparatively melodious Pulitzer Prize–winning Third Symphony.

For all Sopkin's diligence and the Guild's sedulous labors, there were limits to the orchestra's capacity for achieving a degree of musical maturity commensurate with its fiscal majority. To begin with, the ASO was a professional orchestra only in the sense that all its members were paid *something*. But by 1966 the minimum weekly wage was a paltry $135, and principals earned less than $7,000 a year. For an average of more than twenty hours' work per week—five rehearsals and from two to four concerts—few of the seventy-five players earned more than one-fourth of their income from the orchestra. Most were employed as music teachers and in the public schools, colleges and universities, and the rest were musical avocationists; consequently, rehearsals couldn't begin until four o'clock in the afternoon. All were, essentially, amateurs in the truest and best sense of the word. As with the Collegiate

Chorale, Shaw once remarked, "it was their way of loving music." Hardly any of them had sufficient free time to refine their individual skills.

Second, no matter how well the orchestra might have played, it was handicapped by the characteristics of the halls it had to play in. It had begun its history in the cavernous 5,000-seat Municipal Auditorium, built in 1909 as a combination amphitheater and armory. Acoustically and aesthetically it was best suited to spectator sports and revival meetings.

At the beginning of the 1957–58 season the orchestra moved into the Tower Theatre on Peachtree Street. Concertgoers were elated, for the handsome, colonnaded, stuccoed-and-plastered, chandeliered interior possessed the ornate elegance that seemed appropriate to the image of an expensive orchestra and its opulent guest artists. On the other hand, there were serious drawbacks. The reverberation time was appreciably shorter than that of the Auditorium, but there was less sound to reverberate, since most of it went straight up into the flies behind the low proscenium. Worse yet, the seating capacity was only 2,700, and since the average total attendance had been about 4,200, the orchestra had to play each concert twice to less-than-full houses. Paradoxically, when the Tower was remodelled into a Cinerama Theater in 1962, and the orchestra had to move back into the Municipal Auditorium, some 125 patrons declined to renew their subscriptions allegedly because of the return to the less attractive environment.

In the late forties there had been a point when it appeared that Sopkin's dream of a new auditorium designed expressly for symphonic performances would be realized. A few American cities had begun setting up arts councils, patterned in general after Canadian prototypes, which in turn were outgrowths of the Committee for the Encouragement of Music and the Arts established by Great Britain in 1939. Many of the American councils were just *pro tempore* committees of representatives from various performing organizations whose primary objectives were to solve mutual problems of management, scheduling, and audience development. Some of them initiated united fund raising programs to tap new sources of support, which in turn led to coalitions of arts organizations. Several specifically sought to construct public facilities for arts activities.

Early in 1949 the Women's Chamber of Commerce of Atlanta announced the formation of a Fine Arts Foundation, which, drawing upon the Symphony Guild's money-raising ability, was to erect a center to house several of the city's major arts enterprises, including a 2,500-seat concert hall for the Atlanta Symphony Orchestra. Unfortunately, at that particular moment Sopkin and the Guild were embroiled in the great authority crisis, and the orchestra's financial future was in doubt. The Foundation soon sank into oblivion.

By 1955 there were somewhere between twenty-five and fifty community arts councils in the United States—in Grand Rapids, Michigan; in Quincy, Illinois; in Houston; Wichita; and Seattle. Within another few years it was reported that some twenty cultural centers had been opened since 1950, and many more were being constructed, planned, or contemplated.

Moreover, survey after survey provided statistics, replete with graphs and dollar signs, purporting to show that America was being suffused with "culture." Spokesmen for the estimated 1,200 community, metropolitan, and major orchestras crowed over the "fact" that more people were attending symphony concerts than were attending major-league baseball games. Music teachers informed their students that so many hours of concert music were being broadcast on AM and FM radio, and that so many millions of dollars were being spent on recordings of serious music. Fundraisers went forth armed with assurances that American industries were supporting the arts with unprecedented largesse. It was predicted that the Lincoln Center for the Performing Arts, under construction in 1961, would outdraw the New York Yankees by almost two to one. (There were similar hopes for the National Cultural Center, which President Eisenhower had authorized in 1958, though the completion of what was to become the Kennedy Center was then another ten years in the offing.)

"This country is on the verge of an explosion in culture," said Roy Johnson, Director of the U.S. Advance Research Projects Agency and formerly a vice-president of General Electric. "The traditional barriers between artists and businessmen are breaking down. So are the barriers between art and life. Cultural leadership is there for the taking."

The catch-phrase "cultural explosion" resounded across the nation. Chauvinists viewed the phenomenon as a harbinger of victory in the cold war. Certainly, it gave a welcome measure of comfort to those Americans whose well-stocked bomb shelters testified to the common dread of a more deadly kind of explosion.

Some critics, on the other hand, perceived more noise than heat. Harold Schonberg, writing in the *Saturday Evening Post* in 1963, pointed out that the figures were either inflated or irrelevant. There were still insufficient opportunities for American-born and educated performers. Concert life in the provinces was still dominated by the star system, which in turn was still controlled by the musical tastemakers in New York. There was still virtually no federal, state, or local tax support for the arts. "The cultural numbers game," Schonberg concluded, has spawned "a statistical lie."

A fundamental problem was the lack of agreement over the definition of the word "culture." Wherever there was talk of building a "culture center," progressive advocates had in mind a place where musicians, dancers, dramatists, painters and sculptors could all work together under one roof, exploring the frontiers of creativity in a climate of mutual inspiration and encouragement. Reactionaries envisioned a kind of museum dedicated to the preservation of traditional values and modes of expression. Politicians and other pragmatists thought of a glorified social center, as hospitable to conventions, sports events and trade shows as to music, drama, or dance. At best, if a center were actually built, it served to meet only existing needs. At worst, the politicians won the toss.

In Atlanta no compromise was necessary.

When Ivan Allen assumed his duties as mayor in 1961 he was ready with an $8-million urban renewal bond issue that would transform Atlanta from an overgrown country town into a major American city in every visible respect. He conceived a rapid transit system, new schools, improved streets and highways, and a large auditorium and convention center. He was especially fond of the idea of an arts center, to be located in Piedmont Park; an anonymous donor had promised to provide $4 million to start with. "Never," Allen chided a reporter, "think Atlanta should go second class."

Unfortunately, Mayor Allen's proposal was defeated at the polls, a victim of his own miscalculations and of a political skirmish with racist overtones. The next year a much smaller bond issue was approved for construction of a multipurpose Civic Center, which was completed in 1967.

Early in 1962, a trustees' committee of the Atlanta College of Art, headed by Mrs. Hugh Dorsey, had commissioned a study relative to the development of the art school and the High Museum, which shared adjacent property on Peachtree Street and were already institutionally linked under the umbrella called the Atlanta Art Association. The Art Association's board voted to implement the plan, and Richard H. Rich, chairman of the board of Rich's Department Store, was asked to head a drive to raise a few million dollars for it. Rich agreed, provided the plan and the budget were expanded to include a permanent home for the symphony.

Then, on June 6, 1962, a chartered Boeing 707 bringing 106 members of the association home from a tour of European museums crashed on takeoff from Orly Field in Paris. Civic leaders felt that making the proposed art center a memorial to the Atlantans who perished at Orly would be a fitting gesture and would give impetus to the campaign for funds.

The anonymous donor who had offered the large sum for Mayor Allen's aborted arts center in Piedmont Park was Robert W. Woodruff, archon of the Coca-Cola Company, whose father had bought out Asa Candler in 1916 and who had been largely responsible for Atlanta's becoming a hub of commerce and finance. Robert Woodruff wielded immense influence, but he did so unobtrusively, and always with the best interests of the community uppermost in mind. As a black leader in Atlanta once described him, he represented a principle of "progressive paternalism." He assured Rich that his offer still stood, but insisted that responsible management take precedence over social amenities.

To satisfy Woodruff's mandate, and also to attract contributions on the "united fund" principle, the Atlanta Symphony Orchestra, the High Museum, and the Atlanta School of Art merged in 1964 under the aegis of the Atlanta Arts Alliance, a nonprofit corporation governed by a self-perpetuating board of directors and administered by a paid president and staff. The first list of officers and directors comprised a directory of many of the important men and women in Atlanta's legendary "power structure," with Rich as chairman of the board.

The Alliance's first order of business was to secure donations toward the construction of a building containing a 1,762-seat concert hall, an 800-seat theater, two smaller halls for lectures, recitals, or intimate stage productions, an art museum, a large exhibition hall, classroom and studio space for the art school, and all the requisite offices and service areas. The cost, exclusive of most of the land and the small art museum the structure was to envelop, was estimated at around $10 million. By autumn 1965 the Alliance had about $8 million in hand, and was confident of its ability to get the rest. When the construction bids were opened the lowest was nearly $13 million. The expedient move would have been to trim the fat from the architect's design. Instead, the Board of the Alliance decided to raise the extra money. Woodruff came up with another $3 million, and some of his friends chipped in again. Altogether, approximately 70 percent of the cost of the Atlanta Memorial Arts Center was covered by local businessmen, by national corporations with regional offices in Atlanta, and by philanthropic foundations like Campbell, Callaway, and Woodruff. The rest came from individuals.

On the fourth anniversary of the Orly disaster, ground was broken for the new Atlanta Memorial Arts Center. According to architect Joseph Amisano, of the firm of Toombs, Amisano and Wells, the center was to constitute a practical test of the proposition that the arts essentially overlap and nurture one another. Therefore, unlike New York's Lincoln Center for the Performing Arts—the only remotely comparable facility then under construction—the AMAC was designed not only to place various kinds of artistic activity and education contiguously under one roof and to make artists' paths cross—musicians' with painters', dancers' with actors', and so on—but also to enable visitors to enjoy, in a single day's or evening's visit to one convenient location, a concert, a play, an art movie, an exhibit, and perhaps even to observe artists at work in their studios.

When Shaw moved to Atlanta, Maxine dutifully accompanied him, but their moments of happiness together were as brief as ever. In 1970 she moved to Sevendoors on Nantucket Island, and subsequently she and Robert were divorced. For the first half dozen years in his new position, support and encouragement came principally from his close professional associates and a few community leaders such as Robert Edge, Robert Wood, and Charles Yates, who had become friends of his.

Yates had met Shaw in 1938 while visiting his golfing buddy, Fred Waring, in New York. Not long afterward, Waring and Yates, along with their mutual friend Sam Sneed, the golf pro, invited Shaw to join them on Waring's private course at his estate, Shawnee-on-Delaware, Pennsylvania. Shaw had never played the game before, but with cheerful disregard for the caliber of the company he was keeping, he accepted. Unable to borrow a pair of cleated shoes that fit him, he played in his bare feet so as to get a firm grip on the turf with his toes. He broke 100 on the first round.

Ten years later, on October 27, 1948, the Robert Shaw Chorale appeared in Atlanta on its very first tour. The symphony was still in its infancy, and Shaw had hardly begun to dream of having an orchestra of his own. But on each of the eight succeeding visits by the Chorale—on the Atlanta Music Club's All Star Concert Series, or the Flora Candler Series at Emory University—when Charlie and his wife, Dorothy, would entertain Shaw and the troupe in their home, the conversation would often turn to the subject of Atlanta's musical life, and to the orchestra in particular.

In January of 1965, when Shaw was in Atlanta as guest conductor of the symphony, Yates outlined to him the concept of the Arts Alliance, and drove him past the site of the projected Memorial Arts Center. Shaw was interested, and told Yates he'd like to hear more about it when it was finished. The following month, after Henry Sopkin announced his intention to retire at the close of the 1965–66 season, Yates, as president of the Board of Sponsors, appointed a three-member search committee to find a successor. Shaw's name surfaced; it was rumored that he was thinking of leaving Cleveland.

The committee was deluged with suggestions, most of which represented one or the other of two alternatives: either to seek an established luminary from the international galaxy of conducting stars whose mere presence would enhance the ASO's reputation, or else to find a young prodigy who would carry the orchestra with him on his own rise to eminence. Shaw seemed to be the only person in whom the alternatives happily converged, and an invitation was soon extended to him.

He was tempted to accept without hesitation, for it was, as he said, the most attractive opportunity of his life so far, but he had no wish to be "a choice of one in a field of one," so he countered with some more possibilities for their consideration. The list grew to nearly one hundred names, but his kept appearing at the top. Finally, Yates phoned him and persuaded him to take the job.

Shaw was contractually bound to the Cleveland Orchestra through 1966–67, so the ASO's Board of Sponsors engaged a series of guest conductors to see them through until he could officially take over. Meanwhile, brimming with enthusiasm, he began to shape his plans for the ASO's future. In February of 1966 he wrote to Charles L. Towers, president of the Symphony Board:

> I might as well admit that I am getting tremendously excited about the potentials of the Atlanta Symphony situation. Not a day goes by without ideas for programming, personnel and general construction. I have not felt this way about any responsibilities since the early Fred Waring–Collegiate Chorale days, and—come to think of it—even that would take second place to this. Hold on you've got a bair by the teal!

In the first of his annual speeches to the Board of Sponsors, Shaw gave ample clues as to the breed of bear they had by the tail. His premise was consonant with that of the dreamers who had brought to pass the Atlanta Arts Alliance and the Memorial Arts Center: "The arts are not a luxury but a necessity. They bring sanity and wholeness, and purpose and perspective to a society." Similarly, his promises were congruent with their hopes: "In the sort of atmosphere in which the Arts Alliance idea found its beginning, an orchestral association—or an association of the musical performing arts—has responsibilities considerably beyond serving a few hundreds—or thousands—of habitual symphonic—or socio-symphonic—devotees." Accordingly, he declared his intention to foster the development of resident opera and ballet companies, acknowledged the need for expanded outreach activities in terms of education and touring, and emphasized the necessity for an active chamber music program in the interests of breadth in Atlanta's concert life, and the musical well-being of the orchestra's members.

He pointed out the significance of the choral tradition: "The chorus is peculiarly representative not of an *elite*—of skill, or class, or intelligence—but of what Lincoln and Sandburg call *the people, yes, the people.* A chorus reaches deep into community life, crosses all sorts of social and economic lines, and makes a contribution not only to a city's aesthetics, but also its humanity."

He gave assurance that the ASO would continue to cultivate the classic symphonic repertoire: "An orchestra is obliged to make available to a living—a live—audience that which from the distant and receding past continues to prove its pertinence and its communicability. This is the miracle of art—that its ever-lovin' to-whom-it-may-concern crosses not only national boundaries and oceans but generations and centuries. Art becomes a classic not by being written a long time ago—but by remaining pertinent." He also gave notice that from 20 to 30 percent of the orchestra's repertoire would consist of works by twentieth-century composers, including living—and even local—men and women, "to demonstrate that music is not written by pictures in books or busts in a record store, but by dirty sweaty smelly ugly people—like you and me." He warned that a small portion of the repertoire would be drawn from "that sound of this moment upon which one has no right or means of exercising a value judgment: the absolutely absurd, experimental, unconventional, uncensored, inconceivable, unbearable anti-music." No doubt a few of his listeners greeted that statement with silent applause; the rest were either unconcerned—or incredulous.

In a speech to the downtown Rotary Club he elaborated on another point. He wanted greater involvement of blacks in the musical enterprises of the Alliance—as patrons and policy-makers, as performers, and as listeners. "Let's get down to the nitty-gritty," he said, rousing the somnolent assemblage to rapt attention.

What if it were really true that we of white pigmentation are the "deprived" and "underdeveloped" peoples of our time?

What if it really were true that the arts might bring a sanity and a logic and a hope into our too-little and too-late and too-shaky attempts to staunch the flow of wounds too deep and too old?

What if an Arts Alliance were really an alliance of, by and for the people—all the people?

I wish I could describe to you the strange shame of playing a children's concert in Milledgeville, Georgia, for twice three thousand beautiful little children hearing a symphony orchestra for the first time. —And not a single white face in the audience—and not a single black face in the orchestra.

In Atlanta "the arts" have a *chance* to become what the history of man has shown that they should be—the guide and impetus to human understanding, individual integrity and the common good.

They are not an opiate, an avoidance, or a barrier, but a unifying spirit and labor.

Repeatedly he spoke of the need for a large local conservatory in order to attract the best available musicians permanently into the area, give them outlets for their teaching abilities, and thus encourage talented young Atlantans to remain at home to study and work. "There never will be a great orchestra in Atlanta, or a tolerable musical climate, until there also is a distinguished, sizeable school of music functioning on the graduate level," he declared. Reminding his listeners that Cincinnati had recently opened a new $6.5-million conservatory, serving nearly a thousand degree students and fifteen hundred preparatory students, he asked whether Atlanta might not propagate some sort of institution drawing upon the combined resources of local universities and colleges such as Morehouse, Emory, Oglethorpe, Atlanta, Georgia State, Spelman, and Agnes Scott.

Shaw was not unmindful of the cost of all these things, but he was far more concerned with results than with the politics or economics of achieving them.

Economic and political configurations exist to accommodate life, to make it tolerable and occasionally comfortable. Scientific bodies and programs investigate it, in order to extend it in time or space. Religious institutions in the main stream of our era and area are notably more concerned with what happens after it. —But the arts "celebrate" life. In what passes for the communique of the day: It's their thing.

Characteristically, Shaw interspersed his straightforward talks with humor. "This is the first occasion within my short life in Georgia," he remarked offhandedly to the ASO Women's Association, "that has not been opened with an invocation.

—Why, even before a professional football game three weeks ago in the stadium, we were commanded to rise and assume the prayerful position. Of course, it was only an EXHIBITION game, and that may have had something to do with it.

—But then, yesterday, the same thing preceded the Georgia Tech-Texas Christian game. —The outcome of which, according to the scoreboard, would appear to indicate that technique had it over faith—about four to one.

Nevertheless, it should have been apparent to all that Shaw was a no-nonsense conductor and a man of high ideals, strong purpose, and intense communicativeness. In the spring of 1968 Ralph Emerson McGill, the noted columnist and publisher of the *Atlanta Constitution*, observed that Shaw had already become "an influence in the city's mind and conscience and a part of its intellectual as well as cultural future."

10.

The Second Battle of Atlanta

THERE COULD BE no hope of gaining artistic parity with the best in the land unless the ASO became a year-round, full-time, daytime orchestra. The Board of Sponsors took a step in the direction of the first requirement before Shaw's arrival, approving an increase of nearly $300,000 over the 1966–67 budget in order to extend the season from twenty-two weeks and fifty-five concerts to thirty and eighty-five. The change to a new rehearsal schedule at higher pay was postponed until the next season, leaving to Shaw the task of persuading patrons that the same musicians should be paid more money to rehearse longer on the same number of notes that Beethoven's *Eroica* had always contained.

At the kickoff of the annual fund-raising drive in the spring of 1968 he stated his case in terms of analogies drawn from the marketplace and the athletic field, and concluded:

> We have one-half to two-thirds of a sound musical organization about to move from the sandlot to a handsome new park across the street wherefrom, in point of analogy (for the world, in fact, will very much care and long remember what we do there) all of our games are now to be on national candid camera.
>
> The fact that this orchestra plays as well as it does is not due primarily to its present fiscal structure, but to the fact that some very talented people and some variously talented people happen to

be more devoted to their art than any comparable organization in this country. They terribly need somebody to mean business—because they mean music.

Negotiations between the players and the board dragged on for the first nine months of 1967, and toward the end some pessimists doubted there would be an ASO at all. At the last minute a three-year contract was signed, stipulating a $170-per-week minimum salary for the first year, rising to $200 the third, with a gradual increase from thirty-six to thirty-nine weeks per season. Travel allowances, overtime pay, and a two-week midseason vacation were included. The 1971 contract, for forty weeks at $220 per week, provided a group insurance policy. Not until 1976 was a pension plan won.

For a short time the evolution of a resident opera company appeared to be a certainty, even though the Met's annual springtime visit was still the supreme social event of Atlanta's musical season, making competition for broad community support an enormous obstacle. Unhappily the movement expired, a victim of mismanagement, overextension, and a different kind of competition.

The history of the episode began in 1953 with the opening of an outdoor summertime "Theater Under the Stars" using local talent, which endured a tenuous existence for several seasons until a number of civic-minded businessmen led by Mayor Ivan Allen's predecessor, William Hartsfield, brought in a professional producer, Christopher Manos, to head a "Theater of the Stars"—which was moved indoors to avoid losses due to rain. Manos's success led to the opening of a winter season of popular Broadway-type plays, and the eventual establishment of the Atlanta Repertory Theater Company, a thirty-member troupe under the direction of New Yorker Michael Howard.

In 1966 Manos formed, under a single artistic and financial umbrella, the Atlanta Municipal Theater, consisting of the Repertory Theater, the Atlanta Ballet Company, and the Atlanta Opera Company. The professional ballet company, under Robert Barnett, was a direct outgrowth of the first American regional ballet company, started in Atlanta by Dorothy Alexander in 1929. Blanche Thebom was named artistic director of the opera company, and a production of *Aïda* was mounted the first season.

Manos contracted with the Alliance for the rental of the 860-seat proscenium theater and the small experimental theater, plus office space, and announced the intention of presenting a thirty-week season of various theatrical attractions, beginning just as soon as the Memorial Arts Center was ready for occupancy.

Meanwhile, Opera Atlanta, a coalition of the Opera Guild and the Music Club, having abandoned its own plans for production, offered to serve as a promotional agency for the development of opera under the managerial and musical direction of the ASO. Shaw and the Board of Sponsors accepted. When the proposal came before the Alliance, however, the AMT protested, the Alliance conceded, and the symphony had to back down. Subsequently the AMT invited the symphony to participate in its opera and ballet productions, but by that time the coming season's concert schedule had been set, and Shaw was unwilling to dilute his players' energies and loyalties by relinquishing control to another organization and other conductors. Furthermore, he disapproved of the Opera Company's intention to import nearly all of its singers, right down to the chorus members.

The Atlanta Memorial Arts Center was officially dedicated—"to all who truly believe that the arts are a continuing effort of the human spirit to find meaning in existence"—by French Ambassador Charles Lucet on October 5, 1968, with the unveiling of a large Rodin bronze, "The Shade," a gift from the French government. A succession of gala "openings" followed soon afterwards. The art school and the High Museum opened on October 18, with the museum exhibiting forty-nine French paintings on loan from the Louvre and the Petit Palais. On October 19 the concert hall was inaugurated by Shaw and the orchestra before an audience of symphony patrons and their guests; the "Grand Opening" concerts in the regular subscription series were heard a week later.

On October 30 the AMT opened with the first American performance of *King Arthur*, a masque by Henry Purcell, with a cast of one hundred singers, dancers, actors, and instrumentalists, and a lavish *mise-en-scène*.

The entire nation looked upon the profusion of ceremonies with mixed reactions. "As the first owner of a completed and complete arts center under one roof," recalled Chappell White of the *Atlanta Constitution*, "Atlanta had given substance to the then-current talk

of a 'cultural explosion.' The building was both praised and criticized; the concept itself was viewed with varying degrees of fear
and extravagant hope." Locally, there were outbursts of jubilant
pride. Art-life in Atlanta—a city "half phoenix, half peacock," as
someone remarked—had arrived at both a consummation and a
new beginning. When as many as four events were going on simultaneously in the building, and parking facilities proved inadequate,
and the routing of traffic inside frustrated attempts of the security
staff to maintain order, it was apparent that this was indeed, as
architect Joseph Amisano had intended, "an *ACTUAL* center, day
and night, for the people in Atlanta."

It might have been more prudent of Manos to develop a profitable drama season the first year and then add ballet and opera.
Instead, he chose to rely on intensive activity in all three media at
once to arouse massive support. In the first ten weeks of the season, along with *King Arthur*, the AMT mounted nine other attractions, including three ballet programs and Puccini's *La Bohème*.
Manos's budget, based on the anticipation of a $200,000 deficit
(which he failed to cover in advance owing to competition with
the Alliance's fund drive), was woefully unrealistic. A few weeks
after *King Arthur* closed, AGMA shut down a ballet production, and
on January 14, 1969, the AMT collapsed in the agony of bankruptcy.

Although the AMT had been merely a tenant in the center and
not a member of the Alliance, the publicity redounded unfavorably
upon all. Amid rumors that even the art school, the museum, and
the symphony were themselves on the verge of ruin, the Alliance
took over a curtailed drama season and the ballet company resumed its original independent status. Opera was utterly lost in the
wreckage.

During the next ten years Shaw tried to whet Atlantans' appe-
tites for home-grown opera by programming "opera nights" and
concert versions of *Fidelio, Marriage of Figaro*, and *Porgy and Bess*
as part of the symphony's season. In January of 1972 he conducted
the world premiere of Scott Joplin's opera, *Treemonisha*, with
black professionals in the leading roles, Katherine Dunham's dance
troupe from the Performing Arts Center of Southern Illinois University in East St. Louis, a chorus of students from Spelman and
Morehouse colleges, and an orchestra selected from the symphony.
The work was orchestrated from Joplin's piano score by T. J. An-

derson, composer and, at that time, music professor at Morehouse, and the production, made possible by a $25,000 grant from the Rockefeller Foundation, was supervised by Anderson and Wendell Whalum of Morehouse College. Neither entirely home-grown nor entirely professional, it was opera nevertheless—and an immensely important milestone in the civil rights movement.

Joplin's message was that through education blacks could overcome their real oppressors, ignorance and superstition, and find their own way to freedom and equality. By 1972 the social, political, and economic ramifications of the black revolution were far too complex to admit of such a simplistic solution, but the very performance of *Treemonisha*, sixty-one years after it was published by the composer, symbolized a people's burgeoning sense of cultural identity.

Shaw had arrived in Georgia toward the end of the last of the strife-ridden long, hot summers. From early June through late August, 1967, one American city after another had been wracked by vicious rioting, murder, arson, and looting. The reign of terror began in Boston's Roxbury district, then spread through Tampa, Newark, Detroit, Grand Rapids, Waukegan, Washington, Wichita, and beyond. Atlanta, owing to its long-standing coalition of black and white leadership, remained an island of tranquillity in a sea of violence.

Nationally, the conflict was not so much between races as between classes. Gradually, since the late fifties, the civil rights movement had secured for all black people their fundamental Constitutional rights. A few of its beneficiaries had even gained something approaching middle class income and education, which fomented higher expectations within those still disadvantaged. Then, as veteran activists turned their attention toward the immorality of American military "involvement" in Southeast Asia, radical black power advocates and militant black nationalists set out to gain more of the perquisites of middle class white society for their constituents. Crucial issues were equal employment opportunities, integration in the public schools, and the need for black mayors, police chiefs, and school board members. Breaking into the white arts establishment was low on the list of priorities.

White leaders who sympathized with the occasional demands for equal cultural opportunities were often hard-pressed to meet even the most reasonable standards. There was a nationwide trend in the late sixties toward the placing of blacks on directorial boards of arts institutions—in Cleveland, Detroit, Chicago, Dallas—but the ideal candidates had to possess both wealth and influential social position—the first qualification being rare and the second less than universally admired in the black community. The board of the Atlanta Arts Alliance finally acquired three black members in 1969: Mrs. Jenelsie Walden Holloway, head of the art department at Spelman College; Dr. Benjamin E. Mays, retired president of Morehouse College; and bank president Lorimer D. Milton. Wendell Whalum, chairman of Morehouse's music department, had joined the ASO's Board of Sponsors the previous year.

The problem of finding black players for the orchestra was more difficult to solve. The recording and broadcasting of popular music had been an important industry in Atlanta since the early part of the century, and local black youths with musical talent knew that was where the real money was to be made. Just as elsewhere in America, black children who showed interest in serious music received little encouragement from the rest of their community and usually lacked the money to prepare themselves for a career in the field. The few who somehow managed to overcome the obstacles were usually those so exceptionally gifted that they deserved higher salaries than the ASO could afford.

Shaw solicited the aid of the Negro colleges allied with the Atlanta University Center—Clark, Morehouse, Morris Brown, and Spelman—in locating, encouraging, and training blacks who might audition for the ASO, but few were found, and none was able to meet the competition from white applicants until violinist Linda Kay Smith appeared in 1972. The whole situation gave some people who wouldn't have supported the symphony anyhow a good excuse to reject appeals for money.

On the other hand, there was no need to postpone the integration of performers at the amateur level. At Shaw's instigation Spelman College was awarded a small grant from the Rockefeller Foundation in 1967 to establish an Intercollegiate Chorus of students from seven Atlanta-area schools, both black and white, which took part in a performance of the *Missa Solemnis* under Shaw in April of 1968. Choral singers from Spelman and Morehouse participated in the symphony's *Fidelio* in 1971 (with Ella Lee as Leonora and Seth McCoy as Florestan) and *Porgy and Bess* in 1972. Morehouse students have also taken part in Stravinsky's *Oedipus Rex*, Fauré's Requiem, Schoenberg's *Gurrelieder*, and several Christmas programs.

In 1971 Howard Klein of the *New York Times* credited Shaw and the ASO with having initiated a new era in American musical history three years before, when they spent a week in residence at Spelman's Carnegie Foundation–sponsored Festival of Contemporary Music. There, under Shaw, his assistants Michael Zearott and Michael Palmer, and guest conductor Paul Freeman, the orchestra rehearsed and performed new works by fifteen Americans, seven of whom were black: T. J. Anderson, Adolphus Hailstork, Olly Wilson, Frederick Tillis, Ulysses Kay, George Walker, and Arthur Cunningham. The event had focused national awareness on the extent to which black composers of art music had been working unnoticed. Black conductors like Freeman and Everett Lee were invited to feature black composers' works wherever they appeared, and many white conductors began paying as much attention to race as to nationality in their programming. From the Black Music Center at Indiana University soon came a 300-page typescript catalog of compositions by some 850 blacks. The trend was furthered by the Afro-American Music Workshop at Morehouse in 1972, where, in addition to the performance of Joplin's *Treemonisha*, the ASO played works by John W. Work, Howard Swanson, Hale Smith, Stephen Chambers, and Wendell Logan. Ironically, some concerned individuals objected that calling attention to the color of a composer's skin actually reversed what little integration had already taken place.

Atlantans heartily applauded the festival, the workshop, and especially the Joplin premiere. On the other hand, there were mutterings of disapproval when, in 1976, Shaw commemorated the martyrdom of Martin Luther King, Jr., with a performance of Haydn's *Seven Last Words* interspersed with readings from the Reverend Dr. King's sermons and speeches and slide projections of significant events in his career. Some people felt that Shaw had upstaged the famous pianist who appeared in a concerto during the second half of the program.

All of Shaw's plans for the ASO have reflected his untrammeled imagination, his invincible determination, and his kinetic motivation to learn, change, and grow. His efforts in behalf of racial integration have been more than the *cause célèbre* of an obstinately liberal "Servant of Brotherhood"; they have been manifestations of his belief in music as "a community of expression." His programming practices have been carefully planned to further the orchestra's and the audience's maturity and satisfaction. But sometimes the logic of it all has been hard for the casual concertgoer to grasp.

The 1967–68 Subscription Series, which opened with Beethoven's Ninth and closed with the *Missa Solemnis*, consisted in the main of a carefully balanced selection of eighteenth- and nineteenth-century staples, many never before played by the ASO. But observers noted that the most striking aspect of Shaw's programs overall was the number of twentieth-century works they contained, although the bulk of those compositions were products of the older generation of moderns and thus exemplified a comparatively conservative style—Hindemith's *Symphonic Metamorphosis* or Stravinsky's *Symphony of Psalms*; Webern was represented by a preserial work, and Gunther Schuller was the only younger American included. Shaw had judiciously remained within the pattern established by Sopkin.

The second season's repertoire, though still suffused with an appropriate number of standard classics, was a bit more daring in terms of twentieth-century music. It opened with the world premiere of Ulysses Kay's *Theatre Set*, commissioned by the Junior League of Atlanta at Shaw's instigation, and continued with a sprinkling of names not yet to be found in the listeners' guides to concert music: T. J. Anderson and Donald MacInnis (whose acquaintance Shaw had made at the Festival of Contemporary Music the previous year), Eugene Kurtz (a native Atlantan living in Paris), Donald Erb, and Walter Ashaffenburg. MacInnis, then composer-in-residence with the ASO under a Rockefeller Foundation grant, contributed a multimedia work, *Intersections for Tape*

Recorder and Orchestra. Penderecki's *Threnody for the Victims of Hiroshima* and Messiaen's *Et expecto resurrectionem mortuorum* were similarly unconventional. The oldest, most conservative work on the list was Ives's Second Symphony.

To mark the ASO's twenty-fifth anniversary in 1969–70, Shaw programmed a major American symphonic work on all but three of the subscription concerts: Morton Gould's *Soundings* (another Shaw/Junior League commission), William Schuman's Ninth Symphony and Roy Harris's Third, and works by Lukas Foss, Charles Ives, Copland, Thomson, Barber, Bernstein, Mennin, Gershwin, Hanson, Piston, Schuller, and Hovhaness. Five of the compositions had originated in the sixties, and four of those were less than two years old, but the remainder belonged in the category of a "standard American repertoire"—relatively melodious, or dramatic, or colorful works, generally pleasing to the moderately sophisticated listener. In addition, the orchestra played several works by T. J. Anderson, the ASO's Rockefeller Foundation composer-in-residence that year.

Most subscribers might have been unimpressed by the emphasis on American music had it not been for the more than passing or parochial attention paid to it in the press. Robert C. Marsh of the *Chicago Sun-Times* reminded his readers that many conductors of major stature were reluctant to learn American music, except for an occasional premiere of a particularly newsworthy nature, because of its limited utility abroad. Thus, he said, the future of American music lay in the hands of resident conductors like Shaw, whose "pioneering effort" showed him to be "a musician of uncommon imagination and artistic responsibility."

During the same season Shaw also programmed fourteen twentieth-century European works, including the *St. Luke Passion* of Poland's Penderecki, and five more written by Europeans *in* America—Bartók, Schoenberg, Bloch, and Stravinsky. Altogether, the eighteen-concert Subscription Series contained thirty-four compositions written since 1900. On the other hand, many of the twentieth-century works were short in comparison with some of the monuments of older fare—such as the B Minor Mass or the Berlioz Requiem—that were highlights of the season. Figuring on an average of three titles per concert, roughly half the total playing time for the entire season was devoted to the venerable relics of the past. And a respectably remote past it was, considering that the twentieth century was already 70 percent history.

Still, Shaw's menu of modernism was bitter to the palates of the neophobes. Despite earnest and partly successful gambits to capture the interest of the younger generation with Sunday afternoon happenings, informal in both dress and *ad*dress, advance subscription sales and box-office income began to shrink at a discouraging rate.

The symphony's programs for 1970–71 evidenced suitable concern for the bicentennial observance of the anniversary of Beethoven's birth, while twentieth-century repertoire was distinctly international in flavor, consisting of works by Varèse, Ives, and Barber, Britain's Britten, Argentina's Ginastera, Denmark's Nielsen, Poland's Lutoslawski, Greece's Skalkotas, Mexico's Revueltas, Japan's Takemitsu, and Hungary's Ligeti. The box office—like Wall Street that year—was icily indifferent to the blandishments of any such balance-of-trade policy.

In his remarks to the Board of Sponsors at contract-renewal time in January of 1971, Shaw reaffirmed his programming priorities: First, "the masterpieces of the distant and accumulative past"; second, "the clearly demonstrable superior works of the immediate past and near present"; third, the music—"however strange and seemingly un-mannered" —of one's own time; and fourth, the music of one's own place, "both local and national." He also let it be known that he would brook no interference in the domain of his proper responsibilities:

> While any musical director would be a damned fool not to welcome the suggestions and opinions of those dedicated and devoted people who volunteer to market the project and underwrite its deficits, any attempt on the part of non-professionals to *dictate* program materials ought to be resisted, simply to preserve the professional status of the music directorship—in particular his "fire-ability." Any board has every right to fire its music director and hire a new one; but it would be dubious wisdom to diminish the responsibility of the position—unless one wants to hire weak people.

The board suffered the gauntlet to lie there for a full year while Shaw tried out some new ideas. In September, in the first of several engagingly instructive homilies that were mailed to all subscribers, he outlined the salient features of the coming season. The 1971–72 Subscription Series would focus attention upon the music of Brahms (all the symphonies, concertos, and overtures, the *Variations*, and the *German Requiem*) and of Charles Ives, that "irredeemably American salvager, savorer and recycler of folk songs and hymn tunes, red-neck and/or Yankee; spouter and spewer of extravagant truths; America's greatest musical conservationist and innovator." There was to be a generous helping of "characteristic and pivotal works" by early twentieth-century composers other than Ives—who was the only American—and a leavening dash of Mozart, Beethoven, Wagner, and the like. Each concert would commence with a dollop of Renaissance or Baroque preluding—for the aesthetic purpose of either complementing, or contrasting with, some other work on the program, and for the practical purpose of allowing latecomers to be seated before the evening's major work.

The first concert opened with Handel's *Royal Fireworks Music* (1749) and closed with Brahms's Fourth Symphony (1884–85); between them was "Ives, An Introduction," consisting of:

Adagio, from the First Symphony (1892–98)

Variations on "America" (1891)

The Unanswered Question (1906–1908)

From Hanover Square North at the End of a Tragic Day the Voice of the People Arose (1915)

Several days in advance of the first of the three performances of the program, each subscriber received the following missive:

> One of the very interesting aspects of this week's symphony program, to me, is the presence of three thoroughly different forms of musical *variation*.
>
> In a sense, of course, all music is "variational." Even the simplest hymn varies the *text* from verse to verse. —And in any good singing of a folk-song the singer will alter the tune to highlight significant words or situations, and alter the accompaniment for dramatic effect. All of early jazz was *improvisation* (a form of *variation*) around a given tune or, even more importantly, around a commonly understood bass line or harmonic sequence.
>
> —Which leads by the shortest possible route to one of the oldest and most rigorous of "classical" forms: the *chaconne*—represented on Subscription Series No. 1 by the fourth movement of Brahms' Fourth Symphony. According to the Harvard Dictionary (which recognizes something of every musicologist's difficulties in

separating *chaconne* from *passacaglia*) the *chaconne* is "in the character of a continuous variation in moderate triple meter . . . with slow harmonic rhythm . . . and without a *basso ostinato*" (repeated bass line). In Brahms' case what this means is that he has set up an eight-measure sequence of slow-moving and severely restricted harmonies, assigned himself an all-but-perpetually-motored bass line (obviously to foul Fair Harvard), and repeated said sequence *thirty-one-plus times*, emerging absolutely face-eggless. 'Such are *our* rewards of *his* genius.

A second caprice of inventive composers is the taking of some simple, familiar melody (Beethoven took "God Save the Queen," Everyman has tried "Twinkle, twinkle, little star") and its re-costuming in all sorts of unlikely and outlandish musical garb. Without "lyrics" music really offers very few chances to be humorous (Musicians are renowned for their elephantine and clumsy sense of same: In Marlboro, where gather the greatest chamber-music players of the world each summer, frogs in beds and Kleenex ink-balls sling-shotted across the dining room are considered hilarious), and it is small wonder that composers occa-sionally turn to this device to prove they're "only human." If, in Charles Ives' *Variations on "America"* you find him just a bit less than properly solemncholy—eyes cornering to the mini-skirts while old glory climbs over the ball-park—you may just be getting the point.

The third, and most provocative form of variation on this pro-gram is a sort of variation *in reverse*. I'm not sure it's in the theory books, but its psychological potential is extraordinary. It is the *jig-saw puzzle* of variation forms—variation by assembly. As Charles Ives uses it in "From Hanover Square North at the End of a Tragic Day the Voice of the People Again Arose" (How's that for a title? Isn't it worth coming to the concert simply to find out what *that's* all about!) he takes a tune familiar, I should guess, to 97% of our audience, and whispers it in scraps and fragments through a sort of background mumble and murmur; gradually it becomes more cohesive and recognizable; and at last it emerges blazoned and trumpeted in all its shining and sorrowful fullness. —Thus a musical metaphor of Creation: in the beginning, Chaos—variety rampant; but in the end, Identity.

'Almost forgot: bring your "Sunday" voices. You have twelve measures to sing in this one.

R

The fourth subscription concerts, performed on November 17, 18, and 19, consisted of Matthew Locke's *Music for Sackbuts and Cornetts* (167?), Brahms's Serenade in A Major (1859), Bartók's

Cantata Profana (1930), and Bach's *Magnificat* in D Major (1723). Shaw's parish memorandum read, in part:

> Vitality in Bach's music resides not in sonority but in clarity, not in weight but in resiliency, not in mass but in particularity. It's an entrancingly "democratic" sort of music; a host of musical lines and functions, all of them important, all to be heard—simultaneously—and no one line or factor to dominate or suppress the others.
> I find it provocative that richness of detail keeps company with modesty rather than megalomania. (Does anybody else ponder whether Mt. Rushmore's face-lifting was an improvement over the original design?)
> —Neither is Bartók a banger, telling his shadowed, haunting folk-tale in mostly ghostly colors. It's an apprehensive, wistful inconclusive story, full of intimations of mortality—of which the retiring reticent Bartók may have been this century's most obedient servant.
> The *Serenade* is warm walking-in-the-woods-Uncle-Brahms.
>
>   R

The fifth set in the series opened with the *Contrapunctus I* from Bach's *Art of the Fugue* (1749), Vivaldi's Oboe Concerto in D minor ("The Contest Between Harmony and Invention," 1725), Ives's Fourth Symphony (1910–16), and Brahms's Violin Concerto in A minor (1887). Shaw sent all subscribers a copy of the entire "Postface" to *114 Songs*, by Charles Ives, along with a personal reminiscence:

> Dear Friends of the ASO:
> It was nearly twenty-five years ago that I first came upon the enclosed; and in spite of Ives' subsequent high fashion, and except for a limited early edition of recorded songs, I have not seen it otherwise reprinted. We were premiering in New York some of his early choral works, and I was looking for something—*any*thing—which would give us a handle to the man and his music. (He was too ill to be visited—though he aways sent an annual check to keep our amateur chorus in operation.)
> My favorite writers at the time were the lingering enthusiasms of my late college years, many of whom I by then had met and some of whom I knew fairly well: Edna St. Vincent Millay, Robinson Jeffers, Saroyan, Thornton Wilder, Dorothy Parker, Sandburg, Robert Frost and, of course, a list of playwrights and radio writers —all quite disciplined. The Great War had followed directly upon

the Great Depression, and both had mobilized the arts as anxiously, I think now, to *discover* man's humanity as to defend it.

I had been tumbled into and out of uniform and from out of into "the arts" with a speed and reason I could not fathom.

—And here from one appraised then as being on the "lunatic fringe"—a Wall Street arch-establishmentarian—and, in spite of tongue-in-cheek wholly intentional circumlocution, from an all but undiscovered dying genius came the following "Book of Wisdom." In a lonesome nook in the New York Public Library these words appeared in a "Postface" to a book of songs published in 1922. It seemed to me then the healthiest "position paper" I ever had read on the place and function of the arts and man's destiny; and I'll wager that some of you return to specific sentences with wonder and delight year after year after year.

 . . . . Go slow and enjoy.

                R

In addition to the Subscription Series, Shaw projected five concerts of "Romantic Favorites" from France (Franck, Debussy), the Mediterranean (Falla, Ibert, Respighi), Russia (Tchaikovsky, Rimsky-Korsakoff), Eastern Europe (Dvořák, Liszt, Chopin), and Germany (Mendelssohn, Schubert, Brahms). He didn't try to hide his chagrin, however, at having to mollycoddle the ASO's audiences in this way. Prior to the concert of French music he wrote to the subscribers:

> The rationale of this series derives directly from the imbalance statements of symphony orchestras in general and the response of the ASO's trustees in particular, and is simply stated: People like best what they know best—and will pay good hard cash to hear it again. A good common-sense corollary of this dictum—which is equally convincing to players and conductors as to trustees and volunteer workers—is that "the first business of a symphony orchestra is to stay in business."

After a brief discussion of the nature of romanticism and a reference or two to forthcoming delights ("with all this and *much, much* more, we should all be up to our crocodiles in tears"), he grumbled: "Every sunrise and sunset, face in the direction of the Memorial Arts Center, bow low to the ground, and repeat after me, 'Familiarity breeds—Box Office.'" His candor was widely unappreciated. So, inexplicably, were the "Romantic Favorites," judging from the attendance.

Early in February, five of the eight-member executive committee of the Board of Sponsors voted four to one to request Shaw's resignation. On Sunday the thirteenth, in a brief, cordial memorandum, he complied. At rehearsal the next morning he explained to the musicians:

> I am what I have been becoming for better than half a century. This city is what *it* has been becoming for more than a century. This orchestra and its supporters have been forming their character for more than a quarter of a century.
>
> A collision course was set five years ago; and only the fact that we didn't understand one another delayed this day so long. Once we understood one another it was unavoidable.

Beyond that he expressed no regrets, erected no defenses, made no accusations, and refused to discuss details with anyone in public. "Participants," he said to the orchestra, "seldom are competent judges of the events they precipitate," adding—as if to avert further controversy with an innocent sophistry—that "in all probability those involved in the present situation are least responsible." Thus ended the first open skirmish in what *Newsweek* dubbed "The Second Battle of Atlanta." Shaw withdrew to neutral ground. The victors admitted ingenuously that as yet they had no replacement in mind.

Atlanta's musical community was stunned by the unexpected announcement. The Board of Sponsors was completely taken by surprise, so several members demanded that president J. W. Kercher call a special meeting to explain the executive committee's role in "the present situation." The meeting was set for the twenty-first, but adequate explanation was published well in advance by persistent reporters and critics like Clyde Burnett of the *Journal* and Chappell White of the *Constitution*. According to reliable sources, Shaw's "resignation" was the inevitable and irreversible consequence of the diminishing box-office receipts (and poor attendance even by paid-up subscribers), allegedly attributable to Shaw's indiscreet fondness for "modern" music.

In all the advance publicity and in the program books, Shaw had parenthetically indicated the year in which each work had been composed, his purpose being partly to suggest that dissonance and date are not necessarily related, and partly to prove that the majority were·not "modern" at all. Of the nearly one hundred titles on the combined programs of the Romantic and Subscription series, only thirty-four belonged chronologically to the twentieth century. But fourteen of them, plus two dated before 1900, bore the *one* name that, by mid-February, could itself evoke in timid ears an insufferable din, and in tightly closed minds a most delicious loathing: Charles Ives! And still to come were the Third Symphony (1901–1904), the Orchestra Set No. 2 (1911–15), and the schizoid *Seven Sketches for Chamber Orchestra* (1913–16), containing the surrealistic "Like a Sick Eagle" and the singularly opaque "Calcium Light Night."

There were also those who didn't care—or perhaps didn't even know—whether the Ives in question was the Charles or the Burl, but who simply deplored the broader implications of "the present situation." Atlanta had already begun to attract a measure of unwelcome notoriety as the abode of a phalanx of comstockers who harassed local artists until they were intimidated into conformity or driven away. Within recent years there had been an unpleasant flap over the exhibition of some paintings of nudes at the High Museum and another, more sordid controversy over the Alliance Theatre's production of *The Boys in the Band*. If Shaw were forced to succumb to similar pressures from the symphony board, where would a conductor of comparable stature be found who would consider moving to Atlanta?

The board meeting on Monday the twenty-first, which attracted an unusually large turnout of members, was closed to reporters, but afterwards rumor had it that a motion urging Shaw to withdraw his resignation had been tabled for one week pending the outcome of the next skirmish. A half-page advertisement in Tuesday's papers showed where the line of battle had been drawn: "ROBERT SHAW WILL STAY! The Atlanta Symphony will remain great! If . . . Atlanta will back him by selling out the '72–'73 subscription series!"

Immediately following the board meeting a company of ASO regulars, many of them board members, were enlisted under the command of Washington Falk III, who had already distinguished himself by casting the sole dissenting vote in the executive committee's first fateful action—and who had paid for the newspaper ads. One of his lieutenants was the orchestra's venerable founder,

Mrs. James O'Hear Sanders. Their mission was to secure 5,500 twenty-dollar down-payments on subscriptions for the ensuing year.

The campaign spread through the streets, from Kennesaw to Stone Mountain, meeting little or no resistance. By the time the board met again on Monday the twenty-ninth to vote on the tabled motion, 3,500 pledges had been received, more than half of them from new subscribers in parts of the city where supporters had never been numerous. Even if some of the current subscribers refused to renew, victory was certain. Triumphantly, the board voted to offer Shaw a new contract, and he agreed to discuss terms, saying,

> Usually in the struggles between the principals and powers by which institutions are to be guided—amid confusions of honest differences of opinion and obscurities of motivation—usually everybody loses.
>
> This time something extraordinary happened. Everybody won. For the first time in the history of our country the people rose up and claimed a cultural resource as their own.
>
> The mandate is absolutely clear. All of us are now committed to the people to see that this true alliance between all the arts and all the people becomes a living thing.

Showing no outward sign that he had sustained any serious blows in the fray, Shaw sped on full tilt in pursuit of the very same objectives he had outlined on his arrival in Atlanta. For 1972–73, foregoing the deliberate but fruitless caution he had displayed the previous season, he scheduled two concerts devoted entirely to works by such iconoclasts as Anton Webern, Edgard Varèse, George Crumb, Luciano Berio, Elliott Carter, and T. J. Anderson. Consistent with his previous policy, he also laid heavy emphasis on eighteenth- and nineteenth-century works—and not just through repetition of the "standard" repertoire. Typically, in the 1977–78 subscription series, twenty-five of the sixty-nine titles had never before been played by the ASO, yet of those compositions more than half antedated the year 1900.

There were rumblings of dissatisfaction over his programming, but Shaw came to relish the stimulation of the continual "tension and counter-insurgency" between artist and audience. By 1975 the number of empty seats at every concert had once again increased

Photograph by Thomas Beiswenger

to ominous proportions—many of them paid for, Shaw lamented, "at best out of social obligation, at worst in response to social pressures." Nevertheless, the following year the ASO won an ASCAP award for the encouragement of contemporary music.

The price of that award was an exorbitant expenditure of time and energy toward the study of new scores. Shaw has estimated that he must spend about twenty hours in preparation for every hour of rehearsal on a work that is new to him.

Life might have been somewhat easier for Shaw had he joined the fraternity of peripatetic conductors who jet about the globe displaying their finely polished wares to crowds of admiring fans without having to endure the outrageous fortunes of building and guiding orchestras of their own. But he is not interested in getting up in front of a new public and a new orchestra every few weeks. He doesn't need any more fame, and he doesn't like the superficialities of stardom. In fact, it is rumored that one of the hidden causes of the trauma in the winter of '72 was his neglect—or rather, disdain—of the social obligations a celebrity conductor might be expected to enjoy. Certain influential patrons, it is said, were disappointed in him because he acted too much like an ordinary working man.

He simply wants to be a full-time, stay-at-home musical *director* —an artistic conscience and mentor in his community. He does follow the circuit to an extent—a Verdi Requiem in Los Angeles, Britten's *War Requiem* in Houston, a Brahms Fourth with the Philadelphia Orchestra. He made his debut as an opera conductor in March of 1978 with Sarah Caldwell's production of *The Damnation of Faust* in Boston. He also enjoys university residencies of a week or two, where he can share the re-creative process with students and serious amateurs in a more leisurely atmosphere.

Everywhere, the steady crescendo of accolades from critics, audiences, and especially from players in the major orchestras he has conducted, indicates he is fulfilling the prophecy made in the midforties—that if he would combine orchestral with choral studies he could become America's greatest conductor.

On the podium now, his demeanor conveys an almost palpable force, the taut grace and poise of a champion athlete. Hunched over the music desk, dripping with perspiration, arms outstretched as if to embrace the sound, he tastes the line with his fingertips, half sings it through thin lips, his inner ear focused deep within the form—say, the spirit—of the music. The visual aspect of a performance, including his own part of it, is no more essential now than it was when, with his own hands, he would strip a stage of anything whatsoever that might interfere with the *sound* of the Robert Shaw Chorale.

The sound of the Atlanta Symphony Orchestra has progressively astonished its listeners, from the time of its first tour in 1974 to the Kennedy Center and Carnegie Hall concerts in 1976, the presidential inauguration appearance of 1977, and the Western tour of 1978. Its performance of a Brahms symphony has the translucent, intimate quality of chamber music. And it seems as if Beethoven the melodist has never before been heard. The musicians play,

With Caroline, Alex, and Thomas Lawson Shaw

Shaw observes proudly, "as if they love music." Proof can be heard in the recordings released to date, including a *Firebird* suite and some *Prince Igor* excerpts—the first symphonic music to be taped in the United States using the revolutionary new digital, or "pulse-code modulation" system. More and more people agree that the ASO has earned international stature, and that judgment will be confirmed when Atlanta is able to send its orchestra abroad.

Shaw declares that none of this could have come to pass were it not for Caroline, his wife since 1973. As the highly educated and articulate daughter of a prominent Atlanta physician, she knows and understands the community-at-large, and this, combined with her natural warmth and cordiality, has been helpful to him professionally. More importantly, the happiness he has found in his personal life has enabled him to work harder and more productively than ever before, and with a greater sense of fulfillment.

In the spring of 1973 Robert had begun cultivating his acquaintance with Caroline Sauls Hitz, also recently divorced, who at the time was a member of the Board of Sponsors. They would frequently take long walks together, and once, while she was away, he mowed her lawn—she thought the neighbors had done it, while they wondered where she had found "the new yard man." They were married the following December.

Caroline brought to the new family her four-year-old son, Alex, who has affectionately nicknamed his stepfather "Warm." Then, on February 11, 1977, she bore another son, whom they named Thomas Lawson Shaw, after Robert's grandfather, an early California preacher. The audience at Symphony Hall that evening greeted the news of Thomas's arrival with a standing ovation, and a friend congratulated the sixty-year-old father with "My God, Robert, what a memory!"

11.

"Our Yard of Space
—in Our Inch of Time"

THE SECOND BATTLE of Atlanta was only superficially a quarrel between incompatible personalities over unpopular repertoire or social conduct. In a larger perspective it was but one of the more
painfully conspicuous episodes in the unfolding of a problem that
afflicted all professional performance arts organizations in the
country—a problem that a Twentieth Century Fund study in 1966
had described as an economic dilemma and a Ford Foundation
study three years later called an outright crisis.

The cultural explosion was, to be sure, partly a statistical phenomenon, an incidental product of a general "information explosion," a concomitant of the American people's infatuation with
statistics and computer data. But insofar as the statistics reflected
substantial growth in audiences and income, they also portended
cultural self-destruction. In any other sphere of the American economy, higher consumer demand would have resulted in lower production costs; in a labor-intensive "industry" such as the making of
live symphonic music it meant exactly the opposite, and the difference between income and expenses—the "reality gap"—seemed certain to increase annually, and indefinitely, until such a luxury could
no longer be afforded.

As far back as 1957 the Ford Foundation had begun studying the
situation with a view to meliorating it in some way. Nine years

later, in a gesture unprecedented in the annals of American philanthropy, the foundation distributed $80.2 million to sixty-one professional symphony orchestras. Approximately three-fourths was given in the form of endowments, which were to be matched at least one-to-one with private funds and held in trust until 1976; the rest was to be used for various specified development purposes. Altogether, it added up to $195 million worth of support over a period of ten years.

The awards ranged from $325,000 for small orchestras such as the one in Jacksonville, Florida, to $2.5 million for those in Philadelphia, Chicago, Cleveland, Houston, and Minneapolis. Along with orchestras like those in New Orleans, Baltimore, and Seattle, Atlanta's received $1,750,000. The ASO's million-dollar endowment gift was matched easily during an intensive five-month campaign; the balance was spent immediately to add personnel and upgrade salaries.

The foundation's money served mainly to reinforce the recipients' prestige, encourage expanded activity and audience development, and stimulate more generous contributions from local private sources. Regular operating expenses still had to be met, including the new ones created by the grants, and several orchestras nearly foundered on the largesse.

A comparative study of nine "middle bracket" orchestras carried out during the 1968–69 season for the Kansas City Philharmonic recommended that that orchestra's 1969–70 season be cut from twenty-eight to twenty weeks, and even proposed that the playing force be reduced to forty-eight musicians. Moreover, the study predicted that although the Atlanta Symphony Orchestra scored third after Minneapolis and Pittsburgh in artistic quality, second after Seattle in an overall rating that covered income and budgeting practices, and highest of the nine in "community acceptance," it would probably be one of the next to suffer serious financial difficulties. The rest would succumb in due time.

The prophecy was fulfilled by the ASO beginning in the fall of 1971. While ticket sales had increased by more than 100 percent and contributions had climbed to record figures every year since 1967, costs had multiplied threefold as salaries inched upward, services were expanded, and a larger staff was needed to handle the administrative details. The proportion of earned income shrank from 44 percent of expenses in 1967–68 to 36 percent in 1971–72—a depressing statistic, considering that the average ratio for the twenty-seven other American orchestras with which the ASO was keeping fiscal company was about 50 percent. The deficit could not be reduced simply by charging more for tickets, since prices were already as high as the traffic could bear, and a bigger auditorium, enabling the orchestra to reach more paying customers without increasing costs, was out of the question for the time being.

One way to offset budgetary escalation and still foster musical growth was to establish endowments for special purposes: a million-dollar endowment to purchase fine rare instruments for loan to players whose abilities outreached the limitations of their own instruments; a half-million-dollar endowment to pay a semiprofessional chamber chorus that could serve not only as a performing group but also as the "master-classroom" for an international choral arts festival and workshop; a scholarship or sabbatical fund to enable players to undertake occasional study or self-improvement such as a summer of chamber music at Marlboro; fifteen endowed chairs, which would help raise the orchestra to one hundred members. In 1974 a $250,000 gift from Mrs. Howard Peevy, the widow of a wealthy real estate broker, was designated to pay part of the cost of the concertmaster's salary. Unfortunately, the gesture did not start a trend.

Part of the problem was a scarcity of large family fortunes in and around Atlanta. There had never been very many of them, and few were ever in the possession of such dedicated music lovers as Boston's Henry Lee Higginson, Chicago's Elizabeth Sprague Coolidge, or Cleveland's Elroy Kulas. Even Robert Woodruff, who gave seven million to help build the AMAC, two million to preserve the integrity of the block it is located on, and another eleven million to the Alliance's endowment fund, was more concerned with the cultural integrity of the city of Atlanta than with the intrinsic values of the arts. In the interest of civic welfare, and also because of a sincere personal concern, he has spent over sixty million dollars building Emory University into a major regional medical center.

Instead, the city's wealth resides in a great many prosperous business concerns—chiefly insurance companies, transportation and communication giants, and large retailers like Sears Roebuck

—whose high-salaried executives are capable of responding with comparative generosity to the solicitations of the Board of Sponsors, the Women's Association, or the Junior Committee, but who could not afford to make more than an agreeable gesture toward substantial patronage regardless of their personal inclinations.

As a class, unfortunately, affluent Atlantans also lack the long tradition of habitual musical patronage, the *noblesse oblige* deeply implanted in many Northern cities during the nineteenth century by European-born entrepreneurs of the Industrial Revolution who financed the accoutrements of the "cultured generation"—whether out of a genuine love of art, a desire to replicate the social ambience of the old country, a defensive impulse to counter the popular image of the rich as wicked philistines or comic barbarians, or the sheer joy of positive giving. Some say that mercantile Atlantans are also afraid of another cataclysm like the pre–World War I boll weevil plague.

In the spring of 1972 the orchestra requested a direct appropriation of $100,000 from Atlanta's Board of Aldermen (who were already allocating a similar amount to the Alliance) in return for six free "family" concerts in the 4,000-seat Civic Center. The aldermen turned down the request but offered to put up $25,000 if Fulton County (already giving $62,000 to the Alliance) would pledge $15,000, and DeKalb County $10,000. The whole plan nearly failed because the commissioners of DeKalb—one of the wealthiest counties in the entire state—were reluctant to cooperate. One of the commissioners explained that most of the concerned residents in his constituency had already given "at the office."

Throughout the sixties more and more American business leaders came to accept the notion of the arts as civic assets, and tax-deductible gifts, mainly from small, publicly owned local corporations, increased. Beginning in 1967 added impetus came from the Business Committee for the Arts, set up by David Rockefeller to try to persuade executives that their corporations have community obligations beyond paying taxes and maintaining fair employment practices, and that patronage of the arts should be considered part of normal operating expenses rather than a charity. In less than ten years, the results indicated that the appeals were working, and old attitudes were changing.

Nationally, orchestras have received the largest share of such donations. In Atlanta, however, the Arts Alliance initially reserved the right to canvass all corporations and foundations not specifically predisposed to direct their aid to one or another of the Alliance's members. Thus the ASO has been the beneficiary of corporate patronage only indirectly, through receipt of its share of the Alliance's annual operating fund.

Still more support from big business has accrued to the orchestra indirectly through Affiliate Artists Inc. Using funds provided by large corporations like Alcoa, U.S. Steel, and Gulf Oil, as well as by foundations, large service clubs, and labor unions, the organization places individual singers, instrumentalists, actors, actresses, dancers, and mimes, who are specially trained to communicate informally and informatively with audiences of varying tastes, in eight-week residencies as affiliates of existing local institutions such as schools, arts councils, and orchestras. In 1969 the Sears Roebuck Foundation sponsored veteran Shaw chorister and favored tenor soloist Seth McCoy as an Affiliate Artist with the ASO to carry out an audience development project in the Atlanta public schools.

A variation on the residency idea that has been of substantial benefit to the Atlanta Symphony has been provided by the Exxon Corporation, which, first in cooperation with Affiliate Artists and later with the National Endowment for the Arts, has paid the salaries of selected young conductors placed with six American orchestras, enabling them to acquire experience in the broad spectrum of musical and administrative responsibilities connected with a musical directorship. The ASO was chosen to participate in the project because, according to Affiliate Artists president Richard Clark, Robert Shaw epitomizes the organization's concept of the proper relationship between the artist and society. Not the least of Shaw's virtues, Clark told a reporter for the *Atlanta Constitution*, is his desire for all the people to participate in the cultural life of the community.

The ASO's endowment fund grew by more than one-third in 1973, when the John Bulow Campbell Foundation of Georgia contributed one million dollars, and an anonymous donor added thirty thousand, so that after 1976, when the Ford Foundation's original million became available for reinvestment, the interest was covering a little more than a tenth of the operational budget.

Ever since the big, old foundations began giving consideration to the arts in the early fifties, most of them had adhered to the policy of providing—to use the jargon of grantsmanship—seed money for pilot programs that would explore new patterns of action. During the sixties many foundations sought opportunities to encourage activities in the general category of civil rights. The Rockefeller Foundation's grants to Spelman College for the intercollegiate chorus and the performance of *Treemonisha* had satisfied both criteria. The basic policy was premised on the assumption that if an innovation proved viable after a year or two of experimentation, local support would be forthcoming spontaneously. It seldom worked out that way. And when the federal government began assuming some responsibility for patronage of the arts, at about the time Shaw moved to Atlanta, the dilemma remained the same—short-term funding versus long-term institutions.

In 1969–70 the ASO received $50,000 from the National Endowment for the Arts to help carry out an experimental three-year program in chamber music, which eventually was to benefit the entire region. The experiment suffered from uneven artistic quality and inadequate rehearsal time. Momentum faltered when the grant expired, to be revived only temporarily when the AF of M's Music Performance Trust Fund underwrote a chamber music series for the Atlanta public schools during 1974–75. In the meantime there were other grants from the NEA, but none for chamber music.

The so-called economic dilemma, the crisis, in the arts centered around three issues that were deeply rooted in American cultural history: the absence of agreement as to whether the arts ought to be protected as national resources or given the chance to succeed or fail like any commercial enterprise; a reciprocal mistrust between artists on the one side and businessmen and politicians on the other; and the artists' dread of bureaucratic control, reinforced by sordid tales of interference and censorship culled from the history of patronage in Europe.

The issues were debated with rising fervor from the end of the nineteenth century until the middle of the twentieth. In 1937, the year Shaw left home for New York, three bills pertaining to federal patronage were introduced in Congress. One called for the establishment of a separate cabinet position for an arts administrator; another proposed the continuation of the Arts Division of the WPA within the Department of the Interior; the third would have subsumed a Division of Fine Arts under the jurisdiction of the Office of Education. In the early fifties the debate grew more impassioned. James C. Petrillo pleaded for government aid to the arts in the interest of jobs for his union's symphony musicians, while 91 percent of the board chairmen polled by the American Symphony Orchestra League emphatically rejected any such proposal as a threat to free enterprise.

By the early sixties the tide of opposition was in full ebb, and the issue was no longer whether, but when and how the federal government would play its role. In September 1965 Public Law 89-209 was enacted, establishing the National Foundation on the Arts and the Humanities, with so-called endowments for its two administrative branches. The National Endowment for the Arts was authorized to distribute one-to-one matching grants to qualified nonprofit organizations for various purposes, including performances of professional caliber that "would otherwise be unavailable to our citizens in many areas of the country," and to support "workshops that will encourage and develop the appreciation and enjoyment of the arts by our citizens."

It was several years before the impact of the foundation began to be felt in the country at large. The initial appropriation was only $2.5 million, and for the next few years increments were pitifully small, for although the performing arts were now generally acknowledged as important to the national well-being, their priorities were low in relation to those associated with civil rights, conservation, urban renewal, or the war in Southeast Asia. Moreover, the NEA's first director, Roger Stevens, was constrained to proceed with utmost caution, maintaining the highest possible standards under a limited budget, maximizing public confidence and interest, and allaying fears that government subsidy would impede the progress of the arts.

The law's emphasis on decentralization and education fostered the idea of the "residency"—for example, a visit of a day or more by a professional orchestra to an outlying community. Members of the local orchestra are invited to sit in with the professionals for a rehearsal or two, individual players present clinics or master classes, the conductor presents a lecture-demonstration with the orchestra, perhaps for school children, and the whole event culminates in a gala concert by the two orchestras, sometimes featuring a local chorus or soloists. In this fashion every musician becomes a teacher, and music is treated—in the words of the preamble to P.L. 89-209—as "a form of education."

In 1970 the NEA distributed $1.8 million to forty orchestras, mostly for regional touring. The Atlanta Symphony received $100,000 in matching funds for that purpose; the next year the grant was doubled. In 1975–76 the endowment gave the first of two "Bicentennial boosts" to one hundred American orchestras. Grants from the first year's $8.02 million ranged from $5,150 to the orchestra in Kalamazoo, Michigan, to $150,000 to the San Diego Symphony for a summer concert series. The Houston Symphony Society received $300,000 for regional services as well as to enable the orchestra's participation in opera and ballet performances, and to set up a choral workshop with the Houston Symphony Chorale. The ASO was awarded $200,000 for regional touring and for an extension of its summer season.

The ASO's summer season of 1974 attracted the amused attention of the entire country with its unintentionally spectacular production of Tchaikovsky's *Overture 1812*. The sixteen electronically controlled explosive devices installed in the pit to simulate the sound of cannon at the climax produced a dense cloud of smoke that activated the detectors in the ceiling. Scarcely had the applause died away than a company of firemen in full asbestos regalia, axes and hoses at the ready, charged into the auditorium. "As the smoke cleared," Shaw told *Time*'s correspondent, "it became apparent that what I had mistaken in the din of battle as a premature entry of chimes was the smell-all, tell-all alarm that did not know its brass from the principal bass."

Most of the ASO's grants came directly from Washington. Other funds should have been available through the Georgia Commission on the Arts, a state agency established in 1968 under the auspices of the NEA for the purpose of carrying out statewide programs with Georgia's share of the endowment's basic state appropriation. But it was not until 1973, after Governor Jimmy Carter's government reorganization plan created the new Georgia Council for the Arts, that the orchestra received its first money from that source:

$19,000 for "concert development in Georgia"—meaning tours with residencies. For nearly ten years, however, the state agency suffered for lack of financial backing from the legislature. Before Carter left office he had managed to raise the state's per capita commitment to the arts to 8.4¢, which represented a 144% increase over the previous year, but Georgia's expenditure was still far below Alaska's 186.5¢; even Montana, with only a few more inhabitants than Fulton County, was spending 9.1¢ per capita.

Gradually the administrative hierarchy envisioned by the framers of P.L. 89-209 took final shape. In 1975 the Southern Arts Federation was formed to facilitate regional touring by professional performing groups throughout a ten-state region. In all, twelve attractions were made available through the federation—theatrical and dance troupes, folk music and jazz, the Augusta Opera Company, and the Piedmont Chamber Orchestra (established in 1968 by a Rockefeller Foundation grant to the North Carolina School of the Arts at Winston-Salem). The ASO, the New Orleans Philharmonic Orchestra, and the North Carolina Symphony were added to the 1978–79 Regional Touring Program, with local communities offered grants equivalent to one-third the cost of one public performance plus an educational activity such as a workshop, a side-by-side rehearsal and performance, a lecture-demonstration, or a school concert or two.

Forthwith there loomed yet another perplexing dilemma. The NEA's theory was posited on the assumption that the best—that is, the professional—artist should set standards for the amateur. The catch was that the only manageable distinction between the professional and the amateur was the cash nexus. Now, of the seventeen orchestras in Georgia alone, none fit the category of professionalism as defined by the National Endowment except the ASO. The majority are in poor positions to risk the two-to-one guarantee for a contract with a federation orchestra, and those that could afford it either feel they are already operating at full artistic capacity, or else fear that assuming a student role would cost them some of the local prestige they need for their annual sustenance. Thus for the most part the federation orchestras must try to sell performances, not classes.

When Carter became president there seemed to be grounds for the hope that his administration would be more generous toward the arts than those of his predecessors, particularly at the grass-roots level. Carter, a populist, professed a lifelong affinity for music, art, and literature, and demonstrated an exceptional breadth of taste. Shaw found him a "convinced consumer" with "an enthusiasm for excellence."

Carter's political statements about the arts were tactically expedient. In proclaiming Symphony Week in Georgia in 1973 he made a point of the fact that Shaw and the ASO had contributed immeasurably to the musical education of the state's children, and during his presidential campaign he expressed his belief that "if we can educate our young people in an atmosphere in which the arts are an integral part of the everyday world, then we will have built a strong and secure base for the future of the arts in America."

The new administration began auspiciously with what Paul Hume of the *Washington Post* called "the greatest inaugural concert in history." At Carter's behest, the Atlanta Symphony Orchestra and Chorus shared the official privileges which had theretofore belonged exclusively to the National Symphony Orchestra. After the NSO performed its concert of works by Barber, Bernstein, and Copland, under Copland's direction, Shaw led his own forces in Ives's *Variations on "America,"* Robert Russell Bennett's symphonic synthesis of Gershwin's *Porgy and Bess*, and the finale of the Ninth Symphony. Shaw was also asked to arrange for chamber music at each of the seven receptions held in the White House. During a lull between formalities, Shaw related in a letter to the chorus, President and Mrs. Carter sat down to listen to Haydn adagios "alone/together in a roomful of tears."

"Maybe," mused Shaw, "just maybe—some hope."

The federal outlay for the National Foundations rose to $308 million in fiscal 1977. Although the sum by itself was impressive in terms of the average annual rate of increase since 1965, it was still dismally inadequate, considering that the Environmental Protection Agency had to make do with $5.3 billion, and the budget for Housing and Urban Development had to be cut to $7.7 billion. The NEA's portion was $98 million, roughly equivalent to the cost of half a dozen jet fighters. An additional $18 million was set aside for three-to-one matching "challenge" grants to help organizations like the ASO balance deficits or bolster endowment funds. The ASO received a half million dollars from the NEA and another quarter million from the Mellon Foundation.

Alex and his stepfather with President and Mrs. Carter and the Cleveland Quartet in the White House,
1977. Photograph by Charles M. Rafshoon

In the final analysis the real dilemma proved to be not economic
but philosophical—which is to say, political. Hypothetically, if a
symphony board of directors were privileged to orchestrate un-
limited funds from individuals, foundations, corporations, and local, state and federal governments, should the money be spent on
a program of breadth, or one of depth? Who should benefit, the
elite or the demos? The professional or the amateur?

Shaw had held auditions for a fifty-voice Atlanta Symphony
Chamber Chorus as soon as he arrived in Atlanta. Partly to minimize competition with the Choral Guild of Atlanta, which for some
years had performed regularly with the orchestra, and partly to begin building a basis for a permanent international choral institute,
the chorus was set up as a bona fide seminar on rehearsal and performance practices, complete with lectures and with academic

credit available to participants through Georgia State College. In 1970 the Choral Guild gave way to the 200-voice Atlanta Symphony Orchestra Chorus and Chamber Chorus, which were under the charge of various assistants until 1974, when Shaw himself assumed full responsibility.

Typically, week after week Shaw drives his singers to "excel themselves," seldom giving any visible sign of appreciation. Sometimes the relentless pressure has rankled even the most devoted chorus members, one of whom was finally impelled to ask why he was continually badgering them. "Why, I've heard some of those professional wind players make noises like they were blowing through gas pipes," he complained, "and you acted as if you hadn't even noticed!"

"I know," replied the maestro, "but *you* can *do* better."

Although he has mellowed in certain respects, Shaw is just as demanding a taskmaster now as he was forty years ago; his more restrained manner makes his seriousness and determination all the more evident. His "blessed fault," as one friend has expressed it, is his abiding faith in human nature. He still expects the ultimate effort, the extra mile, the final 10 percent from everyone concerned in any endeavor, musical or otherwise. An individual who fails to measure up will more than likely be ignored. If the offender is a whole chorus, Shaw may write a deliberately calm and analytical letter, or else he may "conduct his left shoelace" throughout a rehearsal (of course, he also does that when he is listening intently, and one can't always tell . . .).

The members of the ASOC are intensely loyal. Two singers commute from Auburn, Alabama, a three-and-one-half-hour drive each way in good weather; during a climactic week or more of nightly rehearsals and performances they may log a total of 1,600 miles on the highway. And a certain Atlanta physician, who has sung with the chorus ever since Shaw arrived, has, at the time of this writing, a perfect attendance record.

Once in a great while, however, attendance and attentiveness become too lax to suit Shaw, and he writes a letter to set the record straight.

September 23, 1976

Friends—

I suppose there are two understandings of what is meant by the phrase, "—lived a full life." On the one hand, it could be said of someone who seemingly had encountered almost every available experience. On the other hand I have heard it said of some who departed this life "used up."

Most of us, it seems to me, want to *be made use of*. We want whatever intuitive talent we have, whatever intelligence we've accumulated, whatever energies our genes and the Great Unknown have provided—to be *used*.

That's one of the reasons we're in this volunteer chorus together. (It may be the *main* reason.) We trust that we possess certain aptitudes and understandings that nothing else in our daily lives really uses—touches, utilizes, or "exploits."

Well, let me tell you very frankly that I also come to Monday evening rehearsals as a *volunteer*.

To my way of thinking, this only makes Monday nights *more* important. We're obviously the ones who care.

R

At other times a special letter may be necessary merely "to keep everyone's mind on the warm oats through the barn door ahead, rather than the intransigent mud on this lonesome road."

As usual, most of the letters deal with fundamentals—rhythm and tempo, form, phrasing in Bach's music, score editing, enunciation, and so forth. There have also been letters about works in preparation, such as the requiems of Britten, Berlioz, Hindemith, and Verdi.

> More, perhaps, than with any other composer or oratorio the Verdi Requiem depends upon vocal splendour and authority. The soloists and chorus must soar over the orchestra. Every bit of text must be inflected and fashioned. No tone left unsternum'd as to color, accentuation and dynamics.
>
> Beauty in music is not always quintessential. But Verdi unadorned and unadored is green without gold. His is not a paste-on beauty. No house-pet, quick-change, easy-on-easy-off. No skin-deep.
>
> Think Michaelangelo, da Vinci and Donatello. Think St. Peters, San Marco, La Scala and Pizza Hut. Think Othello, Falstaff and Marlon Brando. Think sunshine, cannelloni, Alps and olive oil. Think Sophia Loren, Arturo Toscanini and Two Ton Tony Galento. Think beauty. And think sub-cutaneously.
>
> Sing same.

R

There have been observations on Mendelssohn and Bach:

> *Elijah* is a remarkable, enjoyable and, perhaps, even instructive "entertainment." One delights in the "cast" of characters—even to earthquakes, fires and still small voices.

But in the *St. Matthew Passion* the chief and ever-present character is the mind of man—yours and mine and Everyman's—as it is
also antagonist, stage, theatre and audience. We have all the lines.
Lordy, lordy, what a difference that makes.

Concerning Beethoven's *Missa Solemnis* he wrote to the Choral
Guild in 1968: "It's a little like setting off a bomb in the brain—
to say nothing of the explosion in the larynx." And of the same
work to the ASOC:

March 11, 1976

The paradox hidden in the question of "final worth" is that, by
some awesome hetero-human balance and justice, that music which
is impelled by ideas and understandings not simply aural, tonal and
temporal in nature, ultimately *is* judged by how well it orders tone
and time in sound. The Ninth Symphony and the *Missa Solemnis*,
whatever their burden of philosophic intent, actually have had to
pass the tests of musical order and craftsmanship.

The pointy head of the paradox (any good paradox has points at
both heads) is that if you're a serious artist (which is to say, a man
or a woman) you're going to be saved neither by purpose alone nor
technique alone—you gotta have both. Each validates the other.

The goodest of wills will not insure the perfectest of symphonies; and know-how without know-what or know-why is in that
longest of runs just another no-know.

May 16, 1972

I am amazed again and again how the mastery of successive
minute technical details releases floods of spiritual understanding.
This must be particularly true of Beethoven, and of this work
which demands such daemonic dexterity.

In every vocal convulsion some truth is struggling to be born.
In every avoidance or diversion of the "natural" (which down-
grades so quickly from the "familiar" through the "easy" to the
"ho-hum") the super-natural finds a voice.

At every instance wherein we achieve this exact balance, or that
unequivocal intonation, or yea rhythmic meshing, or an absolute
precision of enunciation, or an unassailable propriety of vocal color
the miracle happens—the Flesh is made Word, and dwells among
us. We put in muscle and blood and brains and breath—and out
comes a holy spirit.

And a few years later, in January while the *Missa Solemnis* was in
preparation prior to the Carnegie Hall performance, a bit of
parody:

Lines from a condominium—
or it could have been verse:

'Twas the day before New Year's,
And all through Atlanta
Not a noodnik was stirring
Except Nola* and Santa.

The carols were filed
All according to plan,
On surmise that the *Missa*
Would soon hit the fan.

"Fear greatly!" said Frinkly,
"What's wripe to be wrought.
This Missa's a Mothah!
I tidings you not!

"Though it's Missa Impossible—
To psing it or psyche it—
Should the bahstahd be mahstahd
There's nothing quite like it!"

So pledge resolutely
Your blood, tears and sweat.
What Beethoven asked for
He's going to get!
                    RS-anta

When several ASOC members took offense at the rather explicit text—by the Chilean poet Pablo Neruda—of Samuel Barber's *The Lovers*, Shaw excused them from participation, without prejudice, but soberly tendered his reflections on the psychoaesthetic aspects of the work:

January 30, 1975
There is no way to equate the candor, fervor and human commitment of this poetry with public comfort-station graffiti. Irretrievably inappropriate would be the snicker, the wink or the mal jest.

He reminisced about the grotesque sentimentality of the Collegiate Chorale's crooning of "Begin the Beguine" and recalled his "all-time favorite fan letter." Then he concluded:

*Nola Frink, Shaw's secretary and chorus administrator since the spring of 1973, who brought not only administrative ability but also superior musical intelligence to the ever-growing job.

Simply by inventory of the physiological equipment involved, it cannot have escaped anyone's attention that sex is a reasonably private affair. . . . —And it may indeed be that the joys of sex are not increased by singing about it.

No matter what forces may be assembled for the *performance* of music, *listening* to music—even in a public auditorium—is an almost bafflingly private affair. Even when one goes to a concert with the most intimate of friends or beloveds, listening, and all the associations and imagery which it invokes, is so extraordinarily subjective that no other person really hears the "same" music.

The reassuring fact is that just as Neruda's words are personal and solitary, Barber's music is also personal and solitary. He writes from the solitude of his own soul to the solitude of another's soul; and that the event is "inhabited" by many does not qualify the loneliness of the transfer.

The Mahler revival of the seventies brought a hesitant response from Shaw, owing to his own temperament as well as to his background of study and experience with Herford, Toscanini, and Szell. He believed the music of the late romanticists was "better served by conductors who are more familiar with sonority and texture than with line." In the spring of 1978, however, he happily conducted Mahler's Eighth, the "Symphony of a Thousand Voices," with the ASO and the ASOC, assisted by RSC veteran Maurice Casey's Ohio State University Chorus, Clayton Krehbiel's Florida State University Chorus, and an Atlanta boys' choir called The Young Singers of Callanwolde. During the preparation period he entertained his own chorus with a rhymed commentary on his new-found affection for the idiom.

> List'ners rave and rant and holler,
> Zounds! the sounds of Gustav Mahler!
> Jung at heart hail Sigmund's kin,
> "Wolfgang's out and Gustav's in!
> Spartan hearts are infantilish,
> Those on sleeves are much more stylish!
> Rupt your rapture! (not unlikely)
> Muzzle mind, and 'sic 'em psychly!"

> Mean- and erst-while singers panic:
> Tessitura sic tyrannic!
> "Cry to heav'n for what they must have
> To navigate the eighth of Gustav.
> "Half the tempo! Down an octave!

Twice the—! Up the—!" Quel concoctive!
Still and all (as sometimes happens)—
Once the notes are stripped of scrappin's—
It's rather fun, and not unsunny,
To bathe in pools of aural honey.
So, grieve not, Gus! Our new Apollo!
Where you lead us we will wallow!

Late in January of 1976, Tom Pyle died of a heart attack. He had gone on nearly every tour, sung in nearly every recording—often as a soloist—and had been one of Shaw's most trusted aides and confidants. After Shaw's departure for Cleveland in 1956, Pyle became a prime moving force in the choral art in New York City. Together with Florence Kopleff, he founded Choral Associates, Incorporated, a chorus contracting service. They maintained a regular file of around five hundred names, and were able to find work for about half that number during a given season. Many of the singers were Shaw "graduates," but anyone wanting work outside the commercial musical theater could audition. Pyle knew the voices so well he could synthesize any sound a conductor might want. Then he would follow through, seeing to logistical details at rehearsals and concerts, and insisting upon musical standards from his singers that often exceeded the contractor's demands.

Within four days of his death, summoned by no organized means other than one person phoning another, five hundred of his friends travelled from all over America and gathered at the Cathedral Church of St. John the Divine to sing and play the Brahms Requiem under Shaw's direction.

The Atlanta choristers learned of it all a few days later:

February 5, 1976
Picture a gigantic, uncompleted Gothic cathedral all but surrounded by the debris of a disintegrating, dirty, disinterested city; four hundred professional singers—whole sections of "sethmccoys"; the finest free-lance instrumentalists in the city; tables of "covered-dishes" and breads and cheeses and coffee; greetings between friends and colleagues unseen for three decades—always sombre but mostly tearless; a "sight-reading" in German of his favorite oratorio, occasionally with fugues that swarmed and churned the cavernous acoustic, but with lyric portions and sounds and phrasings which almost certainly never will be heard again—

without question the finest chorus ever assembled in the history of Western music—and all bonded together only by love and sense of common loss, common gratitude and common commitment.

Tommy would certainly have been the first to qualify the importance of the particular event which prompted this extraordinary outpouring, to say that beyond the specific death of a specific person there was a "something" which united us all. He was, in the metaphorical, biblical sense, a "prophet"—if not so much by utterance as by life. His connection was closer to the "truth" which all of us have experienced from time to time in varying degree, to which no amount of professional involvement is even relevant, but which we as industrious and dedicated amateurs (literally, "lovers") can perceive nearly clearly, spared, as we are, the harassments and bushwah of the market-place.

I suppose the first scriptural enigma any of us memorize as a child is "God is love." In my case it was some years before I realized that there was a possibility that it said exactly what it meant and meant exactly what it said. Not, "God is to *be loved*," or "God *loves*;" but "God *is* Love. G=L."

At least by analogy (I would say by absolute coincidence) music is love, and so is a chorus, and so is singing together. —And rarely so perfectly demonstrated as by those called together by Thomas Pyle's departure.

I now invite you to realize—with appropriate wonder—that your participation and your "chorus" are not extra baggage, addendum, or post-script, but provide an involvement and commitment which furnish the only light there is. There is no other meaning.

Certainly not in words.

R

Years ago, back in New York City, Shaw was fond of quoting Abraham Lincoln—"I have been controlled by events." Or, as he later expressed it, "I have been sort of picked up by the ears and put someplace and told to 'do this.' "

> The dreams I had for the Collegiate Chorale were displaced by the successes of the Robert Shaw Chorale. And the Robert Shaw Chorale was displaced by my going to Cleveland and for the first time forming a chorus as part of a symphonic organization.

But he has not for an instant been the instrument of blind, "manifest" destiny. His vision, his capacity to imagine the possible, and his willingness to devote himself wholeheartedly to whatever work a given goal might require have already produced three epochal

The Atlanta Memorial Arts Center

contributions to American musical life. The Collegiate Chorale continues to flourish in New York, and its spirit still pervades the American choral tradition; the professionalization of choral performance is an ideal that is still being pursued by a number of energetic and determined individuals; and the symphonic chorus is a firmly established element in our orchestral tradition. Now, the prospect of an alliance of the arts, and in particular the musical arts, which prompted him to accept the invitation to Atlanta in 1967, seems to Shaw more viable than ever before.

To be sure, the Memorial Arts Center is functioning well as a focal point for musical activities in the city and the region. The ASO's season, now running forty-eight weeks, includes an extremely popular summer series in Piedmont Park, presented free to the public as a gift of the city. The orchestra's history came full circle in 1974 with the establishment of the Atlanta Symphony Youth Orchestra. The Atlanta Ballet Company and the successful new Georgia Opera Company contract for the ASO's services, and the Atlanta Virtuosi, an independent chamber music association, selects its players from the orchestra's ranks.

Shaw, however, believing (as do many others) that the symphony orchestra as we have known it is at a dead end, envisions the evolution of a new type of institution—a "musical performance society" of from 150 to 200 professional players under a staff of three to six conductors, continuously and systematically engaged in all conceivable types of musical performance, education, and outreach. His idea is rapidly gaining currency among musical leaders in other parts of the country, but he feels it now has a better chance than ever of becoming a reality in Atlanta first, because Louis Lane, his coconductor, and Stephen Sell, the orchestra's manager since the fall of 1978, share his convictions. "What we're really interested in planning is something for the next hundred years, not for the next few years of our own association—a pattern for the development of a musical performance society in the United States for the next century." If the people of Atlanta take heed, they might soon become the copropagators of a new era.

He speaks of his vision often, and with characteristic fervor and eloquence. In September of 1977, in his annual address to the local media representatives, he reflected upon a recent experience. He and Caroline and Alex had just returned from "a restful and provocative fortnight in Greece," where he had viewed for the first time Delphi and Knossos, the Acropolis and the Agora.

> I padded through and over the ruins
>   finding—as Robert Bridges said—
>   thoughts mostly of myself
>   —and wondering when and if
>   I might catch a frog
>   —with recognition.
> I, in my time,
>   have been more moved by Coventry.
> But now I begin to sense something:
>   Knossos—
>   architectural centerpiece of Crete
>   occupies no more space
>   than the Atlanta Memorial Arts Center
>   Delphi
>   —if you could tilt it until it were level
>   would fit into the outside walls
>   of Atlanta Stadium
>   The Acropolis and the Agora
>   with a minimum of jig-sawing
>   could be accommodated
>   in Lenox Square.

And I wonder if there isn't something
    in the nature of bigness
        —and fame
        —that eats at excellence.
These civilizations have lasted
    longer than ours—
        But even their spans
            are as nothing
        against geological time.
And no man even among them
    lived long enough
    to witness both the beginning
    and the completion
    of a single building.
It amuses me to contemplate that to a world
        removed from ours
        —as ours from theirs—
    Charles Ives and Bach will be sound-alikes.
Truly—Ours is—a Yard of Space
    and an Inch of Time.

His closing words were an enticing challenge to the people of his community:

It is precisely because we are neither
    the megapolis of the East Coast
        nor of the West Coast
That we have a chance
    if we work hard enough—and care enough
    to become our own Knossos
                    or Acropolis
                    or Delphi
    —To make eminently liveable
    our Yard of Space—
    in our
    Inch of Time.

Selected Discography

The following titles are listed in the order in which they were recorded. All were conducted by Robert Shaw unless otherwise indicated. Abbreviations: VC—RCA Victor Chorale; RSC—Robert Shaw Chorale.

1944: Bizet-Hammerstein, *Carmen Jones*—cond. Joseph Littau—DA 366.

1945: Mussorgsky, *Boris Godunov*—cond. Nicolai Beresowsky—VM 1000.

Leonard Warren Sings . . . . Operatic Arias and Sea Shanties— cond. Frieder Weissmann and Morris Levine—LM 1168.

Bernstein, *On The Town* (excerpts)—VC & Orch., cond. Bernstein —M 995.

Hindemith, *Six Chansons*—VC—single 78—#11-8868.

A. A. Milne, *In Which a House Is Built at Pooh Corner*—narr. by Robert Shaw—two 10″ 78s—#V-Y13.

Christmas Hymns and Carols—VC (see 1946).

Malotte, "The Lord's Prayer"; Furber-Adams, "The Bells of St. Mary's"—VC—single 78—#11-9155.

1946: *A Treasury of Grand Opera*—M 1074.

Bizet, *Carmen*—cond. Erich Leinsdorf—M/DM 1078, LM 1007.

Brahms, *Liebeslieder Waltzes*, op. 52—VC with Pierre Luboschutz and Genia Nemenoff, duo-pianists—M/DM 1076 (see also 1965).

Christmas Hymns and Carols (completed)—VC—M/WDM 1077, LM 112, ERA 117, ERB 43.

Bach, Arias from Cantatas 12, 81, 112, the *Christmas Oratorio*, and the *St. Matthew Passion*—Marian Anderson, contralto— M/DM 1087.

Dawson (arr.), "Soon-a will be done"; Shaw (arr.), "Set down, servant"—VC—single 78—#10-1277.

Bach, *Magnificat*—VC & Orch.—M/DM 1182.

Bach, Cantata no. 4, *Christ lag in Todesbanden*—VC & Orch.— DM 1096, LM 25, LM 9035 (see also 1958).

Bach, Cantata no. 140, *Wachet Auf, Ruft uns die Stimme*—VC & Orch.—M/DM 1162, LM 1100.

Blitzstein, *Airborne Symphony*—cond. Bernstein, narr. by Shaw —M/DM 1117.

1947: Bach, *Mass in B Minor*—VC & Orch.—M/DM 1146 (see also 1960).

Poulenc, *Petites Voix*—VC Women—single 78—#10-1409.

Beethoven, *Ninth Symphony*—Boston Symphony Orchestra, Tanglewood Chorus, cond. Koussevitzky—M/DM 1190.

Berlin, "Freedom Train"; Bates-Ward (arr. Shaw), "America, the Beautiful"—VC—single 78—#10-1368.

Brahms, *Ein Deutsches Requiem*—VC & Orch.—M/DM 1236, LM 6004, DV-V-20.

1948: Brahms, *Gesang der Parzen*—NBC Symphony, cond. Toscanini—LM 6711.

1949: *Onward, Christian Soldiers* (8 hymns)—VC—M/DM 1314, LM 85.

Verdi, *Aïda*—cond. Toscanini—LM 6132.

Bach, Cantata 131, *Aus der Tiefe*—VC & Orch.—DM/WDM 1425, LM 1100.

Music of the 16th Century (7 sacred and secular works)—VC—WDM 1598, LM 136.

Poulenc, *Mass in G*—VC—DM/WDM 1409, LM 1088.

Britten, *Ceremony of Carols*—VC Women (chorus identified as "The Robert Shaw Chorale of Women's Voices")—DM/WDM 1324, LM 1088.

Schubert Songs (6; English versions by Alice Parker)—VC—DM/WDM 1353, LM 81, LM 1800 (see also 1950).

Bach, Motet no. 3, *Jesu, Meine Freude*—VC & Orch.—DM 1339, LM 9035.

1950: Mozart, *Requiem Mass in D Minor*, K. 626—RSC, RCA Vic. Orch.—LM/WDM 1712.

Cherubini, *Requiem Mass in C Minor*—RSC, NBC Sym. Orch., cond. Toscanini—LM 2000.

Verdi, *Rigoletto*—RSC, cond. Renato Cellini—LM/VLM 6021.

Verdi, *Falstaff*—RSC, NBC Sym. Orch., cond. Toscanini—LM 6111.

Hymns of Thanksgiving (9, including 4 arr. by Shaw)—RSC—WDM 1559, LM 108.

Great Sacred Choruses (8)—RSC—DM/WDM 1478, LM 1117.

A Treasury of Easter Songs (10, arr. Shaw-Parker)—RSC, plus the Collegiate Chorale in one selection—WDM 1623, LM 1201.

Sweet and Low (8 familiar songs, plus 6 Schubert songs recorded in 1949)—RSC—LM 1800.

Gershwin, *Porgy and Bess* (excerpts)—RSC, cond. Robert Russell Bennett—DM/WDM 1496, LM 1124.

Strauss, *Die Fledermaus* (excerpts)—RSC, RCA Vic. Orch., cond. Fritz Reiner—LM/VLM 1114.

Bach, *Passion According to St. John* (English translation by J. Herford and R. Shaw)—RSC, plus Collegiate Chorale in chorales, RCA Vic. Orch.—LM 6103, WDM 1587, LVT 3000.

Brahms, *Alto Rhapsody*, op. 53—Marian Anderson, RSC Men, RCA Vic. Orch., cond. Fritz Reiner—LM 1146.

Gems from Sigmund Romberg Shows, Vols. IV and V—RSC, cond. Sigmund Romberg—LM 93, DM/WDM 1529, WDM 1600, LM 138.

Margaret Truman—American Songs (10 Revolutionary-era songs, arr. Oliver Daniel)—Margaret Truman, RSC, RCA Vic. Orch.—DM/WDM 1445, LM 57.

Debussy, *Sirenes*—Leopold Stokowski and his orch., RSC Women, cond. Stokowski—WDM 1560, LM 1154.

1951: Verdi, *Manzoni Requiem*—RSC, NBC Sym. Orch., cond. Toscanini—LM 6018.

Bizet, *Carmen*—RSC, RCA Vic. Orch., cond. Fritz Reiner—LM 6102, AVM 3-0670.

Milanov Sings—RSC, RCA Vic. Orch., cond. Renato Cellini—LM 1777.

1952: Beethoven, *Ninth Symphony*—NBC Sym. Orch., RSC, cond. Toscanini—LM 6900.

Verdi, *Il Trovatore*—RSC, cond. Renato Cellini—LM/VLM 6008, LM 7011, AVM 2-0699.

Christmas Hymns and Carols, Vol. II—RSC—DM/LM/WDM 1711, ERA 225 (*Christmas Greetings from Robert Shaw*), ERA 226 (*Merry Christmas from Robert Shaw*).

Gluck, *Orfeo ed Euridice*, Act II—NBC Sym. Orch., RSC, cond. Toscanini—LM 1850, LVT 1041.

1953: Verdi, *La Forza del Destino* (excerpts)—RSC, cond. Renato Cellini and Jonel Perlea—LM 1916.

Mascagni, *Cavalleria Rusticana* (excerpts); Leoncavallo, *I Pagliacci* (excerpts)—RSC, cond. Renato Cellini—LM 1828.

Beethoven, *Missa Solemnis*—NBC Sym. Orch., RSC, cond. Toscanini—LM 6013.

Bach, *Komm, Jesu, Komm*; Schubert, *Mass in G*; Brahms, *Der Abend, Nachtens*, and *Zum Schluss*—RSC—LM 1784.

1954: Verdi, *Un Ballo in Maschera*—NBC Sym. Orch., RSC, cond. Toscanini—LM 6112.

Boito, *Mefistofele*, Prologue; Verdi, *Quattro Pezzi Sacri*, no. 4, *Te Deum*—NBC Sym. Orch., RSC, cond. Toscanini—LM 1849.

Bach Cantatas and Arias—Bach Aria Group, cond. Wm. H. Scheide and Frank Brieff, and RSC, cond. RS in *Jesu nun sei gepreiset* (Cantata 41) and *Am Abend aber derselbigen Sabbats* (Cantata 42)—LM 6023.

With Love From a Chorus (16 Shaw-Parker arrs., including "Jua-nita," "Aura Lee," "Sweet Genevieve," and similarly familiar tunes)—RSC Men—LM/ERB 1815, ERA 256, CC 40.

Saint-Saens, *Samson and Delilah* (excerpts)—RSC, members of the NBC Sym. Orch., cond. Stokowski—LM 1848.

1955: Ravel, *Daphnis and Chloe*—Boston Symphony Orchestra, New England Conservatory Chorus and Alumni Chorus, dir. Robert Shaw in assoc. with Lorna Cooke de Varon, cond. Charles Munch—LM 1893.

1956: *My True Love Sings* (20 Shaw-Parker arrs., including "Annie Lau-rie," "Black, black, black," "Da unten im Thale," "Matona, lovely maiden," "Al olivo," and "Fa una canzona")—RSC—LM 1998.

Eight spirituals, arr. Shaw-Parker (see 1957).

1957: *A Mighty Fortress* (15 hymns, arr. Shaw-Parker)—RSC—LM/LSC 2199, KCS 4032.

Christmas Hymns and Carols, Vol. I (new Shaw-Parker arrs. of contents of LM 1077 [see 1945, 1946] plus arrs. and comps. by Martin Shaw, Peter Wilhousky, Jungst, and Praetorius)—RSC —LM/LSC/ERA 2139, FTC 2026, KCS 4084, CCS 86.

Deep River and Other Spirituals (16 arrs. by Shaw-Parker, Daw-son, Kubik, Miller, and Boatner, including material recorded in 1956)—RSC—LM/LSC 2247.

1958: Bach, Cantata no. 56, *Ich will den Kreuzstab gerne tragen*, and Cantata no. 82, *Ich habe genug*; Mack Harrell, bar.—VC and Orch.—LM/LSC 2312.

On Stage with Robert Shaw (arrs. by Robert Russell Bennett of 12 songs by Gershwin, Rodgers, Porter, Kern, Herbert, You-mans, and others)—RSC, RCA Vic. Orch.—LM/LSC 2231, KCS 6009.

Stephen Foster Song Book (16 Shaw-Parker arrs.)—RSC—LM/LSC 2295.

Bach, *Jesu, Meine Freude* and *Christ Lag in Todesbanden*—RSC, RCA Vic. Orch.—LM/LSC 2273.

1959: *What Wondrous Love* (18 Shaw-Parker arrs. of early American hymns and spirituals)—RSC—LM/LSC 2403.

Operatic Choruses (12 choruses from *Carmen, Faust, Lohengrin*, and 9 other grand operas)—RSC—LM/LSC 2416, FTC 2072.

A Chorus of Love from the Men of the Robert Shaw Chorale (15 Shaw-Parker arrs. of "Vive l'amour," "Turn ye to me,"

"Loch Lomond," etc.)—RSC Men—LM/LSC 2402, FTC 2013, KCS 4038.

Mallotte, "The Lord's Prayer"; Schubert, "Ave Maria"—Perry Como, RSC Men, Orch. cond. Mitchell Ayres—45 rpm single— #47-7650.

1960: Bach, *Mass in B Minor*—RSC and Orch.—LM/LSC 6157 (see also 1947). Grammy Award.

The Immortal Victor Herbert (15 songs arr. Robert Russell Bennett—RSC & Orch.—LM/LSC 2515, FTC 2086, KCS 4082.

Sea Shanties (16, arr. Shaw-Parker)—RSC Men—LM/LSC 2551.

1961: *I'm Goin' to Sing* (16 spirituals, arr. Shaw-Parker)—RSC—LM/ LSC 2580.

23 Glee Club Favorites (Shaw-Parker arrs. of "Whiffenpoof Song," "Gaudeamus Igitur," and songs by Schubert, Schumann, Purcell, Brahms, etc.)—RSC Men—LM/LSC 2598, FTC 2107.

Hallelujah! and Other Great Sacred Choruses—Members of the Cleveland Symphony Orchestra and Chorus—LM/LSC 2591, FTC 2103 (re-recording of *Great Sacred Choruses*, 1950).

1962: *This is My Country* (18 patriotic songs, including Union and Confederate Civil War songs, and a medley of service songs)—RSC & RCA Vic. Sym. Orch.—LM/LSC 2662, FTC 2132, KCS 4090 (subsequently retitled *America the Beautiful*).

Yours is My Heart Alone (12 operetta favorites, arr. Robert Russell Bennett)—RSC & Orch.—VCM/VCS 7023, FTC 2740.

1963: *The Robert Shaw Chorale "On Tour"* (works by Mozart, Schönberg, Ives, Ravel, etc., and one Shaw-Parker arr.)—RSC—LM/ LSC 2676.

The Many Moods of Christmas (17 carols, arr. Robert Russell Bennett)—RSC, RCA Vic. Sym. Orch.—LM/LSC 2684, FTC 2157.

Britten, *Ceremony of Carols, Rejoice in the Lamb*, and *Festival Te Deum*—RSC—LM/LSC 2759. Grammy Award.

1964: *Songs of Faith and Inspiration* (10 songs and hymns by Schubert, Franck, Adams, etc., arr. Robert Russell Bennett, plus one spiritual, arr. Alice Parker)—RSC & Orch.—LM/LSC 2760.

Stravinsky, *Symphony of Psalms*; Poulenc, *Gloria*—RSC & RCA Vic. Orch.—LM/LSC 2822. Grammy Award.

1965: *The Robert Shaw Chorale on Broadway* (11 musical comedy songs, arr. Robert Russell Bennett)—RSC & Orch.—LM/LSC 2799, FTC 2202.

Brahms, *Liebeslieder Waltzes* (op. 52) and *Neue Liebeslieder Waltzes* (op. 65)—RSC—LM/LSC 2864.

Vivaldi, *Gloria* and *Chamber Mass: Kyrie*—RSC & Orch.—LM/LSC 2883.

1966: Handel, *Messiah*—RSC & Orch.—LM/LSC 6175. Grammy award.
Sing to the Lord (16 traditional American hymns, arr. Alice Parker)—RSC—LM/LSC 2942.

1967: *Irish Folk Songs* (16 arrs. by Alice Parker)—RSC—LM/LSC 2992.

1975: *Nativity: A Christmas Concert with Robert Shaw and the Atlanta Symphony Orchestra and Chorus*—Vox QTV-S 34647/48.

1977: Stravinsky, *Firebird Suite*; Borodin, Overture and Polovetsian Dances from *Prince Igor*—Telarc DG 10039.

Acknowledgments

T. J. Anderson
Astrid Arnoldson
Gordon Berger
Jack Best
Dan Burge
Donald Carey
Walter Carringer
Maurice Casey
John Cooledge
Bert Cowlan
Peter Dellheim
Jerry Domer
Lukas Foss
Nola Frink
Franklin Garrett
Walter Gould
Julius Herford
Margaret Hillis
David Hinshaw
George Howerton
Raymond Keast
Florence Kopleff
Charlotte Bieg Krehbiel
Clayton Krehbiel
M. Jeanne Lewis

Glen Lockery
Anne Arant McFarland
Jo-Anne Mussulman
John Naskiewicz
Charles Nelson
Ross Park
Alice Parker
Barbara Permut
Anne Shaw Price
Neil Raber
Martin Sauser
William Schuman
Stephen Sell
Caroline Shaw
Maxine Shaw
William Steck
Peter Stelling
Howard Swan
Fred Waring
Richard Westenburg
Thomas Willis
Ann Woodward
John Wustman
Charles Yates

But when all is said and done . . .
it couldn't have been,
without Jeanne

Index

Italicized page numbers indicate photographs.

82, 89; CC's influence on, 76, 102–103; Shaw's contribution to, acknowledged, 125; RSC's influence on, 163

Choruses, professional, 87. *See also* Robert Shaw Chorale

Chorus of Love from the Men of the Robert Shaw Chorale, A, 170, 254 (1959)

Chotzinoff, Samuel, 57–58, 59, 83

Christian Church (Disciples of Christ), 7

Christiansen, F. Melius, 4, 24

Christmas Greetings from Robert Shaw, 253 (1952)

Christmas Hymns and Carols, 88, 170, 171, 251 (1945, 1946)

Christmas Hymns and Carols: Vol. I, 254 (1957); Vol. II, 253 (1952)

Civic Concert Service, 84–86, 114

Clark, Richard, 233

Cleveland Orchestra: founded, 132–33; educational program, 133–35

Cleveland Orchestra Chorus (COC): praised by Szell, 138; to Festival Casals, 146; records *Great Sacred Choruses,* 148

—letters from Shaw: on Hindemith's *Lilacs,* 66; description of Nantucket, 136; on auditions, 139; on enunciation, 140–41; on amateur choruses, 142–43; on RSC South America tour, 159–60; about *On Stage* album, 173–74

"Cleveland Plan," 133–35

Cold war, 128, 149, 195, 200

Collegiate Chorale (CC), *30;* founded, 21–22; educational programs, 26, 36; wartime responsibilities, 28; fosters American choral music, 29, 35, 65; democracy in, 39–40, 49; substitutes for Jan Peerce, 41; deficits covered by Shaw, 47, 75; records sound track for *The Roosevelt Story,* 54; credo, 62, 68, 70; Choral Arts Foundation, 74–76; influence of, 76, 102–103; early history summarized, 102; continues to flourish, 247; compared with early ASO, 197–98. *See also* Radio broadcasting

—letters from Shaw: on objectives, 28–29, 35, 37, 61; in wartime, 23, 37; on enunciation, 23, 62; on choral techniques, 26, 51–52; "a way of life," 40; on Beethoven's Ninth, 57–59; on form and spirit in music, 70; on transiency of CC membership, 73–74; on Ives's *Harvest Home Chorales,* 77; during first RSC tour, 91; on morale, 94; on inadequacy of stages, 101; parody of Frost's "Mending Wall," 102; on 1953 Choral Masterwork Series, 107–108; on amateur choruses, 108; on San Diego Symphony Orchestra, 118; on San Diego Workshop in the Choral Arts, 119; on John Wustman and Tom Pyle, 121

Collins, Walter, 162

Columbia Artists Management, 144, 146

Columbia Records, 84, 89, 169

Community Concert Service, 85–86, 114

"Community of expression," music as, 108–109, 128–29, 233. *See also* Shaw, Robert (speeches and sermons)

Community orchestras, 113–14

Composers in America, 31–34

Concert booking and management, 84–88

Concert halls, inadequacies of: in U.S., 88, 90, 92, 101; in Russia, 155; in Atlanta, 198